Giving is Good For You

GIVING IS GOOD FOR YOU

Why Britain Should Be
Bothered and Give More

JOHN NICKSON

Biteback Publishing

Royalties from sale of the book go to the Royal College of Music Scholarship Fund and
Insight: Research for Mental Health.

First published in Great Britain in 2013 by
Biteback Publishing Ltd
Westminster Tower
3 Albert Embankment
London SE1 7SP

ISBN 978-1-84954-520-4

10 9 8 7 6 5 4 3 2 1

A CIP catalogue record for this book is available from the British Library.

Set in Adobe Caslon Pro and Bulmer

Printed and bound in Great Britain by
CPI Group (UK) Ltd, Croydon CR0 4YY

'Surplus wealth is a sacred trust which its possessor is bound to administer in his life for the good of the community.'
Andrew Carnegie (1835–1919)

'Am I bovvered?'
Catherine Tate, in her eponymous television show

For Simon, Joyce and Innocent, with love.

In Memoriam

In Memoriam: Sir Anthony Tennant and Garry H. Weston

We all need role models and many are to be found in this book. Many more have inspired me in my work but I am particularly grateful to two philanthropists who are no longer with us.

Sir Anthony Tennant was a distinguished and successful businessman who, as chairman, rescued Guinness from ignominy. As my chairman at the Royal Academy of Arts Trust in the 1990s, his outstanding leadership and unstinting commitment helped to rescue the Academy from a very serious financial crisis and he persuaded many donors to follow his example by giving generously. I much appreciated his encouragement, his friendship and his wit.

Garry H. Weston was one of the outstanding businessmen of his generation but is particularly known for his heroic generosity. Garry gave billions to the family charitable trust and his children continue to give away up to £40 million a year to good causes across Britain. Amongst those who worked with and benefited from his generosity, his empathy and kindness was legendary. Garry served as trustee of the Royal Academy and I will never forget his personal kindness to me.

Acknowledgements

Iam particularly grateful to Victoria Barnsley, Sir Simon
Robertson and Lord Stevenson for encouraging me to write
Giving is Good For You. I would not have been able to so without
their support.

I thank Sam Carter, Hollie Teague and Olivia Beattie of
Biteback Publishing and their colleagues for believing in me
and my mission; Susan Sturrock, my left and right hand during
drafting and writing; Henrietta Bredin for historical research;
Dr Beth Breeze, Centre for Humanitarianism and Social
Justice, School of Social Policy, Sociology and Social Research,
University of Kent; and Professor Cathy Pharaoh, Co-Director
of the ESRC Research Centre for Charitable Giving and
Philanthropy Research at Cass Business School, City University,
London for their advice and support.

I thank all those who gave their time for interviews, most of
whom are named in the book, and to the following who gave
me specific advice, information, encouragement and practical
support: Anonymous, Dawn Austwick, John Botts, Matthew
Bowcock, Scott Colvin, Christoph Courth, Sir Vernon Ellis,
Ruth Finch, Lawton Fitt, David Gordon, Sir Thomas Hughes-
Hallett, Dr Philip Hopley, Jane Livingston, Theresa Lloyd, Fiona
Mactaggart MP, Philippe Narvel, Derry Nugent, Trevor Pears,

Roland Rudd, Kath Russell, Emily Stubbs, Rebecca Williams and the Rt Hon. Shaun Woodward MP.

I owe a debt of gratitude to the following (and I make no distinction between the living and the dead for death has no dominion) who have helped and influenced me in so many ways, and who have, unwittingly, helped me to write *Giving is Good For You*: my mother and father, my family, Alex Beard, Vanessa Bernstein, Dr Ruth Brown, Anton Bruckner, Sir John Burgh, Susan Burns, Sir Trevor Chinn, Dr John Cobb, Sally Ducrow, Sir Nicholas Goodison, Rosi and Anthony Hanson, Russell Harty, Janet Hickson, Joyce Hornsby, Mugyenzi Innocent, Sir Peter Jonas, Penny Jones, Edna Maud McGough, Lois and Allan Pimental, Simon Rew, Dorothy Reynolds and Angus Mackay, Coral Samuel, Sir Nicholas Serota, Kristian Wood and Michael Worrell.

Contents

Part 3: How we might give more

Part 4: Conclusions

Foreword by Robert Winston

Some years ago, archaeologists digging in a pit in Vaucluse, south-eastern France uncovered what appeared to be a very early pre-human jawbone. The evidence suggests that it belonged to a man who was probably around forty-five years old. Using various sophisticated chemical techniques, it was eventually dated to be about 700,000 years old. Because our ancestors had a very different diet, dental decay was not common then so it is rather unusual that all the teeth in that jaw were missing. Bone growth in the dental sockets showed that the teeth had been lost at varying intervals many years before that individual's death. The jaw was clearly the site of multiple dental abscesses which would have been extremely painful and made eating difficult. Unlike modern Provençale cuisine, most of the food then available in this region of France was very tough and hard. Even if fire was used to soften his food, some archaeologists believe that it would have been difficult or impossible for the owner of this jawbone to masticate sufficiently to allow digestion. Yet, most unusually, he had lived for many years with serious dental disease. So anthropologists and other experts have wondered whether some of his comrades in his cave chewed his meat for him before he ate and swallowed it, so that he could avoid the pangs of hunger and survive.

Altruism is a deep-seated instinct and has existed since before human history. In more recent times, charity has been the leading example of human altruism; one might argue it is one of the few traits that distinguishes us from animals. Charity is a moral imperative in human affairs, existing in virtually every culture. In ancient India, Vedic theology expected each person to extend the gods' shelter to others, particularly the protection of children and animals. Today, Hindu families are still renowned for their hospitality for feeding the needy, giving alms and clothing, planting trees and digging wells to protect the environment. By such behaviour they pursue a righteous life.

Three and a half thousand years ago in Mesopotamia, Hammurabi's code recorded a crude form of public charity to protect women and orphans. But monotheistic religions went much further. We know from biblical accounts, charity was well established as a key requirement of the Jewish law, care for the sick being pivotal. The institution of the sabbatical year over 3,000 years ago was designed 'so that the poor may eat' and charity, in biblical Hebrew *tzedakah*, was commonly rated at giving a tenth of one's income. This is still considered indispensable to anybody wanting to live a good life. *Zakat*, the equivalent for Muslims, is recognised in the Koran and regarded as obligatory. It is one of the Five Pillars of Islam. Muslims have a similar word to Jews – in Arabic, *sadaqah* – voluntary almsgiving.

The rise of Christianity led to the establishment of important charitable institutions and activities, initially in Europe. Treating illness and providing hospitality for the destitute and hungry were regarded as universal obligations. One example of such charity is seen with our earliest hospitals in Britain. St Thomas' and St Bartholomew's, established in the early Middle Ages, are great institutions which still lead in the best medical care. Like so many famous schools in England, these foundations were the result of endowment and support by the Church. By the eighteenth century, church support of various medical institutions had been largely replaced by public charity. In the capital, the famous London Hospital, St George's, Guy's and Westminster Hospital were all supported by charitable donations (so-called voluntary contributions), as were many other medical institutions, for example in Edinburgh, Glasgow, Bristol, Birmingham, Cardiff and Manchester. Without such a well-established network, the modern NHS could never have been effectively established.

Although medical causes and medical research remain the biggest recipients of charity in Britain, charity has been vital for so much of what we most value about British society. It is impossible to think of modern Britain without considering what an important part charity has played in our democracy and our sense of values. Education, the arts, our museums, even our special environment are examples of the value of charity to the very fabric of our lives.

Fortunately, the British people have always been fairly generous. Today, well over half of the adult population in the UK (around 58 per cent) gives something to charity each year, and some causes are particularly well supported. Medical charities and the needs of young people still attract relatively large sums of money, and religious foundations receive one of the largest slices of charitable income. There are some curious findings in recent statistics that some people may find rather uncomfortable. I personally find it bizarre that between eight to sixteen times more people donate to animal charities than to the homeless or the arts. Like most people, I am an animal lover, but I can't help feeling human life is more important.

Recently, British people, perhaps because of their imperial history, have been impressively generous with good causes overseas. Just last year, the East Africa Appeal raised over £72 million – the terrible pictures of starving children on television moved vast numbers of people. And, at the time of writing this week, Comic Relief is said to have raised a remarkable £75 million for similar causes.

But all charities are now facing serious shortfalls in the income needed to support their work, and for some this amounts to a deepening crisis. The economic problems we face affect virtually everybody and even the most generous people are tending to give less than in previous years. Against this, there is less money available through taxation to support those less well off for what most of us regard as essential needs. So although donations to charities in Britain amounted to around £9.3 billion last year, there has been a sharp reduction in income. The exact figures are uncertain but charities have received 20 per cent less on average this year. Yet even without the pressures that inflation brings, many important causes depend on charity without any hope of more support from government.

Charity is not merely about giving money, of course. There are many other ways we can all help good causes. Giving time to help as a volunteer for a local charity can make a significant difference. We might consider, for example, helping those in need by serving meals in a soup kitchen, baking and selling cakes, or growing vegetables and fruit in a community garden. Some of us might think of volunteering at a youth club, or helping the reading skills of homeless children residing in shelters. Sporting events can be immensely helpful – I am involved with one relatively small charity that raises well over half a million pounds each year through sponsored bike rides. These events are mostly women-only and take these wonderful, altruistic women to various exotic parts of the world for a guided week-long cycle ride over interesting but sometimes quite demanding terrain. The women work hard to raise charitable funds and also, in many cases, spend months in losing weight, or to get fitter before the rides. Their activity does not only help others, but they themselves also benefit. And they make strong friendships with the other women with whom they cycle. Like them, they seek to see a part of the world in safety that they would never have normally visited.

Unsurprisingly, our wealthiest individuals donate the biggest amounts of money in Britain. Without their extraordinary contributions, our museums, galleries, universities, our health research and our cultural activities could not lead the world. But it has to be said that there are a number of very rich people who give virtually nothing or very little – although of course they are enriched by the presence of these institutions and the good causes which enhance the daily lives of all of us. And though it is uncomfortable to say this, some wealthy individuals do not donate at all, even though there are now considerable tax advantages to richer people when they give to charity. Some of them structure their financial affairs so that they pay what nearly everybody else considers ludicrously small amounts of tax. The tax avoidance schemes that some very rich people use are widely regarded as an affront; the sums that they pay may not reflect more than the tiniest proportion of their earnings. They use our society but try hard not to contribute to it.

Sadly this uncharitable behaviour extends not only to not giving money, but also to avoiding giving in other ways – such as by giving time. We live in an age of celebrity, yet many wealthy celebrities seem indifferent to lending their presence for a mere hour or two to a charitable event. For example, whilst some highly paid Premier League footballers are really generous with good causes, many others seem reluctant to offer their presence even though it would make a massive difference to the profile of the charity. And it is somewhat disconcerting to see really prominent TV performers who appear to have profited from dubious tax avoidance schemes performing on programmes like Comic

Relief. Watched by millions, such admittedly unpaid television appearances are supported by them, perhaps because they are an effective way of greatly increasing a star's personal profile.

I am delighted to endorse this book by John Nickson, who, for many years, has worked assiduously for many different charities. Typically for him, he has arranged for the proceeds to go to good causes. The book is particularly appropriate in view of the economic downturn. If anything, in times like these when so many people are more needy, those of us that can afford it should really be giving more of our income rather than less.

The observation that 58 per cent of all adults give to charity is laudable. But it argues that 42 per cent, nearly half of the British population, gives nothing at all. And although so many of us give some money towards charity, the average sums that most of us offer are a truly tiny proportion of even the most modest earnings of an average working person. Nearly all of us could give more – even a few extra pounds from each of us would go a very long way. This book is timely, because thinking of that age-old moral imperative – to be truly charitable – may hopefully stimulate more people to realise that when they can give to charity, this moral behaviour is as important as being responsible, kind, peaceful, caring and law-abiding.

Think of the owner of that toothless, disease-ridden jawbone, excavated in south-east France. Primitive but important forms of charity saved that individual's life. His early pre-human comrades showed a crucial form of altruism, and their responsible, caring behaviour was an important building block in establishing our own species, *Homo sapiens*. Without that behaviour we humans, with all our remarkable abilities, would never have evolved. We might be no more than the owner of that diseased and painful jaw, the rest of whose bones were lost in the primeval dust long before recorded time.

INTRODUCTION

It did not come naturally: why I had to learn to give

'He who cannot give anything away cannot feel anything either.'
– Nietzsche

How generous are we? Six out of ten of us give an average of £10 a month, about half as much as in the United States but more than most countries. We like to think we are a generous people and in many ways we are. We respond well to disasters and to campaigns such as Children in Need. However, some of us are very much more generous than others.

Relatively, the wealthiest 10 per cent give a far smaller proportion of their income on average than the poorest 10 per cent. Does it matter and should we bothered by it? Many of our most generous donors believe that we should be. In this book I will explain why growing inequality and the low level of giving by so many of the wealthy should concern us. I will also propose solutions and ways of unlocking the generosity of all us, and the wealthy in particular.

I was driven to write this book after more than thirty years as a professional fundraiser because I felt something was wrong. Although I had had the privilege of working with some exceptionally generous donors, I became increasingly aware that the largest gifts were being made by the same people and that many of the names of those imputed with astronomical wealth in the annual *Sunday Times* Rich List were not appearing on donor boards or amongst the benefactors and patrons of our arts organisations. Fellow fundraisers confirmed this and, talking to some of our most generous donors, it became apparent how frustrated they are that the majority of their peers are not giving. Indeed, the exasperation expressed by the wealthy donors I spoke to convinced me that I should write a book making the case for giving. I am doing so with their encouragement.

As I did my research, I was shocked by the vast increase in the wealth owned by the very richest people who live or are based here, and which continued to increase, despite some blips, throughout the current recession. Meanwhile, the great majority of the country grew poorer in real terms and, not surprisingly, some sources show that charitable giving now appears to be in decline, although this is contested by others. There is certainly no evidence to suggest that the proportion of wealth which the very rich are giving is increasing. I was also shocked by the poverty and deprivation I discovered through meeting philanthropists who are doing what they can to address problems to which most of us are oblivious.

I was shocked not because I disapprove of making money and having it. I am privileged and our household pays top-rate tax. Britain needs wealth creators. However, there is now evidence of how damaging inequality can be, as you will discover in the following pages.

I acknowledge the impatience of those benefactors who are angry with those who do not give, but I believe that the most effective way of persuading people to give is to encourage them to follow the exemplary leadership of those who are being generous.

I also wished to demonstrate how philanthropy works and what it means in practice. In order to do this, I decided to embark upon a journey to meet those who give and those who receive in different parts of the country. I wanted to hear first-hand, from people most of us have not heard of and many of whom I had not met before, why they give, how they give and what difference their generosity has made. I found these conversations revelatory and inspiring. I have met people who may or may not be paragons of virtue but who were all united in their belief that they want to do the right thing by following the example of Andrew Carnegie, one of the world's canniest wealth creators and philanthropists, who said that surplus wealth should be used by those who own it for the good of the community.

Some were brought up to give as children, others started in midlife. Some are religious and others are atheists. Every one I met told me that giving had transformed their lives, whether it was the couple funding a refuge and re-education for sex workers in Newcastle, or another couple funding research into poverty, with significant implications for the slum dwellers of Dhaka in Bangladesh and for rural poverty in Zimbabwe.

We learn how people become homeless in Britain; how music contributed to the growth of Manchester as one of the wealthiest cities in Europe, and has transformed the academic performance of primary school children in one of the most deprived parts of Brixton. We learn how philanthropy is helping to save the lives of those with cancer who need oral and maxillofacial surgery and how the death of a young British woman in Afghanistan prompted her parents to commit to those who suffer most in war: women and children. You will discover the relationship between blood and philanthropy. A young British man, brought up in care and foster homes, tells us what it is like to face a life sentence for drug dealing in the US, to survive prison in the UK, and how he came to found his own company which employs ex-offenders, supports the charity that rescued him and which is chaired by a former Conservative Secretary of State for Employment.

Everyone I spoke to, whether they were giving or receiving, spoke to me in the most personal way and with great feeling and conviction. These were all people who are making a difference. They confirmed what I have always suspected: that decisions about philanthropy are rooted deeply in the emotions of those who give.

They also confirmed that the commitment and conviction that is an essential ingredient of successful philanthropy leads to profound feelings of fulfilment. My task is to convey to those who have not yet discovered the joys of giving that they are missing something fundamental. I am driven to do this because I have witnessed how much good people can do.

I believe that giving is good for us. I know it is good for me. I came to this conclusion only recently, despite spending decades asking people for money and serving as a trustee of charities. I am only beginning to understand that giving in its widest sense is fundamental to any concept of what it is to be a human being.

Why did it take me so long to understand this and that being mean makes you miserable? I lived in a bubble of privilege. Neither my upbringing nor my schooling encouraged me to consider the needs of others. My poor father was the least charitable and most unhappy man I have ever known. He retired following a breakdown in his thirties. He had no financial need to work and spent most of his life quietly at home being depressed. One of his many afflictions was a fear that he did not have enough money. Money ruled our family and property was its religion. I have not yet entirely escaped its clutches and understand my father's fear, one that is common amongst the rich.

I learned how to ask long before I learned to give. I also learned how donors think and how effective philanthropy can be. From 1987, I was responsible for fundraising at the British Council, English National Opera, the Royal Academy of Arts and, finally, Tate. This was a period of more than twenty years when the arts in Britain bloomed. Central and local government, the National Lottery, business and private donors worked together and invested in culture as an act of faith as well as for political, commercial or personal advantage. The results were spectacular and have helped to transform Britain's international reputation. In addition to their own intrinsic value, which is beyond calculation, the arts have boosted tourism, attracted foreign investment in Britain, helped to drive the 'knowledge economy' and developed the skills of the workforce. Public investment has been crucial but none of this would have happened without private philanthropy.

Busy asking others to give money, I was too selfish and fearful to think about giving myself until I became a Governor of Atlantic College in Wales. The College is part of United World Colleges (UWC), an international movement which gives a transformational education, based upon the International Baccalaureate and an ethos of service to others, to young people aged sixteen to eighteen from all over the world. Founded in the deep frost of the Cold War as a means of bringing young people together and fostering peace when nuclear war seemed a real threat, UWC is needed more than ever.

Inspired by the possibility of a young Palestinian and a young Israeli sharing a room, learning and serving together and becoming friends at the most formative time in their lives, I became determined to do what I could to support a cause that is devoted to eradicating ignorance and fear and to celebrating difference and diversity. I did not know it but I was about to become a donor.

My moment of epiphany came at an Atlantic College board meeting in 2007. When governors were asked if they could help reduce a shortfall in scholarship funding, I made a spontaneous decision and put up my hand. I said I would support a scholarship for a refugee. I did not know I would be changing my own life as well as someone else's.

That is how I came to meet Innocent, who fled from Rwanda to Uganda aged five, having survived one of the most appalling and infamous genocides in human history. As his parents belonged to the two main opposing tribes, they had to escape massacre by fleeing their country. Innocent was brought up in a United Nations refugee camp in Uganda with a sheet of plastic for a roof, the only one of his siblings to be educated.

When I first met Innocent, who arrived in Britain with few clothes but a big heart and great courage, I told him that I expected to learn as much from him as he would learn from his own life-changing experience at Atlantic College. I had no idea how true this would be. Now at university in the US, Innocent is helping to support his family in Uganda and sends a regular contribution to Atlantic College to pay for the education of others from his own minimal resources. When he left Atlantic College he raised funds to take himself and fellow students back to Kigali in Rwanda, where they worked as volunteers in an orphanage for children who are victims of war.

What I have learned from Innocent is the importance of generosity and the wish to do the very best for others as well as for yourself. He seems remarkably free of self-pity and looks forward with hope rather than looking back with bitterness. Whilst Innocent's life has been transformed, so has mine. I have learned so much more about the world through knowing and supporting him.

Mine is only one instance of many donors whose lives have been enriched by philanthropy. I hope that my experience and those of the people I interviewed will encourage those who are not yet giving to become philanthropic, engaging with the world rather than withdrawing from it and living as refugees as so many wealthy people do. I hope they will be inspired to follow Innocent's example of giving when he has so little to give.

This is a book about values. I fear that our society is becoming more materialistic and selfish, and that our humanity and civil society may become compromised. I am making a personal, emotional and moral case for giving, driven by the example of the two very different refugees I know best, Innocent and my father. Another refugee, Michael Moritz of Sequoia Capital, revealed his deepest feelings when announcing a gift of £75 million to Oxford University to fund students from poor families. Referring to his Jewish parents, who escaped from Nazi Germany, he said: 'I would not be here but for the kindness of strangers.'

John Nickson
February 2013
London

PART 1

Why we should be bothered

CHAPTER 1

Class war?

'There's class warfare all right, but it is my class, the rich class, that is making war and we are winning.'
– Warren Buffett, *New York Times*, 2006

'Am I bovvered?' In the first years of our new century, the comic actor Catherine Tate coined a phrase, in character, which seemed to echo the thoughts and feelings of many. From the expression upon her face, it was clear she was not.

Catherine Tate has summed up an era of debt and, for some, disillusion, disengagement and despair. What kind of people have we become who provide appalling care for the old, the sick and vulnerable, who think nothing of destroying other people's homes and businesses for kicks whilst rioting, and who walk away with six- and seven-figure bonuses despite destroying the wealth of shareholders? What has happened to our humanity, our sense of empathy, respect and responsibility for others? Despite the liberties we have fought for over the centuries and all the wealth we have created, we don't always treat each other very well.

If only in one respect, those who led our financial system to the point of meltdown and caused havoc with the lives of millions in 2008 did have something in common with those who looted our cities in the summer of 2011. They were not bothered about other people.

I believe that not bothering has dangerous implications for all of us. It has undermined faith in the capitalist market economy that has consistently delivered prosperity ever since the Age of Enlightenment in the eighteenth century ushered in the industrial revolution. As a result of reckless speculation, and by spending money we didn't have, we are now in a new Age of Austerity and Anxiety, where prospects for employment, housing, health and social care look bleak for millions, particularly for the young and the poor.

Capitalism has created more prosperity for more people than any other system in the history of humanity, and yet capitalism can only work and be justified if its rewards are seen to be shared. Since the Thatcher–Reagan settlement in the 1980s, subsequently adopted by New Labour, the better-off have become immensely richer, the middle classes are being squeezed and the poor are becoming very much poorer.

There is something wrong in Britain. We are in the midst of the worst recession for generations and yet little has changed for the wealthiest. Expensive restaurants are thriving. Property prices continue to increase as more and more of the international rich take refuge in London. In the part of Westminster where I live, detached houses sell for £10 million or more. However, the poorest ward in London is only five minutes' walk away. Our life expectancy in Little Venice ward is ten years more than in neighbouring Church Street ward, according to my GP. Forty per cent of children in London live below the poverty line. The income of the majority of people is declining in real terms. These simple facts illustrate one of the most serious problems facing Britain today: growing inequality between rich and poor.

Some say that inequality has reverted to levels last seen in

Victorian times, although this may be misleading given that people lived, starved and died on the streets more than 150 years ago. Surely life is not as extreme for the poor now? Poverty is relative. Despite Britain being the world's sixth largest economy, one in five of us live below the official poverty line, defined as 60 per cent of median household income or £359 a week in 2011, according to the Office for National Statistics (ONS). If poverty is defined in relative terms, there will always be those who will be classified as poor. However, it is estimated that over 13 million people, including 3.5 million children, are struggling to make ends meet. Six and a half million are in fuel poverty, meaning that they are spending more than 10 per cent of their income on energy, and the majority of them are pensioners. The average annual fuel bill now exceeds £1,000.

These figures are hard to grasp in the abstract. I find it helps to imagine living on the jobseeker's allowance of £71 a week and looking forward to an increase of 71p in 2013. As Dr Frank Prochaska, a leading authority on the history of philanthropy, reminds us: 'The poor will always have us with them.' It is disturbing that so many of them are in work; indeed, a majority of those claiming benefits are in employment.

Consider this. According to the *Sunday Times* Rich List, the estimated combined wealth of the 1,000 wealthiest people in Britain has ballooned by a staggering 283.5 per cent since 2000.

The collective wealth of the top 1,000 is estimated to have grown from £146 billion in 2000 to £414 billion in 2012. Meanwhile the wealth of the majority living in Britain has fallen as property prices decline outside London and incomes for those in work, except the highest earners, have been squeezed by inflation and pay freezes.

Wealth is news. The headlines and debate have been dominated since the crash of 2008 by stories of greed, fraudulent behaviour and massive tax avoidance by some of the wealthy, including one of Britain's most popular stand-up comedians, amounting to over £4.5 billion a year. Some are reported to be paying as little as 1 per cent of their multi-million-pound incomes in tax.

The exposure of the corporate tax avoidance practised by some of the best-known international brands, such as Google, Starbucks and Amazon, has also caused public anger, made even more intense by the knowledge that the schemes employed by these individuals and companies are legal. There is another reason people are angry. Her Majesty's Revenue and Customs (HMRC) tells us that the gap between tax anticipated and tax paid in 2012/13 could be £32 billion, a sum equivalent to the cost of our armed services, or more than our spending on local government. Meanwhile, the National Health Service has to find 'savings' of £20 billion, whilst 'routine' operations are restricted, and the national welfare bill will be cut by £18 billion with threats of further cuts to come, inevitably causing more suffering to our poorest fellow citizens.

In 2012, the press reported that at least a million old people and more than a million children do not have enough to eat, and Save the Children launched its first appeal to help feed hungry children in Britain.

FareShare is a charity and social enterprise that provides surplus 'fit for purpose' food to organisations working with 'the disadvantaged'. Each year, an estimated 3 million tons of food are wasted in Britain at a time when prices are rising sharply. FareShare's chief executive, Lindsay Boswell, was reported in *The Guardian* during the autumn of 2012 as saying: 'FareShare is about two of the biggest issues facing us now: waste and feeding people.' Holding up a plastic container full of lobster bisque, he said, 'It would be an absolute moral outrage for this not to be eaten when so many people are going hungry.' Without FareShare, surplus food would be poured down the drain; instead it is sent to more than 720 member charities which are Britain's informal welfare net. Boswell says that as the welfare state retreats and the cost of living increases, demand is soaring.

Meanwhile, the press was reporting the resignation of Bob Diamond, CEO of Barclays, after it was revealed that the bank had rigged the interest rate market, thus allegedly profiteering dishonestly and possibly fraudulently at the expense of those with whom it did business. Mr Diamond is estimated to have been paid more than £120 million between 2005 and 2012, during which time the value of £1 invested in Barclays fell to 30p. He also secured a deal whereby the shareholders (of whom I am one) paid part of his tax bill for £5.7 million in 2011, a measure described as 'tax equalisation'. Many other banks were subsequently exposed as having participated in this racket. In 2013, the Royal Bank of Scotland (of which I am also private shareholder) paid bonuses totalling £600 million despite recording a loss of £5 billion. No wonder the normally phlegmatic British are exercised. Since 2008, taxpayers have 'given' £1.2 trillion to the banks, worth £19,271 from every man, woman and child, with no guarantee that the money will be returned.

When the right-wing media rails against the 'underserving rich', the *Financial Times* calls for the reform of capitalism, the Prime Minister and the Chancellor of the Exchequer describe tax avoidance and, by implication, the use of Gift Aid tax relief as 'morally repugnant', and the Treasury describes donors as tax dodgers – something seismic may be happening. Opinion polls suggest that Middle England is deeply unhappy that the rich often pay tax at a lower rate than those who work for them. A poll taken shortly after the Budget in April 2012 reported that a majority of Conservative voters were opposed to the reduction in the top rate of income tax for those earning more than £150,000 a year. We may not enjoy paying tax or approve of how it is spent, but we know tax is the price of civilisation. Many think, including some top-rate taxpayers, that those who believe they are too rich to pay tax are selfish, lack commitment and do not conform to a British sense of fair play.

In better times, Lord Mandelson said that he was relaxed about people becoming 'filthy rich' as long as they paid their taxes. There is a different feeling now. In the midst of an international financial crisis, we see that wealth is increasingly in the hands of the few and we know that growing inequality and poverty leads to social dysfunction. For the first time in living memory, most young people in Britain cannot expect to be as well off as their parents. Privilege becomes harder to justify when some of the wealthy pay so little tax proportionately, and particularly if they do not share their good fortune with others by giving to charity and other causes that benefit society. As the Age of Excess morphs into the Age of Austerity and Anxiety, the behaviour of the elite few will come under increasing scrutiny by the many.

We know that the richest 10 per cent give proportionately less to charitable causes annually than the bottom 10 per cent of the population. There may be disagreement about the specific figures, but no one should dispute that the poor are proportionately more generous than the rich. Before we take up the challenge of persuading the rich to be more generous, we should consider some facts and figures about wealth, poverty and charitable giving in Britain.

According to the Office for National Statistics Report in 2012:

- the poorest 10 per cent had a median value of household wealth of £13,000;

- the wealthiest 10 per cent had wealth of £967,000 or more;
- the top 1 per cent had wealth of £2,807,000 or more; and the wealthiest 10 per cent of households owned more than 40 per cent of overall wealth and were over 850 times wealthier than the poorest 10 per cent of households.

According to Barclays Wealth in 2012, 284,000 people had assets totalling £1 million or more, excluding property.

According to the *Sunday Times* Rich List in 2012:

- the 2,000 wealthiest people living in Britain had personal assets of £34 million or more;
- the top 1,000 owned a minimum of £74 million each;
- the 500 wealthiest people in Britain had assets of at least £150 million; and there were seventy-three billionaires living in Britain.

Before we become too dazzled by zeros, it may help to understand the difference between a million and a billion. We should be grateful to John Lanchester for pointing out in *Oops*, his book about the financial crash in 2008, that a million seconds is less than twelve days whereas a billion seconds is thirty-two days.

The Organisation for Economic Co-operation and Development (OECD) reported in 2011 that the income gap in Britain is rising faster than in any other wealthy nation. The reason the trend is so pronounced in Britain is the creation of a class of super-rich. The share of income earned by the top 1 per cent increased from 7.1 per cent in 1970 to 14 per cent in 2005. At the same time as accumulating great wealth, the rich have seen top tax rates fall from over 90 per cent in the 1960s to 60 per cent in the 1980s and to 45 per cent in 2013.

The OECD says that 65 per cent of those polled in Britain

are concerned by growing inequality. This may well be because
over the past thirty years, the share of national income going
to those on the lower half of earnings has fallen by 25 per cent
whilst the slice going to the top 1 per cent has increased by
50 per cent.

In April 2012, *PeoplePerHour* reported hourly rates of pay
(based on a 37-hour week for forty-eight weeks a year) as
follows:

- Waiter: £3.17
- Nurse: £14.98
- Police Officer: £21.91
- MP: £37.10
- GP: £39.39
- Prime Minister: £80.20
- Jonathan Ross: £562.94
- Premier League footballer: £822.07
- Kate Moss: £3,326.45

According to a report published by Manifest and MM&K,
top executives in the FTSE 100 companies earned forty-seven
times their employees' average earnings in 1998 and 139 times
that in 2011.

The professed justification for the explosion in executive pay
is the need to remain competitive. Any intelligent person can
see that this is a false and ultimately self-defeating premise.
Clearly, many of those who run public companies act in their
own interests rather than for the benefit of their shareholders
but the risks taken by those in the financial sector have become
the responsibility of all of us. Whilst the taxpayer bears the
burden of profligacy in some of the banks, and their shareholders have lost most of their capital and dividends, some senior

executives continue to be rewarded with bonuses unrelated to performance and their pension pots have grown exponentially.

In 2012 we saw the first signs of a revolt against high pay, with shareholders voting against the top pay awards at Aviva, Royal Bank of Scotland, Royal Dutch Shell, GlaxoSmithKline, Citigroup and WPP. Despite a backlash, pay and benefits to top business executives rose by 27 per cent in one year to an average of £4 million in 2011.

In 2011, Charles Moore, former editor of the *Daily Telegraph*, wrote: 'It turns out – as the left always claims – that a system purporting to advance the many has been perverted in order to enrich the few.' At the end of 2011, the *Financial Times* published a leader headed 'Capitalism is dead: long live capitalism', calling for the urgent reform of a system which has become 'unjust' and 'politically corrosive'.

At the CBI conference in 2012, its President, Sir Roger Carr, said:

> We must demonstrate that we are a generation that is focused not just on how much money we make, but how we make money. We must salvage the reputation of business. Businesses' and individuals' standards have been variable, greed prevalent and fairness forgotten in a number of sectors, banking and media at the forefront, but also in other walks of life.

I have met only a very few people who are not outraged by the greed and irresponsibility we are witnessing. I was told by a wealthy friend shortly before he died in 2011 – a former FTSE 100 chairman and chief executive, knighted for his services to industry, an investor, benefactor and chairman of charities – that the current levels of chief executive pay and bonuses were 'monstrous, disgraceful and dangerous'. He also told me that he couldn't understand why anyone should want or need wealth of more than £20 million, which just shows how relative these things are.

Criticism of top pay is not motivated by envy. Many of those expressing concern have more than enough money of their own. The problem is not the making of money but the way it is made and how it is used. We need entrepreneurs to drive the economy and create jobs. We should celebrate them. However, the inequalities in wealth that have grown in the last thirty years are becoming a problem as the majority feel the pinch of austerity and the poor endure real suffering.

What can explain this desire to accumulate more and more wealth? The revolution brought about by globalisation and the implementation of technology must have made a significant impact upon employment and pay and the ability of capitalists to earn higher returns upon their investments. Lower taxes have also played their part. However, some say other forces are at play. In their book *How Much Is Enough? The Love of Money and the Case for the Good Life*, Robert and Edward Skidelsky make much of the notion of satiability. 'Our own view is that it [economic satiability] is rooted in human nature – in the disposition to compare our fortune with that of our fellows and find it wanting – but has been greatly intensified by capitalism, which has made it the psychological basis of an entire civilization.'

The Skidelskys believe the pursuit of wealth is a form of madness because we have lost the link between needs and wants. Noting that the workaholic rich have replaced the idle rich, the Skidelskys maintain that the colossal wealth created and enjoyed by a very few has not always been put to good use:

As we progressed, we lost the idea of the social good as a collective achievement … The logic of contract was sundered from the logic of reciprocity, which in most human cultures and societies has been an integral part of the economy ... Capitalism rests precisely on the endless expansion of wants. It has given us wealth beyond measure, but has taken away the chief benefit of wealth: the consciousness of having enough ... An elite that lives, plays and learns entirely separately from the general population will feel no bond of common citizenship with it ... The greatest barrier to mutual respect in most Western nations is the emergence, beginning in the 1970s, of a permanent body of state dependents ... who are now treated with open contempt. Another barrier to mutual respect is excessive inequality. This destroys respect not just for those at the bottom, but also those at the top, especially if their advantages are perceived as unmerited.

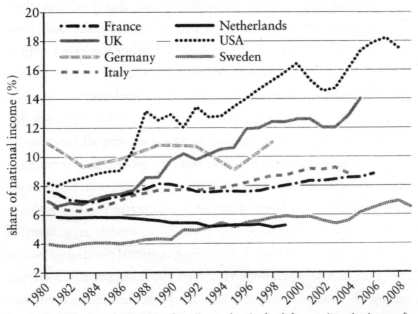

Source: World Top Incomes Database (http://g-mond.parisschoolofeconomics.eu/topincomes/)

In *What Money Cannot Buy*, Michael Sandel argues that we have drifted from a market economy to being a market society in which everything is for sale. In the introduction to his book, Sandel gives a few examples of what may now be bought and sold, including buying life insurance policies off the elderly and then collecting the death benefit when they die. The sooner the old person dies, the more the investor makes. This form of betting on the lives of the elderly has become a $30 billion industry in the US.

Sandel agrees with the Skidelskys that markets have become detached from morals and that it was a moral failing that led to the market triumphalism, greed and orgy of risk-taking that resulted in the crash of 2008. On inequality he says:

> In a society where everything is for sale, life is harder for those of modest means. The more money can buy, the more affluence (or the lack of it) matters ... as money comes to buy more and more – political influence, good medical care, a home in a safe neighbourhood rather than a crime-ridden one, access to elite schools rather than failing ones – the distribution of income and wealth looms larger and larger. Where all good things are bought and sold, having money makes all the difference in the world. This explains why the last few decades have been hard on poor and middle-class families. Not only has the gap between rich and poor widened, the commodification of every-thing has sharpened the sting of inequality by making money matter more.

It is odd that the extraordinary growth in inequality in Britain during the past thirty years did not become a topic for public discussion sooner, and was not a matter of concern to any of the main political parties, none of which was interested or had any idea what to do about it. The truth is that most were distracted whilst the economy was growing and failed to notice that Margaret Thatcher's famous 'trickle down' from the rich to the poor had failed to materialise. Then recession came, with sharp reductions in public expenditure which are quite clearly hurting the poor more than the rich. George Osborne's claim that 'we are all in this together' is implausible and regarded as such by an increasingly alert public. As a top-tax-rate-paying household, my partner and I are struggling to understand how a tax cut of 5 per cent will result in our paying more tax, as the government claims we will. Tax for the rich is largely optional. We may choose to pay stamp duty or not and to claim tax relief or not. Everyone else has no choice but to pay higher-rate tax if the threshold does not increase with inflation or to suffer if disability benefits are capped or cut. This is the absurdity of Alice-in-Wonderland politics, and it is dangerous because it corrodes trust, breeds cynicism and undermines any sense of mutual obligation.

Why does inequality matter so much? I am indebted to Professors Richard Wilkinson and Kate Pickett for their book, *The Spirit Level: Why Equality is Better for Everyone*. Noting that attitudes to inequality will vary according to different political views, the authors have conducted research that has made it possible to compare incomes in a range of countries and within the United States, and this enables us to make an objective rather than a subjective judgement based on whatever prejudices we may have.

Their research shows that where income differences are smaller, there is less violence, physical and mental health is better and life expectancy is higher. Prison populations are smaller, teenage pregnancies are fewer, children perform better and achieve more and there is less obesity. The surveys were conducted in some of the richest developed countries and in fifty states in the USA. The authors concede that inequality may not be the only cause of social ills but say that the scale of inequality is the most important single explanation of why health and social problems are more common in some societies than others.

Moreover, the research suggests that greater inequality has a deleterious effect upon the vast majority of a population. In more unequal societies, the well-paid middle classes are less likely to be healthy, more likely to be obese and more likely to be victims of violence. Their children perform less well at school and are more likely to use drugs and become teenage parents.

Wilkinson and Pickett say that the most important determining factors relating to our physical well-being and mental health are social status and relative income. They point out that the reason the USA has the highest rates of homicide, teenage pregnancy and imprisonment – and comes twenty-eighth in the international league table of life expectancy – is that it has the biggest income differences. By contrast, less rich countries such as Japan, Sweden and Norway, where income differences are smaller, do well on all these measures.

We must, of course, take personal responsibility for our own actions, but an intelligent approach might be to investigate what influences them. Wilkinson and Pickett point out that research has demonstrated that three social factors influence poor health: low social status, weak social networks, and isolation and poor quality childhood experience. Inequality is socially divisive. In the more equal societies, up to 60 per cent of the population agrees that 'most people can be trusted', but this falls to between 15 per cent and 25 per cent in more unequal societies.

In 'Values and Human Wellbeing' by Tim Kasser of Knox College, Illinois, a paper commissioned by the Rockefeller Foundation, the author reports that when people prioritise wealth, status and image above all else, they report lower feelings of well-being, less ability to empathise and a propensity to engage in behaviour likely to reduce other people's well-being. However, those who follow 'self-transcendent' values have a greater sense of affiliation with others and of commitment to community. They also report a greater sense of personal well-being.

Personal well-being would seem to have been a foreign concept to those engaged in the urban riots that shocked Britain in 2011. Why were the mostly young rioters 'not bothered'; why did they seem disengaged and disconnected? Ferdinand Mount, a Conservative and a former Head of the No. 10 Policy Unit writes in his book *The New Few*:

An analysis of more than 1,000 cases brought before magistrates' courts across England found that only 8.6 per cent of those [rioters] going through the courts were either students or employed. Over 90 per cent of them were unemployed. Over 90 per cent of them were also male. And two-thirds were under the age of twenty-five, but only 17 per cent were under the age of seventeen, although the eleven-year-olds caught on camera were so prominently featured and aroused such anguish about the future generation. Thus the rioters were predominantly young adults, male and unemployed. They were not graphic designers or sociology students or commis chefs. They were out of work.

...The truth, I think, is welcome to neither side in the political argument. It is that both Right and Left are more or less correct in their analysis. The collapse of many working-class families, white and black, is likely to leave adolescents in those families even more adrift than adolescents generally are. But it is also the case that young men who have a job to lose are less likely to riot than those who don't have one and cannot see much prospect of getting one. At the same time, the unbridled greed of the oligarchs and their indifference to the normal obligations and restraints do engender a sense that society has lost its recognisable moral shape and, with it, its legitimacy.

None of this begins to excuse riot, thieving or violence … but it does give us a clue as to who is most likely to riot and why. It may also lead us to the intimation that our society may now be fractured in a way that it was not in the past, however severe the poverty and inequality of that past.

For we now seem to have two detached classes, one at the bottom, the other at the top … For what is true of the underclass is, surprisingly, often true of the overclass too: the powerless are as unconnected to the rest of us as are the oligarchs … Neither class pays taxes to any great extent, the underclass because they have no income, the oligarchs because they are non-doms.

Whilst the quality of life in the developed world is incomparably better than it was fifty years ago and our societies have never been so wealthy in material terms, it seems that people are no happier. Moreover, the age of prosperity seems to be over for the foreseeable future. Austerity rules; the numbers of the poor are increasing, as is inequality. For most of our history, the best means of increasing quality of life has been to raise living standards through material growth. The potential for further growth may be limited and if we wish to improve the quality of life further then we must address our social problems and the quality of our social relations – which, as Wilkinson and Pickett point out, are determined by the scale of the inequalities between us.

Reducing inequality will be problematic, not least because there is no political will to impose higher taxes upon the wealthy, and capital is free to roam almost where it will. Moreover, the British people will not vote for the higher taxes to pay for the public services they say they want. The concept that the taxes we pay are for our membership of an educated, healthy, cultured and civilised society was undermined when tax rates were reduced in the 1980s and 1990s. In this climate, it is even less likely that the rich will be willing to pay what some would say is their fair share. A return to the punitive levels of tax in the recent past would almost certainly lead to even greater tax avoidance than we have now and there is evidence to suggest that increasing tax rates leads to lower revenues. Despite some billionaires in the US and France offering to pay more tax and to contribute to the public good, the UK coalition government has scrapped the top rate of fifty pence in the pound and reduced it to forty-five pence on the grounds that wealth creators will be deterred and decide to invest and live abroad. Some may, but there is little evidence that they will be joined in significant numbers. The views of those of us who are not wealth creators, who cannot countenance the idea of living in tax exile, who invest here and pay the top rate of tax, are deemed irrelevant.

We should be pragmatic. Whilst there is a moral case to be made that those who have more should pay more, it is a fact that the wealthy, some of whom pay a lower rate than the people they employ, will not contemplate paying higher tax rates, and there is no political support for insisting that they should. That may change should our economic circumstances deteriorate and if inequality were to increase even further, but for the time being the case for higher taxes is lost, killed off thirty years ago.

One way of addressing the inequality problem – and the sense of anger amongst the majority who have not shared in the increasing prosperity of the wealthiest 1 per cent in Britain – would be to encourage and celebrate more personal giving by the wealthy to causes which contribute to the benefit of a wider public, whether in health, education, science, international development, welfare, sport or the arts. More philanthropy will not replace the reductions in public spending currently under-way, but charitable giving is a means for the wealthy to be a part of, rather than apart from, society and to show a commitment to the common good. It cannot be in the long-term interests of the rich to insulate themselves from a society that is growing poorer. If the public sector cannot grow, we shall need to grow a stronger voluntary sector. And whilst the moral case for charitable giving is strong, philanthropy also offers donors opportunities for personal fulfilment and happiness that the wealthy often find so elusive despite having achieved all the material success they have been striving for.

I have written this book upon the premise that it is a minor-ity of the wealthy who are giving and that there is significant potential for many more of the rich to give a great deal more. The case becomes stronger when we are told that the bottom 10 per cent of the population gives three times more, proportion-ately, than the top 10 per cent. Before making the argument for the wealthiest to be much more generous, let us try to establish the status and condition of charitable giving in Britain today.

CHAPTER 2

How charitable are we?

'Philanthropy is the mechanism through which people express their humanitarian impulses and confirm their membership of a wider society.'
– Theresa Lloyd, *Why Rich People Give*, ACF, 2004

What is the status of charitable giving in Britain today? This is a difficult question to answer because those who provide the statistics cannot agree. According to the National Council for Voluntary Organisations (NCVO) and the Charities Aid Foundation (CAF), the overall amount of annual charitable giving declined by 20 per cent between 2010–11 and 2011–12, but these figures are contested by other authorities. UK and US research suggests that giving falls a bit in recessions but not at the same rate as the economy.

Whilst it is hard to track all giving by the wealthy because they may give anonymously or via private trusts and HMRC is reluctant to undertake more research, we can be confident about giving trends. We rely upon the 'Family Foundations Giving Trends' annual report,[†] 'Coutts Million Pound Donor Report'[‡] and HMRC's record of the number of higher and top-rate taxpayers claiming Gift Aid tax relief. For the record, the

---

† www.cgap.org.uk
‡ www.kent.ac.uk/sspssr/cphsj/documents/Million-Pound-Donor-Report-2012.pdf

most recent annual survey from NCVO and CAF for 2011–12 reports that:

- the overall amount given to charities by adults has fallen by 20 per cent in real terms compared with the previous year to £9.3 billion;
- in real terms, the estimated total for annual giving by adults in 2011–12 is the smallest it has been since the survey began in 2004–05. Both the proportion of people and the average amount given have decreased significantly. The largest amount donated, adjusted for inflation, was £12.6 billion in 2007–08, compared with £9.3 billion in 2011–12;
- the amount given to charitable causes in a typical month decreased over the previous year from a median gift of £11 to £10;
- the proportion of people giving to charitable causes in a typical month has decreased over the last year from 58 per cent to 55 per cent, equivalent to 28.4 million adults;
- donors giving £100 or more a month accounted for 40 per cent of total donations in 2011–12 compared to 45 per cent in 2010–11;
- causes supported by donors have not changed: medical research, hospitals and hospices, and children and young people continue to attract the highest proportion of donors.[†]

The 'Million Pound Donor Report' for 2012 is published by Coutts bank in association with the Centre for Philanthropy at the University of Kent and is researched by Dr Beth Breeze. This report shows that the number of donations of £1 million or more – and the number of donors giving them – has risen to its

---

† See figure 10, UK Giving 2012. NCVO and CAF.

highest recorded level but the overall value of these donations has fallen.

Key points in the 2012 report are:

- 232 donations worth £1 million or more were made by 130 separate donors compared with 201 donations in 2008. However, the value of these donations fell from £1.82 billion in 2006–07 to £1.2 billion in 2010–11.
- The median value of million-pound-plus donations has remained consistent at around £2 million in most of the years of the Coutts survey.
- Thirteen per cent of million-pound-plus donations are worth £10 million or more.
- Fifty-eight per cent of the million-pound donations in 2010–11 were donated by ninety-three individual donors or via personal foundations which gave a total of £763 million. However, the mean amounts given have fallen from £9.8 million in 2009–10 to £5.7 million in 2010–11.
- The distribution of million-pound donations was similar to previous years, the most common destination of donations being made to personal or family trusts for later distribution. However, a smaller share was 'banked' in 2010–11 than in previous years: only 48 per cent compared to 52 per cent in previous years.
- Higher education remains the most favoured cause for individual donors, followed by arts and culture, and international development.

'Family Foundation Giving Trends 2012' is the fifth in a series that annually updates the largest 100 family foundations in Britain. The report is produced by the ESRC Centre for Charitable Giving and Philanthropy at Cass Business

School, London, the Pears Foundation, a family foundation based in London, and the Centre for Charitable Giving
and Philanthropy.

Family foundations are defined as independent charitable
trusts funded originally by family wealth, whether or not the
family is represented on the governing board.

The findings of the 2012 report are that most family foundations are giving more to meet growing demand and despite
depressed asset values. The increase is almost certainly unsus-
tainable in the long term.

- The total giving of the 100 largest UK family foundations was
  £1.33 billion in 2010–11. Although there was an overall real
  fall of 1.8 per cent in giving, there was a substantial increase of
  6.2 per cent if the giant Wellcome Trust is excluded.
- The 6.2 per cent increase in donations bucked the trend for
  the value of family foundations' assets, which were 3.55 per
  cent lower than in the previous year.
- Asset value in 2010–11 was 14 per cent lower in real terms
  than in 2006–07.
- The giving of the largest family foundations has not yet
  returned to pre-recession levels.
- The authors report that the biggest single influence upon
  spending decisions is the reduction in public-sector welfare
  expenditure.
- Some foundations are maintaining or increasing spending
  despite declining asset values in order to meet demand following declining public expenditure. This cannot and will not
  continue indefinitely.
- Independence remains very important to family foundations
  and most see their role as complementing public expenditure
  rather than being in partnership with the public sector.

- Foundations are concerned about what will happen if resources fail to keep pace with increasing demand.
- Over half of foundations think there will be less funding from family foundations in the future.
- Forty-three per cent of foundations surveyed do not think the number of family foundations will increase over the next few years.

For a longer-term perspective of charitable giving in Britain, 'The New State of Donation', a report compiled by Cass Business School, City University London and the University of Bristol, surveyed three decades of giving in more than 205,000 households between 1978 and 2008.[†]

- Average weekly donations have increased over thirty-one years, but the rise in giving has only been in line with growth in the Gross Domestic Product (GDP). As a share of their total spending, households in 2008 were giving 0.4 per cent, the same as in 1978.
- Charitable giving is increasingly dependent upon the elderly. The over-65s now account for 35 per cent of all donations compared with 25 per cent in 1978. The figures are likely to reflect generational factors such as values and belief. The effect of the current recession upon youth unemployment came too late for this survey.

All these reports and surveys confirm that we are entitled to call ourselves a generous nation, although we rank eighth in the Charity Aid Foundation World Giving Index (2012) of the world's most charitable nations, in terms of the percentage

---

† www.cgap.org.uk/uploads/Presentations/SmithCowleyMcKenzie

of the population who regularly donate to charities, after Australia, Ireland, Canada, New Zealand, the United States, the Netherlands and Indonesia. However, according to a Philanthropy UK survey of giving as a percentage of GDP in the United States and Europe in 2006, Britain comes second with charitable giving accounting for 1.1 per cent of GDP, exactly half that of the US where giving accounts for 2.2 per cent of GDP.

Whilst we cannot be sure what is happening to charitable giving overall, we can be confident that the very rich are not giving very much. So who will support the voluntary sector as it struggles to cope with the problems left by reduced public funding? There appears to be no obvious answer. However, one thing is clear. Despite exceptional generosity from a minority, we cannot expect the wealthiest to come to the rescue. This is partly because established and experienced donors are wary of taking on responsibility for public programmes where the state is in retreat. However, the lack of a widespread culture of giving (and gratitude) in Britain, despite considerable reductions in tax rates, has not encouraged the better-off as a whole to be more charitable.

The claim that the poor are relatively more generous than the rich is contested by some on the reasonable grounds that the statistics are unreliable and we often find ourselves comparing apples with pears. Evidence from HMRC, however, convinces me that the sense amongst many philanthropists and fundraisers that the wealthiest are proportionately less generous is true. The only available figures on the use of Gift Aid tax breaks by income band relate to 2003–04 and they indicate that those who earn £200,000 or more give a far smaller proportion of their income to charity than those who are earning £50,000 or less. Those earning £50,000 or less are donating 0.62 per cent of their income compared with 0.21 per cent from those earning more than £200,000 per year.

In summary, this is what the evidence is telling us:

- The wealthy give proportionately less than the poor.
- Half of the richest 10 per cent in Britain do not give to charity.
- The combined wealth of the 1,000 wealthiest has increased by 283.5 per cent since 2000, to £414 billion.
- Only fifty-five people made donations of £1 million or more to other charities in 2010–11.

There is no evidence that the colossal increase in the personal wealth of the few has resulted in more charitable giving in Britain. Indeed, overall giving has only risen in line with GDP in the thirty years during which much of this wealth was accumulated, and it now seems to be in decline.

I believe this is a shocking indictment of the state of Britain today. What do the wealthy who *do* give actually think?

CHAPTER 3

Doing the right thing

'Not giving is bad for you and that is why the rich who are not charitable should be bothered.'
– British philanthropist, 2012

Those who give are the fiercest critics of those who do not. I interviewed more than seventy-five people whilst preparing this book. Fifty of them are philanthropists and forty-seven are resident in Britain and pay tax here. Most of them were highly critical of their peers who do not give and who do not pay tax. Here are a just a few examples of what I was told.

I talked to a leading figure in the financial sector who wished to remain anonymous, not just because of his controversial views and unrepeatable language, but because he gives away millions a year and cannot face being exposed to even more requests for money than he currently receives.

Donor A told me:

There is no moral case for not giving. People like [two high-profile figures from business and one rock star] are c***s because they are so f***ing mean. The fact that one of them transferred a billion overseas to avoid paying tax and was then given a knighthood should be a public scandal. How can I not give when so many people are starving? I couldn't live with myself if I didn't give. I am not that much cleverer and I don't work that much harder than other people. I have been incredibly fortunate in life. When my wealth exceeds a certain figure, I have to give it away and I don't intend to give to my children. People say they won't give because they are not sure about the worth of this charity or that. That is a pathetic excuse. You just do due diligence. You have to take risks in life sometimes. What do people think money is for?

Donor B is a successful and highly respected businessman in his mid-seventies and both he and his wife are philanthropic and have been honoured for services to charity:

In the last thirty years, some people have been making more money than at any time in human history and yet charitable giving has not kept pace with this explosion in personal wealth. I find this shocking when we see much poverty about us, particularly on our doorstep in London. Look at those giving lists and the donor boards in our arts organisations, universities and hospitals. Most of the billionaires are not there. They are not even giving anonymously. I do not understand it. I am not impressed when I am told a billionaire has given 1 per cent of his assets. He is left with 99 per cent of a colossal fortune, money he cannot possibly need.

Victoria Sharp was born in the United States but has lived in Britain for many years, working with Goldman Sachs before founding her own music and education charity, London Music Masters (LMM). She cannot understand how people who are selfish can be happy. She feels provoked by her peers who do not give, particularly those who are wealthier than she is:

Whilst I realise that for some who are newly wealthy, they feel the need to wrap their arms around it, some of those living in London with literally billions are parsimonious beyond belief. They have all the benefits of living here. Whilst they may not use the National Health Service, many enjoy everything else London has to offer and give little or nothing. They are simply motivated by greed. For those of us with millions, it is important to give. For those with *billions*, it is unthinkable for them not to give. We must find a way of motivating them to give.

Sir Simon Robertson, formerly of Goldman Sachs and now chairman of Rolls-Royce, and a major benefactor known for his generosity, told me: 'In these past twenty years, people have become extraordinarily, unbelievably rich. What strikes me about these people, with some honourable exceptions, is how incredibly mean they are. They have no concept of duty, responsibility or obligation'.

Roland Rudd founded Finsbury (global strategic communications firm) in 1994 and, following the merger with RLM in 2011, he now chairs one of the world's largest financial communications groups. Roland also chairs Legacy 10, a charity that campaigns for more legacy donations to charitable causes.

Only a minority of the wealthy are being generous. Also, too many companies are not paying their full tax which is extremely frustrating. It is doubly frustrating that some of the wealthiest are not only not giving but not paying their tax. This is an extraordinary indictment of people who have no shame about opting out of society. Some of those who have been honoured are the worst. I think if you are going to be honoured for being successful, you must also show that you have been generous to others by giving to charity. I think people with money who do not give are both unimaginative and mean.

Donor C is now a philanthropist following a career in fund management.

I was not brought up to give. We were very poor when I was a child because my mother was widowed when I was eleven. We lived on a widow's pension. I went to school with holes in my trousers. That is why I am wired to poverty and exclusion. People tend to have black-and-white views about charities and use them as a defensive ploy to stop any possibility of them being asked for money. People have such a strange relationship with money.

The fundamental point we have to consider is where philanthropy, at every level of giving, sits in the value chain. The poor have a culture of giving. If they don't give, things won't happen. Giving is high up in their value system and that is why they give proportionately more than the rich. I was speaking at a conference and a titled woman came up to me afterwards and said she would give more 'if only they would reduce taxes'. I turned to her and said: 'What do you value more? £50,000 for a new Mercedes or a donation to alleviate poverty?'

Surely that is the most important question we should be asking, but it doesn't get asked often enough. Amongst the upper-middle and upper classes, the priorities are a nice house and staff, a second house, private school fees, several expensive holidays a year and then when we get to the end of a very long list and we see something on TV about Comic Relief or a natural disaster, they think perhaps we should write a cheque, and it might be quite a large one because they feel guilty, but they don't *value* it. People are making frivolous decisions about clothes, cars and holidays. We must find a way of persuading people that thinking about other people and giving is an important and *valuable* thing to do. Why don't people get it?

Michael Oglesby is founder and chairman of Bruntwood, a property company with its headquarters in Manchester. Together, the company and the family foundation are giving away £2 million a year.

People who do not give? That staggers me. I have given a great deal of money over the years. We have huge problems in our country and we cannot ignore them. We must find a way of engaging those who arc selling businesses and are making a fortune. There they are, a new yacht here and a new gin palace there and I think, for heaven's sake! Philanthropy is so much more important and so much more fun than business. Those who are not involved in philanthropy have no idea how much fun they are missing.

Donor D is a well-established philanthropist who gives away several hundred thousand pounds a year.

Consider the unfairness of those who live in Monaco, come back here to their house for so many nights of the year and expect the country to be running properly when they are here, the airport to work, for the police to turn up when they are burgled, these are expensive things that need to be paid for out of taxation. Who do they think has paid for that bit of the M4 between Heathrow and Brentford before they cruise in to Knightsbridge? Some of them may give the odd million here and there but it won't be the same as 50 per cent of their income. They are possibly 'giving' just 5 per cent of their income.

What has gone wrong is any sense of responsibility. The real problem is this non-dom business. The United States has it absolutely right. If you want a US passport, you must pay US tax wherever you are. This non-dom problem is causing such inequality and such bad feeling in Britain. Everyone should pay tax and then be given the instruments to be more charitable. We currently have a system that positively encourages tax avoidance and we do not have a tax-efficient system that encourages people to be charitable.

We should be encouraging people to make money but giving them the means and incentives to give money. That is the state's job and it has to be more imaginative about its role in encouraging giving. Philanthropy achieved a lot in Victorian times, but children were still dying in the streets. We don't want to go back to that, but we can grow our charity sector more whilst the state maintains its commitment to the NHS and the common good.

Our problem is that not enough people are committed to the concept of the common good. The NHS and the service it offers to everyone is a hallmark of Britain today. You can choose to go to a private hospital if you are rich, but if you pay your taxes you are contributing to the NHS and to the wider common good. The rationing of treatment is therefore wrong if you are not paying your taxes.

I don't think being mean and being unimaginative are the same thing. Mean means mean and some people are very mean indeed. Not giving is bad for you and that is why the rich should be bothered. By not taking up the possibility of giving, some of the rich are generating a culture in which they are despised. If we continue to have a society that encourages unfairness and a lack of responsibility, if some of the rich fail to engage and to contribute, then we are heading for trouble.

When thinking about writing this book, I talked with colleagues and some of those benefactors I have come to know and was surprised by the strength of the feelings they expressed about those who do not give. They are fed up because a majority of their peers will not accept that they have a responsibility to contribute as donors and taxpayers. However, I have been struck by something much more important. Without exception, everyone I have spoken to who appears in this book and at least 90 per cent of the philanthropists I have worked with over thirty years are driven by a desire and a determination to do good for others rather than for themselves. The most common refrain about giving is: 'It seems the right thing to do.' They are making a moral commitment and they mind when they see a lack of morality in their peers.

Our purpose is to persuade and encourage those who are not giving to explore and discover philanthropy, to understand that those with wealth may use their power for good, that they can help to change the world and in doing so find personal fulfilment and pleasure. We will not succeed in recruiting more philanthropists simply by attacking those who do not give. Having expressed our frustration, we should follow the example and optimism of Eglantyne Jebb, founder of Save the Children, who said the world is not ungenerous, merely unimaginative. So before we hear first-hand stories of those who are giving now, let us try to stimulate the imagination of those who are not by exploring what giving means, how it has helped our species to survive and grow, and how it has helped us to create the civilisations of the past and the civil society we enjoy today.

CHAPTER 4

Why we give and why we don't: a brief history of philanthropy

'It has always seemed strange to me … the things we admire in men, kindness and generosity, openness, honesty, understanding and feeling are the concomitants of failure, and those traits we detest, sharpness, greed, acquisitiveness, meanness, egotism and self-interest are the traits of success.'
– John Steinbeck

We are in Afghanistan. It is the night of 8 October 2010. Fourteen members of a US Navy Seals Team dropped from two special forces helicopters to mount a rescue mission. The attempt failed. Linda Norgrove, a young British aid worker who had been kidnapped by the Taliban, died.

Later, I watched an interview with her parents, John and Lorna Norgrove, on *Channel 4 News*. Lorna said:

We certainly don't want to enter the blame game … We are just immensely proud of what she was doing in Afghanistan and we want to continue her work in some way. She knew I wasn't keen on her going back but there was no way as a parent that I would stop her doing that. I knew she had grown to love Afghanistan and loved the people and I knew that was where her heart was.

She wanted to do humanitarian work there and I think that was what was important to her. And what she felt she had to do. We feel the need to move forward to something to help continue her humanitarian work.

John Norgrove continued: 'So we are setting up a charitable foundation, the Linda Norgrove Foundation, the aims of which are to undertake humanitarian work, initially in Afghanistan aimed at helping women, children and families.'

The Norgroves, who live on the Isle of Lewis in the Hebrides, are not particularly wealthy. However, they donated £100,000 to the foundation. This was matched by £100,000 from the Scottish government, and with further donations from Linda's employer and the public, nearly £340,000 was donated in the foundation's first year.

I was mesmerised by the interview with the Norgroves, by their dignity, composure, compassion, empathy, selflessness and generosity. I am very grateful to John and Lorna for giving me permission to write about Linda at the risk of intruding upon private feelings. I was transfixed as I watched and listened to them. Later, I realised that this moment was the genesis of an idea to write a book about giving. John Norgrove told me: 'We are all in favour of trying to get people to give more. We firmly believe one of the main problems today is people focusing on what they think they need rather than looking outwards.'

The Norgroves made me think about what giving means, why people give and why they don't. Giving is clearly important, and it is a word we use on countless occasions daily without thinking.

Are we wired to give and has the altruistic gene been as important as its egotistical twin in our evolution? Has cooperation, sharing and generosity been the key to human survival? We learn from research that monetary rewards and charitable giving activate a primitive part of the brain that also responds to food and sex. Research also shows other circuits are stimulated, relating to social bonding, suggesting that giving as an expression of altruism is not just a superior moral factor designed to suppress selfish, destructive urges, but that it is hardwired into us and designed to give pleasure.

So it would seem that empathy and emotional intelligence gave us an evolutionary advantage by encouraging us to work together as well as to compete, and to live in social groups. We became more social the more we understood each other.

The earliest hunters apparently signalled their ability, power and reproductive prowess by holding large feasts and sharing food. One could argue that not much has changed. Women were supposed to find altruistic men more attractive because they were more likely to share meat with them and their children. Claims have been made that because we are only the species that cooks, cuisine is the foundation of civilisation as we know it today. Rituals around the preparation and sharing of food have been central to our behaviour as social animals.

As human society developed, gifts were used to buy peace, to express affection, loyalty and unity. A sense of social obligation began to emerge, a need to give and to repay backed up with sanctions of moral enforcement, namely shame, guilt and dishonour. So we can see that exchanges and giving in these societies were not primarily economic. They had moral significance. They were also not always altruistic, sometimes being used to reinforce status, power and wealth. Nevertheless, we can see that we developed a biological need to help others because this was the best way to sustain and prolong life. Evolution has shaped us by favouring altruism as well as ambition and the urge to compete. And so we learned how to serve others and to be generous to strangers.

I doubt if theories proposed by neurobiologists, psychologists and anthropologists do justice to Linda Norgrove and her parents except to say that what moved me and others I know who saw their television interview was that it was such a powerful and perfect demonstration of humanity. I realised what an exceptional experience that is and I began to wonder if we are in danger of losing it.

❦

'Would you give blood to a stranger?' I asked a friend. 'Of course', she replied, 'why ever wouldn't you?' I have never given blood and, to my shame, I realise that it was probably that I couldn't be bothered rather than squeamishness.

Writing this book has led me into unexpected territory and to a remarkable book, *The Gift Relationship: From Human Blood to Social Policy*, by Richard Titmuss, who writes:

> There is a bond that links all men and women in the world so closely and intimately that every difference of colour, religious belief and cultural heritage is insignificant beside it. Never varying in temperature more than five or six degrees, composed of 55 per cent water, the life-stream of blood proves that the family of man is a reality.

Titmuss's chapter on transfusion is an inspiring, poetic read and reminds us that 'the very thought of blood, individual blood, touches the deepest feelings in man about life and death'. Our interest in blood here is in those who give theirs and their reasons for doing so. In Britain, blood is given, whereas in some other countries, blood is bought and sold. Titmuss was fascinated by the gift of blood because it is offers donors a rare opportunity to make a moral commitment to those outside the family or a circle of friends and colleagues, to what Titmuss calls 'the universal stranger'. Those who give their own life force are motivated by a concept of fellowship.

Here are a few of the results from a survey of almost 4,000 people conducted in 1967, quoted by Titmuss. They were asked to say why they first decided to become a blood donor.

'Knowing I mite be saving somebody's life.' [sic]

'You cannot get blood from supermarkets and chaine stores.' [sic]

'No man is an island.'

'I thought it just a small way to help people. As a blind person, other opportunities are limited.'

'Just to help the hospitals.'

'I get my surgical shoes through the NHS. This is some return as I want to help people.'

'To help babies that are born with bad blood.'

'Some unknown person gave blood to save my wife's life.'

'My husband collapsed and died aged 41, without whom life is very lonely so I thought my blood might help to save someone the heartache I have had.'

'Feeling guilt at having received so much in life and having given so little.'

'Sense of duty to the community and to the nation as a whole.'

'No money to spare, plenty of blood to spare.'

❧

We know, of course, that not everyone is charitable. Why do people not give? I am indebted to a report published by the Institute for Public Policy Research (IPPR) in 2002. In

'A Bit Rich? What the Wealthy Think about Giving', the authors discuss Stanley Cohen's book *States of Denial*. Cohen demonstrates that denial is a natural instinct, a way of making difficult truths easier to live with. 'There is implicatory denial (it's not my responsibility or I don't have trust or confidence in charities), interpretive denial (I am not wealthy, I am just comfortable) and literal denial (I do give, meaning only small change in a tin).'

Here a few quotations from wealthy non-donors who are in various states of denial. I doubt if many are blood donors.

'There are people begging on the streets but they are not homeless so I don't give money to them or to homeless charities.'

'You have made your money; you do what you want with it.'

'You bury your head in the sand, you know, when it's almost as if there are so many problems that it is easier not to think about them and you don't bother.'

'People who are poorer, they come into contact with people that need help more and therefore they relate to it better. They might know someone who is homeless or someone who has got some hideous illness and cannot afford the treatment … whereas people who are rich don't talk to people like that.'

'The welfare state is crumbling. Things we used to be able to rely upon we cannot any more therefore we have to pay out of our own pocket, like education, health cover and pensions. We are forced to be selfish to cover our own needs. You think of your own needs.'

'I resent giving to charities when it shouldn't be charities supporting whatever that need is. Charity should not be stepping into the breach; it should be done by taxation and good government.'

'I paid £27,000 in tax last year, which is sort of giving to charity in my view. I am paying more than other people. The welfare state is a safety net for people who cannot support themselves ... I have never had anything out of it.'

'To me charities are just mercenary systems for generating income for a whole bunch of administrators who will charge whatever they bloody well please. Whatever ends up in the actual hands of the people to whom you have actually contributed, it's an incredible stroke of luck as far as I can see.'

'For me the most efficient form of charity is to find a project that might actually benefit mankind ... that is far more effective than feeding billions of people who don't contribute very much but stagger along killing each other half the time.'

'I am jaded.'

Towards the beginning of my fundraising career, I was advised by one of my trustees that the world is divided between those who give and those who don't, the implication being not to waste valuable time upon people such as those quoted above. This is almost certainly sound advice when dealing with pessimists, but I am an optimist, which is an essential quality for those who have to raise money.

My optimism compels me to persuade those who could be persuaded that giving time and giving money can make a meaningful difference to the lives of others as well as to our own. To be persuaded, the doubters need evidence. We are genetically programmed to be philanthropic and we are in danger of taking a wrong turn, in evolutionary terms, by becoming more selfish and creating more and more inequality. Perhaps those who are yet unconvinced need to know rather more about who philanthropists are, what they have achieved in the past as well as the present, why they became philanthropists, what motivates and guides them and what kind of people they are.

Theresa Lloyd wrote *Why Rich People Give* in 2004,[†] the first British research report into attitudes of wealthy people towards philanthropy. She is writing a sequel (to be published in 2013), with Dr Beth Breeze of the University of Kent, author of the 'Coutts Million Pound Donor Report', to reflect current circumstances and in the context of a huge increase in private wealth despite recession. Amongst Lloyd's prime concerns in 2004 was to find out why people in the United States appear to be more generous than those in Britain and why the younger generation of those who had made fortunes in finance and IT were not giving. As data on giving by the wealthiest is limited, she interviewed eighty-six donors, who remained anonymous, from a range of ages, backgrounds, sources of wealth and approaches to philanthropy. The majority of those interviewed were worth between £5 million and £100 million, with incomes between £100,000 and £2 million, although some had much greater wealth. Those interviewed reported their giving as between 5 per cent and 10 per cent of income, although it actually ranged from under 1 per cent to 25 per cent.

Lloyd identifies five main motivations, incentives and rewards:

1. Belief in the cause is the strongest motivator, and choice of a cause is often influenced by a wish to effect change in line with a particular interest or belief;
2. 'Being a catalyst for change' is the next strongest motivator and includes 'making a real difference' and 'getting value for money';

---

† London: Philanthropy UK, Association of Charitable Foundations, 2004; www.acf.org.uk

3. 'Self-actualisation' covers personal development, applying expertise in a different sector, learning new skills, directing money which might otherwise go to the government, addressing causes with a personal connection and defining a place in history;

4. 'Duty and responsibility' is about the satisfaction of conscience, the obligation of the privileged to those less fortunate and the desire to 'put something back';

5. 'Relationships' encompasses the fun, enjoyment and personal fulfilment of involvement with people, including the senior staff of charities, beneficiaries and other donors. Donor networks are important, as is a desire to join them.

I wanted to know more and so I also talked to seventy-seven donors, volunteers, charities, their trustees and those who have benefited from other people's generosity, most of whom agreed to be on the record. However, before interviewing, I needed to gain context by finding out how philanthropy began and what influence it has had upon the way we live now.

※

The first indications that doing good might be a good thing are found in the Egyptian *Book of the Dead*, where it is reported that a smooth passage to the afterlife may be guaranteed by a record of benevolence. From the start, religion determined the moral foundations of philanthropy. In Greek mythology, the first philanthropist was Prometheus, who shared the gift of divine fire with ordinary mortals although he suffered at the hands of the furious gods. Hermes, Eros and Dionysius were considered philanthropic for their gifts of protection for travellers, sexual desire, and alcoholic liberation from anxiety.

The concept of charitable status began in sixth century BC Greece when tax exemption was offered to hospitals, orphanages and schools. Wealthy citizens were encouraged to fund temples, armouries, city walls and granaries. Philanthropy became a badge of pride, an emblem of civic loyalty and commitment. Groups of the wealthy, no doubt inspiring their successors at the National Theatre, Glyndebourne and the Royal Opera House, commissioned plays, funded productions and supported festivals of drama.

In ancient Rome, Emperors were expected to win the support of the public by providing public baths and gladiatorial games, even free haircuts and olive oil, and funding art and literature. In Greek and Roman society it was understood that benefactors would receive public recognition in return for their generosity. Marcus Aurelius, who was Roman Emperor between AD 161 and 169, made a law that gifts of legacies may be made in perpetuity, providing the legal framework for our trusts and foundations today.

The concept of charity and concern for others lies at the root of most religions. Jewish philanthropy continues to make a contribution in Britain out of all proportion to the number of Jews who live here. We owe a debt of gratitude to the Rothschild, Wolfson, Rayne, Sieff, Hamlyn, Clore and Pears families in particular. This is partly because one of the guiding principles of Jewish life is *tzedakah*, or justice. Meaning more than charity, *tzedakah* instructs that one should do what is right not because it is good but because it is just. Poverty is considered an injustice and it is also important that the dignity of those who are helped must be respected. Because of the importance of *tzedakah*, a highly developed sense of community and obligation is at the heart of Jewish culture.

Christianity developed the Roman view that giving was

obligatory for the wealthy and powerful and taught that charity was an expression of love and of humanity. A good Christian should help anyone. When Christianity grew from being a fringe cult into a state religion following the conversion of the Emperor Constantine in AD 312, its principles and practice formed much of our world as we now know it. It is striking that Roman society, from the top to the bottom, adopted a religion that seemed to promote the transfer of wealth from the rich to the poor, particularly as at least 90 per cent of the population lived in poverty and the wealthy minority enjoyed abundant luxury. However, the Empire would not have survived so long if it had been unable to feed its people. The Roman tradition of bread and circuses was founded upon the need to maintain power, often the main ingredient in the earliest manifestations of philanthropy. Subsequently, a more sophisticated culture of giving developed as the wealthy financed an expansive programme of building churches. And whilst the wealthiest may have engaged in competitive acts of generosity, those of modest means too found ways of contributing to an immense building programme that also provided employment. Gradually, giving morphed from transfers of wealth from the very rich to the very poor to an extraordinarily successful fundraising campaign for the church. The rise of the church depended upon the redistribution of surplus wealth until the point came when it grew so powerful that the exercise of religious power and state power became indivisible.

By the Renaissance in the fifteenth century, the church was growing ever more powerful, fuelled by the sale of indulgences – a form of investment designed to offer insurance against spending perpetuity in hell not only for sins committed but for those that might be committed in the future. The church's accumulation of colossal wealth coincided with the rise of banking and an age of extraordinary cultural patronage of which the infamous Medici family were the supreme example. Five hundred and thirty years later, there was an exhibition staged in Florence in the autumn of 2012 called *Money and Beauty: Bankers, Botticelli and the Bonfire of the Vanities*. The Medici Bank failed, but their patronage of great artists lives on in the world's great galleries and museums, as does the Catholic Church, which remains immensely wealthy but somewhat diminished in terms of temporal power.

Philanthropy had more modest beginnings in Britain. St John's Hospital in Malmesbury is mentioned in a charter dated AD 939, the date of its foundation being unclear. Benedict Nightingale reports in his book *Charities* that the hospital now consists of three flats for the elderly. This was known as 'parish pump charity'. Nightingale describes The Hospital of St Cross near Winchester where visitors would ask for 'wayfarer's dole', which was a loaf and two pints of rough wine. 'It might have included a place at dinner in the great hall that evening. Now, it has been reduced to a postage stamp of bread and a few sips of beer; but it is still free and still available to all, impecunious or not.'

Philanthropy grew and helped to establish the foundations of society as we know it today. In the twelfth century, London's oldest hospital, St Bartholomew's, or Barts, was built, being funded mostly by the Bishop of London and Henry I in the form of a gift of land. As early as AD 325, the Church had agreed that bishops should be responsible for running hospitals in all cathedral cities and in AD 511, it was decided that they should devote a quarter of all church revenues to the relief of poverty, the first manifestation of a form of welfare state. At that time, the rich gave to the church primarily to pay for prayers after their death. However, St Francis of Assisi and his mission to serve the poor became more influential, leading to the founding of hospitals and almshouses throughout Europe. By the fourteenth century, cities became the major centres of wealth with the growth of a new merchant class that made money from trade and banking rather than land ownership.

In fifteenth-century France, Nicholas Roulin, Chancellor to the Duke of Burgundy, founded a hospital, the Hotel-Dieu de Beaune, or Hospice of Beaune, its mission being to support the poor and sick. Roulin was not of noble birth but he became one of the most powerful men in the Duchy through his philanthropy in the wake of the Hundred Years' War. The splendid buildings of the Hospice and its collection of art are still standing in Beaune today, although the hospital has moved to the outskirts of the town. Five hundred years later, we may continue to support the charity and find great pleasure in doing so by participating in the annual auction of top-quality burgundy harvested from the vineyards bequeathed to it.

In England, the system of Poor Laws was first formalised between 1587 and 1598 and, subject to amendment in 1834, these remained in place until the welfare state emerged after 1945.

In the intervening period, an increasing number of philanthropists helped to define the way we live now.

Many who attend fundraising gala concerts may not know that amongst the first to pioneer this often successful if exhausting form of philanthropy was the composer George Frederick Handel. Handel was a patron and governor of the Foundling Hospital, founded in 1739 by Thomas Coram, a shipbuilder, the first of its kind to care for the homeless children he found living and dying on the streets of London. The suffering of these children can barely be imagined. In 1749, Handel gave a benefit concert to fund the completion of the chapel. The concert, attended by the Prince and Princess of Wales, included a newly found work, the 'Foundling Hospital Anthem', which concluded with the 'Hallelujah Chorus'. Such was the success of the concert, another was arranged for the following year and Handel gave a benefit performance of *Messiah* every year until his death in 1759. In addition to donating an organ to the chapel, Handel raised over half a million pounds for the Foundling Hospital. All of Handel's warmth and compassion, as well as his wit, is apparent in his music.

The artist William Hogarth was also an important supporter of the Foundling Hospital. He donated his own paintings to decorate the walls of the hospital. Other artists followed his example and so the first British art gallery was founded. The collection is on view today in the Foundling Museum in Brunswick Square, London.

So much of what we take for granted in almost every aspect of our lives – the works of genius that have determined what we know, what we think, what we see and read, what we say, hear and sing, and what we do – began with an act of creation that was often nurtured by patronage and philanthropy, whether by the state, the church or the rich and powerful.

Modern philanthropy and the growth of charities evolved with the start of the industrial revolution in the eighteenth century and the rapid expansion of the British Empire in the nineteenth century, when Britain became the wealthiest and most powerful nation upon earth. By the 1890s, government was spending about 5 per cent of GDP and philanthropy was at a peak. By the 1960s, government was spending over 50 per cent of GDP, much of it on the welfare state, and philanthropy and volunteering appeared to be in decline.

In order to grasp the significance of these developments, I visited Dr Frank Prochaska, a history don at Somerville College, Oxford. Prochaska is the author of a number of acclaimed books on philanthropy and social history. We talked about the changing relationship between the government and the people in that time. The Victorians held their governments in esteem but expected little from them in terms of solving social issues. In a Christian culture they believed that poverty could be banished and that this could be achieved by voluntary service. A century later, an opinion poll suggested that 90 per cent of the British believed that there was no longer a role for charity because the abolition of poverty was the responsibility of the state, along with health and education. Responsibility for welfare provision resided in the political process.

In a lecture Prochaska gave in 2012, he posed a paradox:

With the rise of collectivism, the payment of taxes had become the primary civic duty. Individuals could take satisfaction from paying their taxes, but they were in many ways more impotent in an age of universal suffrage and parliamentary democracy than their disadvantaged ancestors had been under an oligarchic system. Paradoxically, there was more social connectedness in the age of Queen Victoria, with all its class distinctions and fear of representative democracy, than in modern Britain, with its New Jerusalem egalitarianism. Those very distinctions and fears made social contact within and between classes essential. Self-governing institutions, from lowly mothers' meetings to the mighty voluntary hospitals, had connected citizens to their communities and gave them a measure of direct control over their own affairs. In an era of religious commitment, limited government and strong local allegiances, social responsibility was not simply a corollary of privilege but a corollary of citizenship.

I had not appreciated the significance of the role of women in philanthropy or understood the importance of working-class philanthropy. Prochaska told me:

A level of emancipation of women came about through their involvement in charitable causes. It was something they were free to do and a means of expressing themselves. By the middle of the nineteenth century, women were founding their own institutions. These were often middle-class women, many living quiet country lives, who would have little to occupy their time otherwise. The law defining married women's property rights meant they could give away their own money.

Women had fewer opportunities for self-expression than men in the nineteenth century, and charity offered them an outlet for their talents as well as an opportunity to develop interests in education, health, law, prisons and both local and national government. As members of charities, women established their right to vote in terms of deciding how funds should be allocated. Through philanthropy, women who had been involved in charities became prominent in the suffragette movement.

Many of the great reformers in the eighteenth and nineteenth centuries were women. Elizabeth Fry (1780–1845) was a member of the Gurney family, Quakers who founded Gurney's bank, and her mother was a Barclay. She used her banking fortune to further prison and social reform. Octavia Hill (1838–1912) became a pioneer in the provision of social housing and insisted the working classes were represented on her committees. She is most renowned for founding the National Trust. Josephine Butler (1828–1906) campaigned for the welfare of prostitutes. Angela Burdett-Coutts (1814–1906) became the wealthiest woman in Europe when she inherited a fortune of £3 million in 1837, most of which she spent on scholarships, endowments and the relief of poverty. Most notably, she established the National Society for the Prevention of Cruelty to Children and was influential in the founding of the Royal Society for the Prevention of Cruelty to Animals. Burdett-Coutts's philanthropy was recognised by Queen Victoria in 1870 when she was granted a peerage. She was buried in Westminster Abbey.

Other great Victorian philanthropists have made their mark on our century. Joseph Rowntree (1836–1925) made a childhood trip to Ireland and witnessed the effects of the potato famine that killed over a million people. He dedicated his life to eradicating poverty and improving the lives of others. After taking over the family confectionery business, the Quaker philanthropist was not content to be the King of Chocolate but transformed business practice, set up a model village for the poor and provided his employees with one of the first pension funds, free education, a library, doctor and dentist. In 1904, he gave away half his wealth to set up three trusts, one of which became the Joseph Rowntree Foundation, which today spends more than £10 million a year funding poverty studies.

In 2012, the Rowntree trustees described their mission as follows:

We are a Quaker Trust which seeks to transform the world by supporting people who address the root causes of conflict and injustice.

Joseph Rowntree was always very clear on one thing: for your efforts to have any lasting benefit, you must tackle the roots of a problem. If you only treat the 'superficial manifestations' of poverty or social injustice or political inequality, then you will ease the symptoms for a time, but make no lasting difference … We want to engage in philanthropy which changes the existing power imbalances in society to effect real change.

We place ourselves deliberately at the cutting edge of difficult and contentious issues and we want to support change towards a better world … Our interest is in removing problems, not in making them easier to live with.

Joseph Rowntree's mission is as relevant today as it was more than a hundred years ago and his commitment to finding lasting solutions continues to inspire donors and charities. Others who also made a lasting impact were George Cadbury, William Hesketh Lever, Henry Wellcome and George Peabody (1795–1869), an American banker who transformed the prospects of the poor by building the Peabody estates in London. At that time, conditions for the working classes were so bad that basements were awash with sewage. Upstairs, the dead lay with the living and both were tormented by rats. As many as thirty people might share a room, lying on stinking rags. There was no central water supply and there were frequent outbreaks of cholera. The Peabody Trust was amongst the first to provide decent housing for the poor of Victorian London and George Peabody was hailed in his lifetime as 'the most liberal philanthropist of ancient or modern times'.

Frank Prochaska reminded me that philanthropy and volunteering were not only the preserve of the very rich but were deeply engrained throughout Victorian society, including the working classes.

The assumption that the working classes are not charitable is quite wrong and very damaging. If the twentieth century may be described as the age of collectivism, the nineteenth century was the age of Societies.

Historians often take the view that charity is a form of social control, which confirms the power of the rich and keeps the poor in their place. I take a different view, which takes into

account the philanthropy of the working classes, which is a
subject that has eluded most historians. Perhaps unconsciously,
historians who see philanthropy in conventional class terms
have tended to perpetuate the view that working men possessed
little feeling or humanity, when in fact egalitarian benefi-
cence came naturally to the poor and was essential for their
domestic economy. As a cleric in south London remarked in
1908, 'The poor breathe an atmosphere of charity. They cannot
understand life without it. And it is largely this kindness of the
poor to the poor which stands between our present civilisation
and revolution.'

Hospitals were amongst the charities supported by the poor.
More than half the income of several hospitals in the north
of England came from 'workmen'. Miners funded hospitals in
Wales. Royal patronage became a means of encouraging philanthropy from the working classes. The League of Mercy was
founded in 1899 to establish a large body of voluntary workers
which would assist with the establishment and maintenance of
voluntary hospitals. The league raised £600,000 from 'artisans,
tradesmen and humble subscribers' for the voluntary hospitals
before they were nationalised in 1948.

The records show that they [working people] established
their own Sunday schools, charity schools, soup kitchens, wash-
houses, temperance societies, Salvation Army shelters, boot and
clothing clubs, servants' institutions, navvy missions, sick clubs,
mothers' meetings and visiting societies. When they cooperated
with their wealthier neighbours, as in hospital provision, education or the arts, their philanthropy acted as a springboard into
the existing social system.

To many people in Britain today, the very idea of Victorian
philanthropy has an air of quaintness about it. But as we reject
the piety and social hierarchy of our forebears, we tend to forget

that benevolence and neighbourliness, self-help and helping others were amongst the most urgent of Victorian values. We also tend to forget how much of Britain's idealism and democratic culture grew out of these values.

Most of us, particularly readers of Charles Dickens, would not wish to return to those grim days, however much we may admire the dynamism, ambition and optimism of our forebears. Poverty and the problems it spawned became too much for the voluntary sector to bear. Demands for state action grew, adopted by the Liberal Party initially and subsequently by the Labour Party in the first half of the twentieth century. The welfare state was established after the Labour Party won a landslide election victory in 1945, voted into power by a people battered by two world wars and a determination not to return to the poverty, deprivation and inequality of the previous 100 years.

Prochaska told me:

A contentious issue is whether the welfare state made life more difficult for the voluntary sector. After the Second World War, a great many voluntary traditions disappeared altogether. During the 1930s, there were over 50,000 female voluntary district visitors and by the end of the war there were almost none. The tradition of that sort of social work had collapsed. If you read histories written in the 1950s, you will come across a profound lament for a tradition destroyed by the government, but the romance of the ideal of the NHS has meant this has been largely forgotten, even a hostility from the Labour left because they saw everything in class terms. They forgot about the working-class tradition and friendly societies.

There was no need for children to be taught the concepts of

citizenship and civil society when we had a Christian ethos that taught we should serve our fellow men. Social stability requires looking after other people. That began falling apart towards the end of the nineteenth century when growing segregation of the classes posed a problem for philanthropy and threw the working classes back on their own resources.

Philanthropy is an individual tradition. There is no easy matching-up of voluntary giving with state provision. In the US, the philanthropic tradition is more robust and somehow more old-fashioned, but I don't see Britain going back to a nineteenth-century model. We need to find a companionable solution and there needs to be some tension so that people are convinced of the need for philanthropy.

The idea of the Big Society is extremely misleading because in a sense it should be called the Small Society. David Cameron says he wants more localism and parish solutions but all governments want to consolidate rather than cede power. Margaret Thatcher trumpeted Victorian values but she did not always promote them. Under the guise of Victorian Liberalism, she carried forward the very collectivist agenda that she had disavowed, which won her few friends in the voluntary sector.

Prochaska's world view poses exactly the kind of intellectual challenge we need as we find ourselves struggling in a world where nothing seems certain any more. Libertarian and sceptical, his perspective suits the times when Gordon Brown whilst in opposition described charity as 'a sad and seedy competition for public pity', but only a few years later launched the Giving Campaign as Chancellor of the Exchequer in the first New Labour government. Whither philanthropy when religion is in decline, the state is in retreat and its role is disputed, we are crippled by debt and most people are poorer in both cash and time? Are the newly super-rich prepared to offer the leadership shown by their predecessors in centuries past?

We are, however, ahead of ourselves. We should first hear from those working for charities and from those who are giving now as to what they believe personal generosity may achieve in the most difficult circumstances facing us for generations. We need to find out whether or not the spirit of humanity, as embodied by the Norgrove family, is flourishing in our country and what we may learn from the selflessness of Linda's parents, who urge us to look outwards rather than confusing our wants with our needs.

PART 2

The way we give now

'I resolved to stop accumulating, and began the infinitely more serious and difficult task of wise distribution.'
– Andrew Carnegie

CHAPTER 5

The challenge

'Let me tell you about the rich. They are very different from you and me.'
– F. Scott Fitzgerald

'Yes, the rich have more money.'
– Ernest Hemingway

The challenge is this: whilst the richest in Britain increase their wealth and the remainder grow poorer, how do we reverse the decline in charitable giving? How are we to persuade more of the wealthy to give and to give more? How do we engage the rich and convince them that they should be following Andrew Carnegie's example and acknowledging that they have a duty to the rest of us? What, if anything, do the rest of us have to do to persuade the wealthy that we need them to contribute to civil society to ensure its health and vitality, and that by doing so, they may find fulfilment? What should the government be doing on our behalf to encourage more philanthropy? How do we motivate all able-bodied people to be more charitable, by giving their time as well as money? What must we do to create a better society, if not a big one, whilst the state is in retreat?

To find the answers, I put these questions to a spectrum of

exceptionally generous donors who represent a variety of religions and none, and who also hold a range of political views. I
asked them why they believe giving is important, what motivates them, where they give their money and why they find
philanthropy fulfilling. Almost everyone I spoke to is resident
here and pays UK taxes and their view may be summed up by
two anonymous remarks: 'I have a visceral dislike of the idea of
living offshore for tax reasons.' 'You shouldn't scarper if you have
been honoured by the nation.'

Motivation and an understanding of what drives it is fundamental to any effort to increase philanthropy. Too many people,
notably in government, the civil service and the media, have no
idea or no interest in what moves people to give. My interviews
were conducted in the aftermath of the 2012 Budget when the
government tried and failed to limit tax relief on charitable
donations. The message from the Treasury was that donors were
deliberately avoiding tax and were therefore motivated to give
to charity for personal gain. This calumny was taken up by some
in the media. The language used betrayed a staggering degree of
ignorance, prejudice, myopia and political ineptitude, and a worrying lack of empathy with those most likely to fund the growth in
the voluntary sector which the government wishes to encourage.

Before we begin our tour of philanthropists and charities, it
might be helpful to hear an alternative view so that we can keep
a sense of perspective. I am passionate about philanthropy and
believe it is a power for good. Others have their doubts, so I talked
to someone who has expressed them in public: Polly Toynbee,
the author, journalist and charity trustee. I asked Polly for
her take on charities and philanthropists:

I couldn't imagine a society without charity. If you looked
behind the Iron Curtain from 1945 to 1989, you could see

societies without charity and it was appalling. The idea of no civil society and good people not getting together to address terrible poverty and its fallout was one of the most dispiriting things we have witnessed. When the USSR collapsed and there was no state to pick up the pieces, there was nothing, nowhere for people to turn to and no civil organisation. The Soviet state would have regarded charity as threatening because it would have been a buffer between the state and the people – a good thing.

There is no doubt at all that the idea of charity and of organisations addressing particular needs is a positive one. Charity is at its best when it acts as a beacon and as a pioneer, seeing and doing things no one has done before. Look at Camila Batmanghelidjh who works with the most disturbed teenagers. The system is not able to cope with them. She knows what works and how to do it and so she set up Kids Company in London. But she doesn't think she is a substitute for the state. She is showing the state how to do it. She fills the gap as best she can. But no charity will ever have the resources to do this on a large scale. However, showing how to do things better is very important and charities have always had this function.

I asked Polly why she is worried by philanthropy, or aspects of it:

I think there is a way in which the very rich try to justify the grotesque injustices in society by saying, 'We give lots to charity and we wouldn't give so much if we were not so rich.' They don't stop to think whether they are giving a reasonable proportion. Also, why should they be the ones who decide where the money goes? They may give it to the cats' home or to their son-in-law's charity or some passing fancy by whim. If that is what they want to do, they are not necessarily supporting whatever and wherever there is the greatest public need. Yes, the state is forced to pay into whatever charity the rich choose. Through tax relief, we taxpayers contribute to donors' charities of choice, regardless. So for me, the idea that it is better to have very large sums spent whimsically, maybe according to the vanity of multimillionaires, is unacceptable.

I responded by saying that, in my experience, the vast majority of donors are not vain and self-indulgent but serious, concerned and committed to doing the right thing. I believe that there is a different and potentially more damaging problem in that it is only a minority of the wealthy who are being generous. I also said that I believe it is the responsibility of charities to make a much stronger case for philanthropists to support what is in the public interest. Indeed, the most professional philanthropists insist upon public benefit being defined before they will consider supporting a project. Polly countered:

The Charity Commission is in a dubious position on deciding what is of public benefit. As long as people are giving to donkeys' homes and getting tax relief from all of us then public benefit is going to look ridiculous. All the Charity Commission can do is be a custodian to ensure that charitable donations are not spent corruptly. I think taxpayers' money should only go to causes that the state approves of. I don't think taxpayers' money should be dragged in according to the fancy of donors.

I would abolish tax relief. The government could set aside a sum for charities and would distribute to its chosen charities, matching donations of private money pound for pound. The incentive for the donor would be that their charitable gift would leverage in public funding, but only on what the government has selected. This doesn't stop people giving to the cats' home but it does eliminate donors' whims as a factor in decisions as to how public money will be spent. The government is democratically elected and entitled to decide how public money should be used to support publicly chosen priorities.

The Charity Commission cannot decide what is worthwhile. They can only decide what is honest. They shouldn't be involved in decisions about whether money is going to Eton, Odin or cats – and donors will always be free to give to whoever they like, but not with our money added.

There is an awful lot of vanity in big donations. I don't mind what people give to as long as I and other taxpayers are not paying for someone to sit in the Royal Box and have a lovely time in the Royal Opera House in return for having their name all over the place and being loved and admired.

And donors often want to control the causes they want to donate to. Camila at Kids Company spends nearly all her time raising money and it drives her mad because the donors are trying to control what the charity does. Donors say, 'Oh, I can run a charity or an academy, appoint all the governors, choose the head teacher, that would be really fun. That is what I will do now that I am bored with making money.' Some of these people think they are good at everything and are treated like princelings as if they really had this expertise.

I told Polly that I didn't recognise her description of most donors. Any reputable organisation should be able to see off those seeking self-glorification at the expense of a charity's mission. I have only had one notable experience of this, when I was at English National Opera. An elderly woman from Japan offered us £50,000 to mount a performance of *Madame Butterfly* in which she would sing the title role. We turned her down but Polly thought we had perhaps made a mistake given how much money we could have made.

Polly may or may not have been right about *Madame*

Butterfly, but is she right about whim, vanity, self-glorification, not to mention tax relief and definitions of public benefit? Let us find out.

❦

I began by talking to two men who have chaired two of the charitable organisations I worked for as head of fundraising.

Previously chairman of Tate and the Aldeburgh Festival, as well as Pearson and HBOS, Dennis Stevenson (Lord Stevenson of Coddenham) is unusual in that he started giving when he was very young. Dennis's family belonged to the Church of Scotland and he was a grandson of the manse:

> I was born to it. I was brought up to believe that giving to charity is what you do. It is like brushing your teeth, non-negotiable. I started giving money away as a teenager and continued through my twenties when I was earning very little.
>
> I agree with the Dalai Lama. You give for selfish reasons because it makes you feel good about life. As in business, you give both 'sweat equity' in terms of time and effort and you give financial equity. I do both, if imperfectly, but the important thing is to do it. Trust me, I have discovered that giving money can be a huge source of satisfaction. That may be selfish but I think that is acceptable if the job is well done and you can show that you have added to the sum of 'human happiness'.
>
> I have a simple message for all those who are able to give but do not: giving truly makes you happy. Another source of satisfaction is that giving can enable you to interfere. That is what human beings like to do: exercise power and make a difference. I am forever doing it and that is fine as long as the motives and outcomes are demonstrably good.

The Stevenson family, including his four sons, make collective decisions and focus their giving upon the arts, primarily music and the visual arts (Dennis was chairman of Tate when the commitment was made to build Tate Modern), medical charities, particularly mental health and epilepsy, and local charities in Suffolk, where they have a home, and Sierra Leone. Dennis and his wife reckon to give away at least 20 per cent of their post-tax income and have been doing so from a time when they were not well off.

I was a poor little kid and now I am not so poor. I am a very lucky boy. It seems perfectly obvious to me that in our circumstances, now is the time both to pay tax and to be generous. I can understand families struggling on median incomes and resenting paying tax but when you have more than you need for the basics, of course you pay tax *and* you give it away. I wouldn't feel comfortable if I wasn't contributing to roads, schools and hospitals. What is the matter with these people who are so rich and cannot bear the thought of paying tax? I just don't get it.

It also seems clear that that the extraordinary wealth enjoyed by about 25 per cent of the world, which has only existed for the last fifty years, has not made us any happier. One of the great errors of our time is the failure to come to terms with the problems created by too much material wealth, growing inequality and poverty. Giving is our own small way of trying to deal with that.

Dennis, one of life's great enthusiasts as well as a man of charity, sits on the crossbenches of the House of Lords. Sir Simon Robertson, my chairman when I worked for the Royal Academy of Arts, now chairman of Rolls-Royce, has his own investment company as well as many charitable commitments. He shares with Dennis a belief in using private wealth for public benefit.

Unlike Dennis, Simon was not born into a tradition of charitable giving, but his motivation is equally straightforward. Despite a successful career in the City, he did not earn sufficient money to do more than give relatively modest sums via Gift Aid. When Goldman Sachs was floated in 1999, Simon knew he would receive a multi-million-pound windfall.

> I started giving large chunks of money after the flotation relatively late in life, because I knew I was extremely fortunate. I happened to be in the right place at the right time. I didn't feel guilty about having so much money but I did feel that it was the right thing to do to give some of it away and to continue to do so.

The concept of giving back is fundamental to many donors. For Simon Robertson, this reflects his acknowledgement that he owes his good fortune to others and that people in his position should respond to the needs of others.

> Becoming rich is often the result of being lucky. You may have inherited or had a clever idea of your own, in which case you have probably made your money on the back of other people's capital or labour. I am also conscious that I should be supporting aspects of our civil society that might not flourish without private support. In many ways, we have a stronger civil society than in the USA and I am determined to do my bit to ensure that continues.

He is a major benefactor to both the Royal Opera House and the Royal Academy of Arts.

> I buy into the idea that that the arts are important to the well-being of our society. Even the Communists acknowledged that,

and arguably invested in a higher standard of education than we have. The arts bring pleasure to millions and we need to nurture creativity if we are to be happy as people and successful as a society. The Royal Academy has no state funding so needs people like me. I like the idea of helping the Royal Opera House to be elitist in the best sense of the word and that we can afford to enable people to enjoy excellence at a price for half the seats which is less than the cost of attending a football match.

Simon Robertson and his family also give to medical causes and charities supporting socially disadvantaged young people, particularly in Hampshire where he lives. He made a significant donation to the Eden Project, of which he has been a trustee for ten years, attracted by the importance of promoting understanding of the habitat in which we live.

Simon's other motivation for giving is that it makes him feel better.

People ask why I am supporting the arts rather than the health service. I *am* supporting the NHS because I am paying top-rate tax. However, in addition, I am also using my own money to give to cancer charities. I much prefer the idea of giving my money away than giving it to the government but I am also perfectly happy to pay my taxes. I believe I have a duty to do both. I happen to think I am more efficient about spending the money I give than the government is and that makes me feel better!

I know from first-hand experience how much time these two men devote to their charitable commitments, worth even more in value than the millions they have given away. Inspired by their enthusiasm, I took the train to Newcastle to discover what is happening, metaphorically speaking, at the coalface.

CHAPTER 6

Philanthropy and community: the view from the north-east

Lyn and Trevor Shears

W alking down a street of elegant late-Victorian villas in Gosforth, just north of Newcastle, I could not see anywhere that might be the home of a couple who give away £800,000 a year. The scene was prosperous rather than grand, understated and discreet, which is, I guess, how Lyn and Trevor Shears are. They are, however, an exceptional couple, not simply because of their wealth but because they are so generous and imaginative in supporting unconventional causes, such as helping sex workers find new employment. They had responded warmly to my request for an interview, being keen to encourage others to follow their example and learn what they have learned. The Shears also introduced me to other donors and to the Newcastle-based Community Foundation serving Tyne & Wear and Northumberland, of which more later.

The Shears established their charitable foundation following the public flotation of the transport company in which they had a large stake in 1994. The Shears Foundation started with a donation of shares representing about 40 per cent of their wealth, and the endowment now stands at £14 million. They are in their mid-sixties.

Lyn: 'We had too much money. To me it just seemed obscene. We couldn't keep it all. So we gave half of it away, putting 40 per cent into the foundation and 10 per cent for our family. That still leaves us with an enormous amount of money.'

I asked the Shears what else had motivated them to be charitable. Trevor:

We were charitable before we sold the business but not to the extent we are able to be now. My family was middle class but our roots were working class. There was compassion in the family but there wasn't enough money for philanthropy. The decision to float the business encouraged us to think about what we really wanted in terms of what our life should be. Much as I enjoyed my job, I felt we wanted more out of life. And we came to realise that we wanted to put back into the society that had created the wealth.

We created a charitable trust still not knowing what to do with the money. The first thing we supported was pioneering work at Bradford Royal Infirmary on cochlear transplants for deaf children. This really fired us up as the NHS didn't have the resources. We then started to receive applications but we still didn't have a focus for our work. We then supported a local hospice which brought us to the notice of the local Community Foundation. Through that relationship, we learned how to become proactive as philanthropists and some of the pitfalls.

The Community Foundation for Tyne & Wear and Northumberland supports charitable giving in the region by matching philanthropists with projects. Trevor was a trustee for six years.

I asked Trevor and Lyn if they had any other objective for their philanthropy.

Trevor: 'We want our giving to be about raising awareness and educating and helping people to understand in the widest sense what is possible, how they can improve their own lives and "change the world", even in quite modest ways.'

Lyn:

In the last couple of years, we have done much more to try to tackle issues around deprivation because of the recession. We have a project with The Sage Gateshead [music and arts centre] for sixteen- to eighteen-year-olds who have been excluded from school, who can barely read and write and who seem to have no chance of achieving anything in life. They would never dream of going into a place like The Sage Gateshead as they believe it is for posh people and not for them. They go to the old coal staithes behind The Sage, where they used to dump coal. In that place, they can do whatever they want, whether it is graffiti or to play their own music, but gradually they gravitate into what is on offer in The Sage itself, where they can experience every kind of music imaginable. We have helped to give them somewhere they can go and learn through their own music. If you can encourage them to belong to something and to learn how to spread their wings, they have a much better chance of being able to fly.

The Shears Foundation now has clear criteria for funding cultural, educational, environmental, health, medical and community projects and is supporting an eclectic range of causes, including the refurbishment of the Live Theatre in Newcastle and its education programme to encourage young playwrights; The Woodland Trust; the recently refurbished Tyneside Cinema with its focus upon young people; furniture recycling in Northumberland; Alzheimer's Research UK; bursaries at Bradford Grammar School; the Open University Scholarships; and encouraging young opera singers.

I asked Trevor and Lyn if they had encountered any particular problems and challenges.

Trevor:

There is a problem in much of society about what we are doing. This is the view that has been expressed to us: 'Why should you have all this wealth to decide whether you are going to support this or that? Wouldn't it be better if the state was organising that? Increase the taxes on the wealthy and then the government can decide what is in the public interest. Why should they get tax relief on charitable donations?' I believe this is what a lot of people are saying. Look at the row about tax relief. It is a bit perverse to think that we go to the trouble to give away £100 in order to get tax relief worth £40 or £50! And do we really believe that the state or local government would fund the kind of things we are doing?

Lyn:

For example, we are supporting Girls Are Proud (GAP). Not many people know about this project but we have learned so much through it. Apparently there is no red-light district in Newcastle and everything is behind closed doors, leaving the girls far more vulnerable than most prostitutes. Now they have a centre they can go to where they can talk about the problems they face, which are usually drug-related or with the men who manage them. The centre is where they can be given support and learn skills to enable them to give up prostitution and find other work, but only if they actively choose to change.

Trevor: 'And people say to us, the state won't fund this because it isn't considered a priority, so who are you to decide you should divert your money from the state because of low tax and use it do something which is not a national priority?'

Lyn: 'Initially, two of our trustees opposed our wish to support GAP because they disapproved but when we explained how the charity works and what it does to support these vulnerable young women, they could see the need.'

Trevor:

GAP is part of The Gap Project, which deals with homelessness, not just prostitution. They did a pilot project with prostitutes to see if they were interested in a self-help project. The centre is there to provide shelter if they want to leave that work and find the training they need. But they have to want to do it.

Lyn: 'We also support the West End Refugee Service in Newcastle. Most of the users are waiting to hear if their applications for citizenship have been successful, so they are feeling vulnerable and need a boost.'

Trevor:

When we first started this, we did agonise over dealing with ethnic minorities. We decided we didn't want to support work that overtly kept immigrants and refugees separate from society, we wanted to support projects that encouraged them to become British. We believe that one of the beauties about Britain is the immigrant influences we have had over the centuries which have all been absorbed to create our own particular society. I don't necessarily support an open-door immigration policy but for people who are here and want to be British, then we want to encourage that.

Lyn:

One of the hardest things we have had to learn and had to face is not so much deciding what we want to support but what we do *not* want to support. We don't support religious charities, partly because we are atheists but also because many religious charities are pursuing another agenda over and above the stated objective.

Initially, Trevor and Lyn were shy about publicity for their philanthropy.

Lyn:

We wanted to be anonymous because we didn't want people to think we were showing off. We changed our mind because it could have seemed as if we were ashamed of giving and the only way we could persuade others to give was by talking about what we are doing. But we are wary about coming over as holier than thou.

And then, by going public, they had to face hostility.

Lyn:

When the Community Foundation set up the Acorn Fund for donors who could only give relatively small regular amounts, the reaction from some friends was extraordinary. They were aghast. To quote: 'We are not rich. How dare you ask us? Why should we give to people who are on benefit? They haven't helped themselves so why should we give?'

The Shears are concerned that the philanthropic message is not widely heard and understood.

Trevor: 'There isn't anything in society that is saying to the children of privileged families that philanthropy is the right and good thing to do. If only we could find some way of that percolating into the education system.'

Lyn:

One way for children to learn about philanthropy would be to meet people who are being generous and for them to hear their stories at first hand. Our grandchildren are becoming philanthropic. We have one family board meeting a year and the eldest grandchildren attend. They were amazed at the amount of money going through.

Trevor:

We have involved our children and their children in what we are doing. They don't have time to be trustees yet but they will take over in due course. They are involved in or are in the know about the decisions we are making and that is how our grandchildren are learning about what it means to give and why it is important.

I asked Trevor and Lyn if they had a specific message for people who aren't giving.

Trevor:

The best advice we could offer to people who are thinking about being philanthropic is to go to your local Community Foundation. They will set you up and help you to become professional. The Community Foundation Network is the national body. They will help you work out your priorities and how to implement them. As for those who don't think about giving, you cannot tell people what to do with their money. You cannot imply that we are right and they are wrong. However, we are convinced that we get more satisfaction from seeing what happens to our money than the people who receive and benefit from it; it does indeed makes us feel good.

❧

Rob Williamson and the Community Foundation
of Tyne & Wear and Northumberland

Dennis Stevenson told me that whoever invented Community Foundations should be given a knighthood. Prior to my visit to the north-east, I had wondered why, and why I had never heard of them. Trevor and Lyn Shears had been adamant I should investigate and I began to understand why when the foundation's Head of Philanthropy, Derry Nugent, offered to organise what became an inspiring few days in Teesside as well as in Tyne & Wear.

Community Foundations were born 110 years ago in the United States. They bring together funds from a variety of private- and public-sector sources and match them with groups seeking finance for projects designed to benefit the needs of local communities. The Tyne & Wear Community Foundation, Britain's first, was created twenty-five years ago and now has an endowment of £45 million, giving away more than £4.5 million a year in a huge area embracing 1.8 million people. Derry Nugent explained:

We are focusing on philanthropy rather than charitable giving. We position ourselves as philanthropists rather than as grant-givers. We ask philanthropists to think about what they are giving to and why. This is a very important part of our job. There are now sixty-eight Community Foundations across the country. We are greatly helped in this by matching funds from the government. The coalition is supporting us through its Community First fund so that every £2 from a donor is matched by £1 from the government.

Now I understood why Dennis Stevenson is so keen. A private donation of £20,000 becomes £30,000 with the help of the taxpayer. Donors love matched funds and leverage. I explored further with Rob Williamson, the foundation's charismatic chief executive:

It is a very positive thing that philanthropy now seems to be back in fashion but we have been talking about it for twenty-five years, despite the preponderance of the public sector in the north-east. We only became a conduit for public money during the New Labour government. We didn't undertake this lightly, but we were in a good position to distribute public money because of our networks – but it came at a cost, namely our perception with donors. Public money was also helpful in providing overhead funding for the Community Foundation to grow nationally but it is now time to refocus on private giving.

We position ourselves as philanthropy hubs as well as grant-makers. This is a very important message to give to existing and potential donors. Our outcomes are charitable and our role is to support the community but we are also here to support philanthropists.

The key to our success and our ability to thrive in the north-east and overcome the challenges the region has had to face over the past twenty-five years is a strong sense of community. It is a cliché rooted in truth that there is a strong sense of community in England's periphery, and this is reflected in the commitment of people and businesses. Current philanthropy has been created on the back of a long tradition of giving and mutual support. This has enabled us to focus on the needs and interests of donors who want to respond to local needs.

We do not say: 'Please give us your money and then go away.' We say: 'Please come in and become engaged with what we are doing, join our membership.' We make sure we have the right people around the table: grantees, donors, businesses and local government. We have brought everyone together with no sector dominant. This is very attractive to new donors who want to join our network of the influential. Why are we not better known? If we compare ourselves to the US, their movement has a history of more than 100 years. It is not surprising we are not a household name after twenty-five years. We have had to grow slowly out of local networks. We can see this happening already in Essex, Bristol and Scotland, and now London has its own Community Foundation. We are now able to demonstrate that we are a very effective way of giving money.

Rob welcomes government support via matched funding but he shares the concerns of most philanthropists about the lack of consistency in the approach of ministers:

The current government is schizophrenic about philanthropy. The Department for Culture, Media and Sport does one thing and the Civil Society team does something else. For example, matched funding through the Arts Council's philanthropy incentive Catalyst scheme matches £1 donated with £1 from the DCMS. The Community First scheme via the Office for Civil Society offers a £1 match for £2 donated. We think the DCMS is keen to attract major donors where the OCS is obsessed with small donations. Why is there not one consistent approach?

Government is obsessed with irrelevant innovation at the expense of tried and trusted work. Some of this innovation will simply shift donations from buckets to cash machines or supermarket checkouts. This is just displacement activity which will not increase the amount of charitable giving.

Government doesn't understand that if you really want to get major gifts out of people, you have to have a relationship with them which becomes so close that you need to be able to see the whites of their eyes. You cannot do that at a supermarket checkout. We have calculated that it takes two years from starting a relationship to receiving a significant donation. It can be quicker but rarely is.

I asked Rob if he has a message for government:

Philanthropy is now on the agenda and we are pleased that some ministers have been talking about it. That is good. We welcome government support for Community Foundations through the Community First programme. This is all very positive and matched funding is brilliant. However, the government must trust us to make the best use of these challenge funds and not hamper us with restrictions that limit our freedom and flexibility to make the best use of the money. These make it much harder to do a deal with donors because they take the pleasure and the fun out of giving.

Of course we have to account for public money but we do know what we are doing and these Treasury conditions are counterproductive because they disincentivise donors, thus defeating the original objective.

You might think that with talk of the Big Society, our moment had come but no one in government came to experienced organisations in the regions like ours before talking about it in public. I think government, or parts of it, may be equivocal about us because we cost money. They don't really understand professional philanthropy and professional fundraising. They think we should all be volunteers.

✻

Fiona Cruickshank, SCM Pharma

'I am a drug dealer but legal.' These were almost the first words from Fiona when we met in the Community Foundation's offices in Newcastle where she is a trustee. Fiona is forty-six, founder and non-executive director of SCM Pharma, a member of the advisory board of the University of Newcastle's Business School and a former North-Eastern Woman Entrepreneur of the year. She created her first pharmacy business, The Specials Lab, in 1999 and was awarded an OBE in 2010.

I asked Fiona, who now gives away more than £50,000 a year, when she first started giving and why:

There is not a religious bone in my body but my father is a Franciscan and my mother is a lapsed Catholic so I guess altruism was always around. I was brought up in a small rural community and to believe you support your own community, and that is exactly what I felt I needed to do when I started my first business. I am a scientist by training. I started with nothing in 1999 but by the time I sold my first company for £20 million in 2008, I was employing more than 170 people.

Fiona intrigued me because she is such a dynamic and larger-than-life person who is clearly and successfully focused on her business but she had some difficulty in coping with her wealth and deciding what to do with it.

> I started to think about what to do with the money. My giving beforehand has always been very reactive, a pound here and a pound there. When I was financially successful I realised I could do something to help others. I would not have thought about that if I had been an employee.
>
> Charitable giving started through the business when lots of people began knocking on the door and I wanted to hide under the stairs. Business decisions are easy. Giving was difficult. I couldn't handle it. Then someone introduced me to the Community Foundation and I thought that was a brilliant idea. I didn't have to make a single decision and just had to write a corporate cheque. We were giving away about £20,000 a year to support the local area and specific rural communities. Life is really tough up here in remote parts of Northumberland. I just set the agenda, which is to support social need.

Fiona may have thought she had solved the problem of how to handle her charitable giving and business success but, the more successful she became, the more the pressure grew.

> More people were banging on my door assuming I had cash but I was living on a basic salary because we were ploughing profits back into the business. So I was turning charities down. Then, in 2007, I was invited to be a visiting professor at the Newcastle Business School. There was a fee which I didn't want to take but it was funded by an endowment and I realised I had to. However, I couldn't spend it and decided to start my own personal rather than corporate giving through the Community Foundation. Then I topped it up because it wasn't enough.

Setting up her own personal fund encouraged Fiona to think about what really mattered to her and this, she realised, was women in business and women in science. She had made considerable capital by being a woman running her own technology-based business and had already started giving time as a mentor. The company was already supporting the government's Primary Science initiative to encourage primary school children to take up science.

> I set up my own personal fund to help young people and young women in science and asked the Community Foundation to manage it. We set up an after-school science club so that primary school children could experience whizz-bang-wallop science and have some fun. We also started an outreach chemistry lab at Newcastle University that the kids could use as a summer school. They worked with adults and lab technicians so they think that science is really cool. And the kids were also intrigued that I was involved and putting money into it. So we developed a narrative about what we were doing together and the kids loved that. This was good for the kids and good for science.

Fiona also started funding bursaries at the university, enabling additional studies and research outside the university curriculum for science and medical degrees and in time was supporting science initiatives from primary schools to postgraduates. She also invested in start-up businesses and was giving outside the Community Foundation as well as within it. Then she sold her business. I asked Fiona what she plans to do next and whether she has any advice for people in her position who are not thinking about giving.

I now have £50,000 a year of my own money to give away. I am still learning and I am still instinctual. I need to get a bit more focused. I don't need everything I have. If I sell my next business, I will do a lot more giving than I do now but I don't yet know if I will change direction. I am only interested in accumulating money to do something better with it. I don't really want more stuff. Shiny things don't work for me.

What would I say to someone in my position who isn't giving? It really depends upon what their personal values are. I would ask, Why aren't you giving? Do you really know what you want? Being obsessed with stuff is madness but if someone is obsessed then persuading them to give will be a hard sell. Some people are simply me, me, me. If they say they don't know why they are not giving, perhaps there is some hope.

I don't think about what I get out of it. It seems the right thing to do. I am emotional about my giving. It is a bit like creating a business. I just want to see it grow. And it is so good to know that something useful is being done with the cash. What else are you going to do with it? You might as well try and do something creative with it and try to make things better.

And I don't mind paying the tax because that means that I have earned it. I guess I am a serial investor and I just want to make something out of nothing. It is not about me. I am just trying to encourage others.

As I left this big-hearted woman, I wanted to give her a hug but thought better of it. I wish I had. I told her that I was off to Middlesbrough the next morning to meet Andy Preston. You will like Andy, she said.

Andy Preston, Green Lane Capital, Middlesbrough and Teesside Philanthropic Foundation

I did like Andy, very much. I had read about him in the *Financial Times*, and about the work he is doing to support his local community in Middlesbrough, which suffered badly when local industries collapsed within a very short period of time. Andy is the founder and chair of the Middlesbrough and Teesside Philanthropic Foundation. He used to work in London as a financial markets trader. He built and ran a number of trading businesses for international financial organisations and then created and managed a large hedge fund group for a European bank.

After moving back to the north-east, Andy founded a property and investment business, Green Lane Capital. I met Andy in Green Lane's offices, a haven of cool behind Middlesbrough railway station. I had to wait some time as I watched an elegant man in his forties pacing up and down talking on his mobile. I could have been in London. However, once our meeting started, it was immediately clear we were anywhere but London. I asked him how had life been growing up:

I was brought up in a Catholic, working-class environment in Middlesbrough with a strong sense of community and everyone went to church. Everyone knew everyone, there was a strong sense of belonging and we lived according to working-class tradition. The church did interesting things. So the priest would say: my cousin Father Kelly is in Uganda trying to raise £300 for a new well. We all felt a responsibility to do something. It was nothing to do with being generous. It simply was the right thing to do. And the wrong thing not to do it! We were brought up to believe that giving was important and essential. We were not poverty-stricken but we certainly were not rich. My dad was a steelworker who went to night school to become a teacher. But everyone gave something.

I am now an intellectual agnostic and a 'cultural Christian'. But for me, Catholicism was about going after the lost sheep. You look after each other. I suppose it was socialism, community, pulling together, giving what you can. This was left-wing in its ethos and ideology at a time in the 1980s when the Zeitgeist was 'make as much money as you can, borrow as much as you can, just buy another car if you feel like it'. This was a very selfish time, all about money and self-aggrandisement.

Andy went to Edinburgh University and moved to London in the 1990s. He prospered, as he is good at making money. He went to charity events which raised a great deal of money and was struck that those who gave were praised extravagantly even though some of them were so wealthy they could hardly have noticed how much they were giving. And he also noticed that the beneficiaries did not seem to care where the money had come from. In 2002, he became one of the first patrons of ARK (Absolute Return for Kids), famous for raising many millions of pounds at its annual gala:

That opened my eyes as to what was possible. Let's not get too carried away. Not everyone involved will be going to heaven, but it was good work. What I learned was that the giving I grew up with, which was quiet, discreet and about taking personal responsibility, is very good. The giving at ARK is about self-promotion, back slapping, demonstrating leadership. It is very different and in some ways better from the point of view of the recipient. This kind of giving may not be as virtuous but it makes more impact and is more efficient in terms of the sums raised.

This was a revelation to me and I started to write personal cheques which seemed enormous compared to my previous giving. I could afford it, but I had never known anyone who could write cheques like that. It felt so good. And it felt good that people could see I was doing good. Because of my background, my inclination was for my giving to be private but I was persuaded to go public in order to encourage others.

Andy used his influence and his experience with ARK to get some of the money up to Middlesbrough to a charity called Fairbridge, now part of The Prince's Trust, that supports marginalised young people. This is a national problem but the problems facing the young were particularly bad in the north-east. The funds helped to transform the Fairbridge Centre in Middlesbrough and persuaded Andy to do more locally rather than nationally, and he decided to try to recreate something along the lines of ARK, where the local people who can afford it are the cornerstone of the charity's finances. He had by then left London and returned to his roots.

By now, the austerity measures were being announced. Many great community resources were being cut and this was the spur for me to do the local version of ARK. I recruited my co-founder and then started knocking on doors. I approached all my contacts who might have a local interest and asked for a minimum donation of £5,000 to enter this new 'club' and become its patrons. I asked twenty-nine people in our first year and twenty-four said yes.

We raised £200,000 in our first year. We were not going to change Middlesbrough with that, but we could preserve community assets for another year, keeping going an old-age pensioners club or a boxing club or developing the Powerchair

Football Club so that our town can compete in the national league. I am not hugely wealthy but I am solvent. Actually, time is the most valuable contribution I can make. I am trying to set an example and show that it is possible to do something. I am not particularly talented. If I can do this, then lots of others can as well. Part of being a human being is to want to help. Someone just has to show leadership and start the ball rolling.

I asked Andy how we could persuade more people to follow his example. He thinks charities need to work harder to make themselves more relevant:

When I was a child, charities seemed as if they were about doing good work, but now they are big businesses with highly paid senior executives and large legal and marketing departments. They sometimes manipulate their figures to show how much they give away, but I think their running costs are far too high. I also get really cross with charities when they complain about the recession without any obvious sign that they have tried. I know it is tough but the money is out there if you look hard enough. People need to understand the benefits of giving, which can be personal and psychological, and not all charities know how to promote these. They don't have the right leadership and they don't know how to use networks.

Andy believes that local people must try to address their own problems rather than rely upon others. He is helping to organise the world's biggest art competition, Care Where You Live, based in Teesside. He is expecting up to 20,000 entries. There will be prize money worth £41,000 to help charities, schools and local organisations.

In this town, we have a legacy of a small number of massive employers. Everything had seemed secure with jobs for life. You lived all your life in the same place, had lifelong relationships and everything was mapped out. It ended very quickly and there was nothing there to replace it. The state provided a basic buffer but that is not the solution as to how to create a life. We are trying to show the way. Look how social media can help people brand themselves and create their own employment. We have to be creative today.

This is now entrenched in my psychology. If you go out into the world with a spirit of openness and generosity, the world is generally generous back. Giving means leadership. Giving is doing something positive, about taking a stand and sacrificing something for a greater good. That should be a message for anyone who is a manager.

With a final blast of charisma from Andy, it was time to leave the north-east. I reflected upon what I had experienced and what I had learned. I realised even more profoundly than I had before that there are limits to what the state can do. My concern is whether philanthropists are able or willing to fund what the state cannot do or decides it can no longer support. My conversation with Wendy Hodgson of the Outpost Housing Project in Newcastle brought things into perspective. Outpost Housing provides shelter for gay, lesbian and transgender teenagers who are homeless because they have been rejected by their families. Living in London and having spent most of my working life in the cultural sector, I had become immune to the problems faced by vulnerable young people elsewhere. These problems will not be at the top of every donor's priority list. Outpost Housing enjoys support from the voluntary sector with the help of the Community Foundation. There is local authority funding, but for how much longer? The worst of central government fund-ing cuts to local authorities have yet to be implemented and Newcastle City Council has announced it is planning to cut its budget for culture by 100 per cent. Will the voluntary sector and local philanthropists come to the rescue? The Tyne & Wear and Northumberland Community Foundation will not be short of work for the foreseeable future.

However, having met some extraordinarily generous and empathetic local philanthropists in the north-east, my optimism remained reasonably intact as I returned south to my next desti-nation: Brixton.

CHAPTER 7

Education: from primary
schools to postgraduates

Victoria Sharp, London Music Masters
and Jessop Primary School, Brixton

Concern for the young and their education is evidently a priority for many philanthropists. Appropriately, Victoria Sharp
began giving at an early age at school in Connecticut, USA.

This was the way we were brought up. Giving was inculcated
very early. We were organised to do things for the community
as part of our school activities. For example, some of us went
to read to old people in a local home. I was very young when I
went to an empty bed and realised that the person I had come
to know had died. I was forced to think about other people and
their needs and that I had a responsibility to others as well as to
myself. That is a big thing for a child. We also supported poverty
programmes overseas by collecting money at Hallowe'en for
UNICEF and became quite competitive about it.

Victoria eventually joined Goldman Sachs and came to London
where she met Richard Sharp, her now ex-husband, and
together they formed the Sharp Foundation, through which

they supported various charities. She continues to do so independently for several organisations including the Royal College of Music, where we both sit upon the governing council, and the London Philharmonic Orchestra, which she chairs. She now works full-time in the non-profit sector, where she gives most of her time and a significant proportion of her disposable income to a small charity, London Music Masters (LMM), of which she is the unpaid chief executive.

LMM's music education programme, the Bridge Project, was founded in 2008, primarily to change the lives of disadvantaged young people and their families by introducing entire classes of primary schools to formal classical music tuition and giving them all the opportunity to play and to perform with professionals. LMM also offers several three-year awards providing performance opportunities, mentoring and a bursary to professional violinists at the start of their careers. Part of their programme includes working closely as role models with the Bridge Project primary school children.

I asked Victoria how and why LMM's Bridge Project was conceived:

I was struck by the criticism of all the conservatoires that their intake was not sufficiently diverse. We realised that as centres of excellence, conservatoires should by definition take the best students who apply. Diversifying the pool of applicants requires widening access to high-quality music tuition at grass-roots level, something the school system was not doing in any uniform way to reach all children. We began a four-year pilot project by targeting two inner London primary schools, where a large percentage of the children are from very diverse backgrounds and are on free school meals. The initial results, which show raised social skills and academic attainment as well as strong musical outcomes, are tremendously encouraging. Very young children from difficult backgrounds can now concentrate in class, cooperate with others and are achieving more academically. It is also terrific that their families get involved. Through our partnership with the London Philharmonic Orchestra, the Royal College of Music, Wigmore Hall and the Southbank Centre, our young students' aspirations, their view of life and the part they can play in it has been transformed. They have new role models and can meet and perform with them. They feel the Royal Festival Hall, for example, is not just for the privileged but is for them too.

I attended a concert given by some of these children at the Royal Festival Hall and I have to report that scores of little ones playing 'Twinkle, Twinkle, Little Star' in unison on their tiny violins is a powerful and emotionally testing experience. I have also visited and attended classes at both Ashmole Primary in Lambeth and Jessop Primary in Brixton and was impressed by the smiling faces, the dedication of both pupils and teachers, the patience shown by the children and the evident pleasure shared by everyone involved, all in an ambience of relative calm and order.

I was at Jessop Primary on the day Benjamin Grosvenor, one of Britain's most outstanding young pianists, visited in his capacity as an ambassador for LMM. He played for the children who sat transfixed, expressions of ecstasy on some faces, amusement on others. Afterwards, I asked Lillian Umekwe, Jessop's head teacher, what impact LMM's Bridge Project was having on the school:

I have been head here for five years and I have been on such a long and extraordinary journey. When I arrived, the buildings were in such a state that it was impossible to learn. Parents voted with their feet and we had only 180 students. Each class had fewer than ten students in it. The school was one of the worst in the country. The parents who brought their children here could not be bothered to find another school. When I arrived, the school was in special measures and on the verge of being closed down.

I took on the school because I have always enjoyed a challenge. I believe every child has talent, however disadvantaged. There must be something that they are good at. You have to dig it out. Most of the children here are very deprived. That was then. We now have over 400 children from forty nationalities. English is the second language for the majority and most are so poor they are entitled to free school meals. But we are now above the national average, having been bottom of the league, and our most recent OFSTED report rated us as 'outstanding'.

What happened? I met Victoria Sharp. She told me that Jessop was exactly the kind of school she wanted to support. I am passionate about music. I was brought up with it so I know that if we can get the children to concentrate, their lives will change. The most important thing is to capture the children at the right age. Most of the children here have few opportunities in life, certainly not to go to the Royal Festival Hall, which we have now done. I knew that if we could get the kids to sit for half an hour learning and listening to music, they could do the same for other subjects.

It is hard to find the words to describe the impact LMM has had on the children. This is now the school of choice. The parents say, 'I want to see my child carrying the violin.' Previously, this was a privilege for the private, independent schools. The parents do make a small contribution but our children have been *given* an opportunity. They learn valuable technical skills which does wonders for their self-confidence. And they have the privilege of learning together. The children learn so much from that. They also learn social skills and how to build their self-confidence as well as how to trust and support each other.

Music has also brought children and parents together. The parents are supporting their children, not something that can be taken for granted, and they are coming to events, including going to the Festival Hall for the first time. Even some of the staff have started learning the violin.

Not all these children will be musicians but because we have given them this experience, music has enhanced their achievements across the curriculum because these skills are transferable. They now have such self-confidence that they believe they can achieve. All this is because the commitment of the music teachers is outstanding. They have an impact on everyone here, not just upon the children but upon me and my colleagues. They have become our family. They have helped us all to believe in ourselves. They are so patient. They so obviously enjoy what they do and the children know this. They now know what commitment is.

What has been the impact upon me? I am so happy! I am overcome with goose pimples. This is a music school now. The greatest impact on me is to see the children doing so well, to see them then and now, to realise that some of these children would have been excluded and thrown on the scrap heap. Now they are flourishing. We would not have been able to achieve any of this without music and London Music Masters. They should be in every school.

LMM wish every school and every child had the opportunities enjoyed by Bridge Project students at Ashmole and Jessop, but there are a number of challenges to overcome. Firstly, it would not be feasible for any one non-governmental organisation alone to work with the 20,000 or so primary schools across the UK. Secondly, the charity can only expand the number of schools where it operates if it diversifies its sources of private funding. This is already starting to happen. Thirdly, LMM realises that growth must be carefully planned, funded and executed in order to maintain standards. Victoria Sharp and her team are, however, interested in working with other partners to roll out their model to a larger number of schools, particularly as they become able to demonstrate that LMM is more cost-effective than its competitors and achieves high impact. However, there are other concerns raised in the process. Victoria continued:

I do worry about spending on education and music education in particular. If improving the state of the nation depends on raising educational standards then, logically and above all, there should be increased spending on education, and the arts should play a significant role in the holistic education of our youth. High-quality music tuition has demonstrable impact on academic attainment and social development. It would be a critical error to cut it. There is an expectation that the private sector should fill the widening funding gap for something which has clear positive social and educational impact as well as artistic, cultural benefit. Not to overlook the enormous contribution to the economy from the music industry and the wider arts sector. Unsurprisingly given the nature of things, there is a tendency to look for a quick fix for issues that require patience, commitment and long-term investment.

I am proud to be a patron of London Music Masters and have been privileged to see its work at first hand. The potential for rolling out the highly effective music education it espouses depends upon its ability to mobilise more private-sector support but the role of government is also crucial. Philanthropists such as Victoria Sharp, who give so much time as well as millions of pounds to improving the quality of life for the disadvantaged, are doing extraordinarily valuable work in the national interest. The government says it values this kind of work and wants more of it, but its actions belie its words. Moreover, I know Victoria did not enjoy last year's spectacle of the government's attack on donors who use tax relief to make their money go further. London Music Masters is a shining example of private initiative and money working with the public sector to secure a better future for our young people. That is in the interests of all of us.

✣

Lord Nash and the Pimlico Academy

Academy schools arouse strong feelings. Originally conceived by the New Labour government, the first academies achieved striking academic results. The number of academy schools has spiralled since those early days, encouraged by the coalition government. There are some who work for academies who backed the original concept but believe the current government is on a dangerous path. The original academies were formerly failing schools in areas of deprivation and they were established to support regeneration. Critics are suspicious of the trend for increasing centralisation by Michael Gove, the Secretary of State for Education, and fear that the original mission for academy schools will be lost. I am going to step to one side and not join the argument here because it is not part of my brief. All I am trying to do is demonstrate to potential philanthropists how it is possible to use capital creatively to make a real difference and to transform the prospects of the young.

One of the valuable things I have learned during my research is to reject stereotypes, to have few expectations and to be prepared to be surprised. John Nash, who sponsored the creation of Pimlico Academy, has a reputation in certain parts of the press. In 2007, *The Observer* published an article under the heading: 'Venture capitalists go on the school run: Tycoon and philanthropist John Nash is turning his hand to academies. But should private equity be in the classroom?' The article goes on to describe him as the barbarian at the gate and a donor to the Conservative Party. Even a friend of his told me he could be arrogant.

The reality was very different. The answer to the question: should private equity be in the classroom must be a resounding 'yes'. The facts speak for themselves.

I met a modest, quiet and reflective man in the offices of Sovereign Capital, who had clearly learned a lot from the formative experience of setting up an academy against considerable opposition. Our meeting was held before John Nash became a government minister and before his elevation to the House of Lords. I asked John why he had decided to invest in the Pimlico Academy and what had led up to his decision:

Everything started a bit later for me. I am now sixty-three. I didn't get married until my mid-thirties but after a lifetime of making money, it seemed natural to start giving it away and my wife and I set up a charity called Future about seven years ago when I was in my fifties. I have always been interested in education, so that became our focus. I don't think of it in terms of giving back. I am much more interested in problem solving. There are a lot of problems around young people and I wanted to help do something about it.

We had heard about the Academy programme but were initially wary because it was so high-profile. However, I was introduced to Andrew Adonis who I think is a super man. We knew about Pimlico. Both my wife Caroline and I used to live there and we knew the school. We were keen because it was local. We pitched to Westminster Council and they liked our vision, which is that every child can succeed whatever their circumstances and that we must not lower our sights about the potential of the young, however disadvantaged they may be.

Our vision is driven by the fact that both Caroline and I had unsatisfactory education experiences and I didn't have a happy home life. My mother died when I was quite young. Although my circumstances were not as difficult as those for many young people today, I do feel able to identify with their problems. Most people who I have met who are outstanding have a deep personal driver that motivates them. So this is quite personal for Caroline and for me. We do identify with the young and the problems they face in their education and in their home life.

The Pimlico School has a deep tradition of being left-wing. It was founded by Harold Wilson, and Jack Straw was chairman of the governors. The teachers leaned to the left and although we were seen as very right-wing, my views on education are to the left. However, the school did not want us, they didn't want to be an academy and they didn't want to be taken over. People saw a wealthy couple taking over a school and they were very wary. I can understand that, it did look odd, particularly as academies were brought in by a Labour government. There were rumours that we were going to pull the place down and build flats. When we visited, the kids lined the entrance with rows of coffins labelled Future. It was very unpleasant and quite a formative experience!

Once people got to know us, they realised our hearts were in the right place and that we were not pursuing some deep and dark agenda. It is depressing in this country that people cannot see philanthropy for what it is and think we are all on some evil mission.

We took over a school that was failing by any measure. Morale was low, the children wouldn't look you in the eye, behaviour was very poor and a few years previously there had been a riot. The teachers had also had nine days of strikes in the year before we took over. The worst thing is low expectations. Some of the kids were doing courses that were below them. There was a massive noisy concourse in the middle of the school and we put down decent tiling and brought in sofas that people said would be trashed, but they weren't.

Staff morale is so much higher because we hired an inspirational Irish head, Jerry Collins, who is very driven and really cares. He has been so good at turning round the staff. The kids are very savvy. They soon worked out that we were on their side. Behaviour turned round with the application of some clear rules and boundaries. The teachers were more visible and literally came out of hiding! In order to raise expectations and to introduce the students to people outside their social strata, we have invited up to 300 speakers in the last four years. The idea is to introduce role models and the relentless message that you can achieve whatever you want if you put your mind to it and do the work. This has undoubtedly lifted horizons.

I asked John what he has learned from his involvement with Pimlico and what messages he might want to give to other potential sponsors as well as to government:

I have founded a lot of companies and businesses over the years but this is undoubtedly the most rewarding thing I have been involved with. 1,200 kids are a big responsibility. Our focus on education has been so interesting. Rather than go off and found new schools, we thought we should concentrate on Pimlico and ensure that we really understand the complex issues involved. Being a teacher is not easy. It is a very challenging job.

Experienced business people tend to underestimate the judgement calls required when working with charities. The issues are often complex. Some business people think charities are a bit woolly but the quality of people working in the sector is much higher now and there are some outstanding leaders. What business people can do is help with strategy and empowerment and give management a shoulder to cry on.

I pressed on about how we can persuade more people to become involved by volunteering as well as giving:

We are at a stage in life where we can give lots of time, but that is not the case for everybody. However, no one has yet turned down an invitation to speak at the academy and that is clearly a very valuable 'gift'. Improving trustee boards and recruiting with good networks will help to persuade more potential sponsors to get involved. People don't want to sit on a board of plonkers. Governance is key. So many school boards have fifteen or more members and are just talking shops. We have six very bright governors at Pimlico who really know what they are talking about. We should also remember that people are perfectly entitled not to give. The best way to entice people is to ask them to support specific projects that are likely to appeal to their interests.

I think the younger generation are becoming more public spirited. The kids at Pimlico are volunteering and supporting charitable projects. All schools should make this a rite of passage and teach the young that they need to be imaginative and compassionate. I think people are becoming more public spirited. We can see this in the quality of people becoming teachers and the calibre of people leading charities. All this should help to improve volunteering and giving.

I asked John how we might resolve the conundrum of how to reconcile the private interests of donors with public need:

But I am interested in public need and the public interest! We cannot begin to compete internationally unless we improve education in this country. Seven per cent of the country is educated privately and to a very high standard in internationally competitive terms. Ninety-three per cent are educated in the state sector where standards are variable, sometimes excellent but too often average compared with schools overseas. The issues are not really party political. They are blindingly obvious. Read Andrew Adonis's book *Education, Education, Education: Reforming England's Schools*.

John Nash had a parting shot for government, a refrain I was to hear over and over again:

Politicians do not understand how rich people think. People of my age are thinking of giving away all their income and sometimes their capital at a time when they are no longer earning. They should be encouraged to do so, but if tax relief is withdrawn, donors will react negatively and stop giving. Messages coming out of government are confusing because no department seems to have a brief for philanthropy.

I left John with his words returning to me over and over again:

'We should teach the young that they need to be imaginative and compassionate.' These are not the words of a barbarian.

※

Jerry Collins, Principal, Pimlico Academy

I was looking forward to visiting Pimlico Academy and meeting its principal, Jerry Collins. As I waited in the reception hall, I had time to take in the cool, clean lines of the new building, the academic achievements mounted on the walls, the warmth of my professional welcome and the smartness of the students. I was formally greeted by an enthusiastic and immaculately dressed Jerry Collins.

I asked Jerry to describe the ethos of the academy and without prompting and spot on cue, he told me:

We try to imbue a sense of compassion in our students. We want them to have a very clear work ethic, to be highly literate, to be knowledgeable, independent and ambitious. In a way, compassion is almost the most important. We want them to be the kind of children who will hold out a hand and help others rather than just look out for their own needs.

I am always conscious that we sometimes say things and then do not follow up by fulfilling them. These values have to be entwined in the fabric of the school to make them meaningful. So we have divided the students into four houses, Apollo, Athene, Hero and Zeus, and each house is linked to a charity. One of them is The Abbey Centre for local senior citizens. There was one project when the older people came to talk about the Blitz during a history lesson. This is turned out to be hilarious when the women talked about what they got up to in the ruins! The students then taught them how to use the internet. All the students have to be involved in working with charities and they get a lot out of it.

In year 11, the students take part in the Youth and Philanthropy Initiative [YPI, a charity to promote volunteering and giving, see Chapter 13] and that works really well. We are very much engaged with it and there are some moving stories. All students have to develop their own projects that involve research into local charities and then report back to the whole school in assembly. We know this is making an impact because more and more students are coming to us after YPI to say they want to fundraise when they move into the sixth form.

I asked Jerry about the school's academic record, the changes brought about converting to an academy and the role of its sponsors, John and Caroline Nash.

I started here in 2008. Since then, GCSE results in Maths and English have improved by twice above the national average over the last four years. Our A level results have gone up from 67 per cent to 82 per cent, and last year 83 per cent of the students who left went on to university and over half of these went on to the Russell Group of universities.

Eighty-five per cent of our students come from the poorest 30 per cent of wards in the country. Thirty per cent come from the most deprived wards. Twenty-five per cent are white British and sixty languages are spoken. Forty per cent are on free school meals. There is a lot of deprivation and many of our students come to us without the educational attainment, including reading, expected of most children of that age.

Caroline Nash has led the development of a knowledge-rich curriculum. Teachers worried initially that it might be too difficult for inner-city children but is it has been a revelation. There is a particular emphasis upon learning history chronologically, making sure that our students have a really deep understanding of the country they live in. We took them on a trip down the Thames, and they learned about the Globe, the bridges and how they were built, St Paul's, the Tower of London, the National Maritime Museum and other features related to core subjects. They had a wonderful time. John and Caroline financed the trip and came on the day. It is very unlikely that the children would have had such an experience without their initiative and support.

The students now have a sense of purpose and direction. They understand that we are supporting them and helping them fulfil their potential. Learning was not at the centre of the previous school and that is now very different.

The new building has made a tremendous difference. We had nine strike days the year before I was appointed. I started about five months before the new school officially opened and it was a difficult time. We had to cross picket lines. The old building was infested with mice and cockroaches. There was no evidence of the children's work, no displays and poor uniform. I was struck by an overwhelming sense of demoralisation that oozed from every corner. At break times, there was sometimes serious violence. Anything seemed to go. There was a school youth club and we had to manhandle some of the older boys out of there because the violence was so bad.

Neither the students nor the staff had any belief in themselves. I remember someone visiting after we had sorted things out and she asked how we had managed to get rid of all those violent children and find these young people and I had to tell her that these were the same kids she had seen before. We just treated them with respect and encouraged them to believe in themselves.

Regarding our sponsors, John and Caroline Nash, it was a bit like two worlds colliding. There was much suspicion and animosity amongst the staff and parents and I found the union extremist in its approach. There were some good teachers who operated inside cocoons and are still with us. I think this was all very difficult for John and Caroline. The situation needed careful management and I knew I had to move quickly to improve morale. It took me some time to persuade the teachers that the Nashes were a force for good. There was a lot of understandable suspicion, but we got there by making sure that everything was funnelled through me in that I dealt directly with the union and any issues with staff. This enabled John and Caroline to focus on the big picture and once staff could see this they bought into it.

The staff now understand that John and Caroline are truly aspirational for the school and that the children had been denied such things as a decent curriculum, opportunities to go to university and experience things outside the world they knew. Now we see the children reaping the benefits and that has convinced the teachers. I must say that despite all the considerable difficulties, working with John and Caroline and with everyone who came together to make Pimlico Academy what it is has been the most positive experience of my life.

Jerry Collins looks, and so obviously is, a happy and fulfilled man. Having been on the inside and, more importantly, at the centre, he understands the importance and meaning of giving time:

There is a misconception about philanthropy. It is not just about money. John and Caroline's contribution in terms of time is far bigger than the money they put into the school. The amount of time they give is extraordinary and it is this that has made the difference and given the school a new sense of direction, not the money. The staff are better practitioners and teachers because of what the Nashes have done here. Interestingly, the students who are most keen to fundraise here are the most deprived. If we can somehow get communities to help themselves, that would make a tremendous difference. If philanthropy is just the remit of the rich, you are then cutting out many people who wish to contribute and who have the will to do so.

As I left Pimlico Academy, Jerry said: 'One of the great things the Nashes have done is to ask regularly "Why do you do that?" Too often, the answer is: "Because we always have." I now know that is not the correct answer.'

❦

Sir John Madejski and the John Madejski Academy, Reading

During more than twenty years as a director of fundraising and as a trustee of charities, I have encountered a small number of donors who are monsters. However, contrary to the view of some, the great majority of philanthropists are not vain, self-indulgent and self-regarding tax dodgers. Most are generous, imaginative, concerned, highly respected, committed and serious people. Many are delightful and a few inspire great affection and devotion, even love. One of these is Sir John Madejski.

John Madejski is a prime example of a self-made man exceptionally loyal to his roots in Berkshire. From an inauspicious start, leaving school with no formal qualifications, he was wealthy by the age of forty-nine when he donated £500,000 to the Falkland Islands Memorial Chapel in Pangbourne, a timely donation which was crucial in enabling the chapel to be built.

John became really rich in 1998 when he sold his share in his publishing company for £174 million.

He was to make a habit of rescuing good causes at a local as well as national level.

> Reading Football Club was broke in 1990. I was not prepared to see our local team and the fourth oldest football club in Britain go bankrupt. I wasn't a huge football fan but the club is synonymous with the area. Saving the club was something I felt I could do for my community.

John donated most of the £25 million cost of a new football stadium and, in his twenty-three years as chairman, has poured millions of pounds into the club which was back in the Premier League in 2012. He also gave £3 million to the Royal Academy of Arts in 2002 to enable the completion of the restoration of Burlington House. 'I knew that my donation was crucial in ensuring that the historic Fine Rooms could be restored and opened to the public for the first time. I liked the idea that paintings and sculpture previously hidden in the basement could now be exhibited, with free entry.'

John also gave generously to the Victoria and Albert Museum. 'The V & A was able to create a new garden, a tranquil place for contemplation just off one of the busiest roads in London. I did get a kick out of helping to create something uplifting for people to enjoy.'

John is revered because, although he now describes himself as *nouveau pauvre* since the recession, he can be spontaneously generous. I witnessed this at a spectacular party we organised at the Royal Academy of Arts on behalf of all the arts to celebrate the Queen's Golden Jubilee in 2002. This was a highly spirited and, for a few, bibulous occasion, funded in its entirety by one very private anonymous donor. We had just managed to carry an unconscious literary dame down the main staircase moments before Her Majesty left. As we waved goodbye to the Queen, I turned to John and thanked him for helping me in a failed attempt to persuade someone to give £3 million to restore the Fine Rooms. I asked John if he could think of anyone else who could give that amount. 'Yes,' he replied immediately, 'me.' Unfortunately, I had to rush off immediately to a dinner for some of our American benefactors and John shouted after me: 'What's the matter? Don't you want my f****** money?' All turned out well.

John Madejski has a highly developed sense of obligation and community.

The fundamental thing about life is that we enter and leave with nothing. What we have when we are alive is merely borrowed and money exists to be used. What is the point of dying rich? I believe in sharing my good fortune with my fellow citizens. I believe in doing some good whilst you are here and enjoying the difference you can make. I think we can all help other people and there is a role for everyone whatever their circumstances. Most people can give time or expertise and those who are best suited to making money should give their surplus funds away.

I worry that our sense of community, and the sense of obligation to it that seemed so strong when I was young, has broken down. This is a serious problem with serious implications for our country. Community is very important to me.

John describes his donation to found the John Madejski Academy (JMA) as the best thing he has ever done.

Leaving school without any qualifications made me realise how vulnerable young people are. I was lucky and had whatever it takes to be an entrepreneur. Not everyone is so lucky. I thought I was well aware of the problems facing young people in Reading and didn't need to be convinced that I had a role to play in helping to revitalise run-down schools and give youngsters a better start in life. After we had opened JMA, I asked the head to describe the beginning of the school day which she said started with an eight o'clock breakfast club. We are not running a hotel, I remonstrated, until she explained that for some kids, the first meal of the day – and sometimes the second – may not be provided at home. Hungry children do not make either good or happy pupils. Giving children a start in life takes on a new meaning.

Most of us are so ignorant and so stupid about the reality of life today. I was amazed when I discovered what was going on and how people live just down the road. The depth of ignorance amongst the middle classes is truly shocking. I am very grateful that I have been able to do something to help make life better for our kids locally. We couldn't get them to attend school and now we cannot keep them away. The kids are very proud of their school. They clearly enjoy it. They are more confident, there is eye contact now. And they are achieving academically. The change the academy has brought to south Reading is dramatic. Education has been the key to helping the underprivileged, education is the key to effecting change, nothing could be more important.

I was very flattered when I was invited to Downing Street and was personally asked by Tony Blair to fund an academy in the East End of London. I refused. My commitment is to Reading because I knew how big the problems were in south Reading and how much we needed to do something for young people there. I doubt if I could have made the same commitment in terms of time and energy if I had agreed to support something in London, however deserving the cause. I had to decide where I could add value and make the most difference and only I could do that.

John Madejski spends half his time on charitable projects, much of it on public speaking, visiting schools and mentoring young people. He is also Chancellor of the University of Reading and is proud of founding and funding the John Madejski School of Reputation at Henley Management College.

Since we started twelve years ago, we have become the leading authority on business reputation. This is a poignant moment as we contemplate what is happening now. The behaviour we are seeing in the banks, the way those who own businesses, the shareholders, are being fleeced by managers who pay themselves too much without any justification. It is not practical, not logical, dishonest and wrong. Good companies depend upon reputation. If everyone was more mindful of reputation, we would not be in the mess we are in now.

John Madejski enjoys a high media profile and his name is attached to many of the philanthropic projects he has supported.

If you have had a tortuous upbringing and you start off with an inferiority complex, giving is a way of redeeming and feeling good about yourself. If that involves publicity and national recognition through the honours system, then I hope what I have been able to do and the public recognition it has attracted will encourage others to believe that they can also make a difference and that they are entitled to enjoy it whilst they are here.

Nicola Maytum, Principal, and colleagues, the
John Madejski Academy, Reading (JMA)

On arrival at JMA, the new building is a bit of shock, 'high-tech' in the midst of a run-down suburb in the poorest part of Reading. Nicola Maytum, JMA's dynamic principal, agrees.

> The new building helps. The local community is so proud and the visual impact is so important. There were two predecessor schools on the site and the buildings were horrible. For the community to have someone believe in them and to create this 'eco' building with state-of-the-art IT, that lifts spirits and makes people feel proud.

Going back to school after nearly fifty years has proved to be another kind of education for me. Head teachers and schools have changed since the 1960s. Nicola has been teaching for twenty years, often in challenging circumstances. I asked her why academies have been successful:

> The key to the success of the original academies is funding. We had the resources to invest in the right number of people to support the students. Most academies have smaller class sizes and we can afford to invest in family work, mentoring and support for children with special needs. We can afford a longer day, one-to-one tuition and funded trips. From the start, we were free to think differently, we could look at the specific circumstances of a particular area and respond to its needs.
>
> What has changed? We have a breakfast club where up to 300 of our 1,000 students have breakfast each day and we encourage the staff to join them. There are literacy, numeracy, science and sports clubs. Sport is our speciality. All that happens first thing

and sets them up for the day so all the kids are engaged before they go into formal teaching.

JMA has been open for six years and the results are encouraging. Before, only 7 per cent of students got five GCSEs including English and Maths. Last year 35 per cent achieved that. This year, we expect that figure will be 50 per cent. Eleven students are going to university this year and that has never happened before. This has been achieved by the pupils' own sense of belief, encouraged by the conviction of the teachers.

We teach citizenship and every student is involved in electing their own school council so they know about voting. They also get involved in charity fundraising. We believe it is important to stop a dependency culture which is so easy in an area like this. We teach the children to give. We celebrate the raising of even small amounts. Working together to achieve something gives everyone a sense of pride.

I asked Katie Royle, Head of Sixth Form, how JMA develops student knowledge of the outside world and encourages them to think about their future.

We teach a discrete subject called personal development which covers crime, drugs, careers and political education. We also offer a personal curriculum designed to meet the needs of students. For example, we work with the University of Reading Law School to hold 'street law' sessions. We also work closely with the Law School to hold a debating competition every year, and that allows students not only to develop a range of skills but also to discuss topical subjects.

We encourage the students to have a national and global perspective as well as knowledge of local issues and charities. We also work with Resolve Mediation. Each year, Resolve works with at least eighty students on a nine-week programme to develop their emotional literacy and conflict management skills. We also work with agencies such as the Police Community Education Officer and other agencies to deliver messages on knife crime or teenage pregnancy, and charities that bring in ex-prisoners to talk to students frankly about the reality of life in prison.

I asked Nicola Maytum about John Madejski's role in establishing JMA and his relationship with it:

Sir John Madejski's money and his vision were the catalyst to bring all this about. People know that he cares passionately about the community. He wanted a school in this part of Reading so that the local people can believe that they are worth it, and to believe that their children can achieve.

He gives so much time to the school and uses his network so generously. The students are able to visit different businesses all because of him. His initial gift has changed everything and has proved transformational for everyone, including Sir John. When Tony Blair opened the door of No. 10 to him, it opened so many doors for so many others. Through Sir John, we have a partnership with the University of Reading which is working with us on a literacy programme and a teacher development programme. A partnership with Reading Football Club has helped us to develop an elite sports programme and he has helped us to take over the local leisure centre which was going to close.

We are so proud of what we have achieved together and what John Madejski has achieved for us. This has been, and is, the best job I have ever had because it is so fulfilling.

What you are reading is not propaganda. I am simply reporting reality, telling true stories about what is possible when talented, professional and committed people come together to do good, inspired by the leadership of philanthropists who are visionary and care about their fellow citizens and communities. I will leave the last word to a student at JMA:

JMA is such a great school which cares about every student, including me and my family, and when it's time to leave I will be very disheartened. This school has helped me so much when it comes to a lot of things like sports and academics. Being an athlete, I have to train hard in becoming better at what I do and the school has helped me in every way. Financially, I found it very hard to keep up with all the demands of my sport and the school were the first to help me. Without them, I don't know how I would be able to continue doing what I love. Also, I found it hard when it comes to something like GCSE Maths which isn't easy for me, so my teacher held after-school sessions for me. I am very thankful. Some good memories have been made here.

❦

Jill Longson, Vice-Chair UWC Atlantic College and Vice-Chair UWC International (formerly known as United World Colleges)

Between April and July 1994, the Hutus of Rwanda slaughtered up to a million of their fellow men, women and children from the Tutsi tribe in one of the world's most notorious genocides. The situation was particularly dangerous for those Rwandans who intermarried. One Hutu-Tutsi family managed to flee across the border with their five-year-old son and were eventually settled in a United Nations refugee camp in Uganda where the family remains.

Eventually, the boy was sent to a United Nations School, many miles away from his family. His fees were paid for by the occasional labouring jobs his father was able to find. He did not see his family for months at a time. His siblings remained behind in the camp in conditions unimaginable for most readers of this book. The boy was intelligent and did well at school. When he was sixteen, he was told to go to Kampala, the capital, to take some examinations. Later, he was told that he had been chosen out of 400 other young people to receive a scholarship to attend UWC Atlantic College in Wales where he would study for two years. However, he must not tell anyone, not even his parents, where he was going as the previous successful candidate had been murdered by a rival.

The boy, now seventeen, eventually set off for Britain some time after the start of term because of visa delays. He said goodbye to his parents, who had no idea where he was going or when they might see him again. He arrived at Heathrow airport on a chilly autumn day with only two shirts, a pair of trousers and a battered pair of shoes. He was met and driven to a remote twelfth-century castle perched above cliffs on the coast of south Wales. This was the United World College of The Atlantic and would be his home for two years. A day or two later, I received a phone call from the College's development office to tell me that Innocent had arrived safely, for I had funded his scholarship. They told me that he didn't have many clothes, and the rest is history.

I have enjoyed a close and rewarding relationship with UWC Atlantic College since 1990 when I was recruited at a dinner in London by Jane Prior, wife of Jim Prior, the former Tory politician, and soon to be the college's chair. Jane did such a good job that I was on a train to south Wales in days, although, in my ignorance, I was deeply suspicious that UWC Atlantic

College might be part of some right-wing operation funded by the CIA. I was wrong. I walked into a haven of liberal values and tolerance. Like everyone who visits, I was seduced by the intelligence, maturity, integrity, enthusiasm and obvious fulfilment of the students, mostly aged between sixteen and eighteen, young people from all over the world who were clearly enjoying the experience of growing up together. I went on to become an adviser and then a governor before retiring from the board in 2010. I have also served on the board of UWC International which represents the Colleges worldwide and chaired its fund-raising committee.

I asked Jill Longson, vice-chair of the college, why it matters. She now spends a great deal of her time supporting the college's effort to raise scholarship funds for those young people who have little or nothing. I asked Jill about her background and what it was like to be at the college:

Both my parents were involved in various charities in Jersey, where I was brought up. We were brought up in a family with a definite set of values and taught to think in terms of helping and giving to others.

I won a scholarship to attend UWC Atlantic College when I was sixteen. I applied more because I heard it would be an outward-bound adventure, not really thinking about the values I would learn there. However, the cultural differences I encountered made an immediate impact upon me. Jersey is a very insular place and the college really opened my mind and my eyes to the world. Atlantic College is the founding member of a remarkable international movement (UWC, formerly United World Colleges), founded by Kurt Hahn in 1962 to promote peace and understanding between nations.

I was immediately aware of how very generous other people

had been to enable UWC Atlantic College to be created and to fund the scholarships for most of the student body. This began to change my thinking about wanting to make a difference in life and what kind of contribution I could make.

After leaving college aged eighteen, Jill went to India as a volunteer and, after university, where she read economic development, she went to Thailand for a year as a volunteer in a leprosy hospital, working as a fundraiser. She then undertook a master's degree and subsequently worked in sales, planning and marketing in the travel industry. In 1997, Colin, her partner, sold his company:

Our lives were transformed by this and we decided to live in Spain. I knew it was time to give back, not just money but energy and commitment too. I realised giving money to Atlantic College wasn't enough because I also wanted to shape the future of something I so strongly believe in.

Colin and Jill started giving on a modest scale with a specific idea. They decided not to support big charities because they wanted some control over how the money was spent. They thought about who had energy, time, passion and commitment but no resources, and the answer was obvious: young students graduating from Atlantic College:

We came up with the idea of GoMAD or go and make a difference. We fund student applications from Atlantic College who want to develop and run community projects anywhere in the world that will make a significant impact. This happens during the summer holiday and before they go on to university. So far, we have supported thirty-five projects in thirty countries. At

£1,000, the awards are small but the leverage is extraordinary. More than 200 students have taken part in those projects having raised the additional funds they need from elsewhere. Many go to countries in continents they have never visited before, doing very hard community work, transforming the lives of others and their lives too. Innocent went back to Rwanda with eight Atlantic College graduates to work in a hostel for orphans. That must have been a truly remarkable experience for all of them, one they will never forget.

Jill joined the governing board of Atlantic College and became chair of the college's capital appeal:

I became more and more involved and have given so much time and energy because I feel so passionate about the cause. Our world is riven by conflict and a lack of understanding between people, nations and cultures. If we can educate the young to be more globally aware, have a value system rooted in humanity, if we can give them the right tools and skills to go out and make a positive difference in the world, and if we can help ignite their passion to do something they truly believe in, then we have a chance to make the world a better place.

I asked Jill about some of the students who have attended the college recently and the role some alumni go on to play:

Our first female Afghan student arrived at Atlantic College in 2008 and her scholarship was funded by consortium of alumni from my year. Not only did this two-year experience transform her life, it transforms the lives of others around her, her fellow students at Atlantic College and at the leading American university she is attending and where she is vice-chair of the

International Relations Society. She is a catalyst for change and provides a bridge to understanding.

A young woman from Peru arrived at the college as a child worker. She has now set her sights upon a career in politics in Peru. Aged twenty-two, she has worked for EOTO, a human rights activist group, she has worked as a social welfare analyst in the Peruvian parliament and is studying for a master's in political science.

Our alumni survey enabled us to see the alignment between mission and reality. The survey company said they have never seen such a close alignment in an educational institution. Many of our alumni go on to do remarkable things. Many work in NGOs, in the diplomatic service in countries in conflict, in the United Nations, in positions of government from Spain to China, one is at the forefront of malaria research, one is the founder of Nokia and another is the CEO of Voluntary Services Overseas.

The college has taken another pioneering step forward, which I believe could play an important role if adopted widely in the UK, in developing a culture of giving. Students may now leave with the Atlantic Diploma as well as the International Baccalaureate (IB). The IB was developed with the help and support of Atlantic College, which was the first to adopt it in the 1970s:

The IB is an excellent qualification but we believe our students are learning something in addition to a specific curriculum, an extra piece of magic. Our mission is about using education to unite people in a more sustainable, socially just and peaceful world and the new diploma is designed to reflect this and the experience the students have as well as their academic achievement.

The college has four new faculties that are on a par with the IB faculties: Global, Environment, Social Justice and Outdoor. Each faculty is led by a member of the academic staff. All students have to be involved with all four faculties and specialise in one of them. Every six weeks, the college stops all academic classes for two days and holds a conference. A recent conference was 'Young Voices In The Middle East', attended by a Jordanian journalist, a Palestinian cartoonist and an Israeli diplomat, giving the students a rare opportunity to examine one of the world's most complex and challenging problems in depth. Students visit the local prison, offering support to the foreign prisoners there and the college also has a link with a charity for refugees in Cardiff. The emphasis is upon personal responsibility and the students are driving much of what they do.

I asked Jill what we might learn from the Atlantic Diploma, given that the Secretary of State for Education is keen on a core curriculum biased in favour of attainment:

> We are committed to providing a value-based education. If you don't have a set of values that drive every aspect of school life then what is the point? The values of respect, service, a sense of idealism, personal challenge, compassion, the celebration of difference and an appreciation of international and intercultural understanding – these values are absolutely fundamental to the ethos of Atlantic College and the new diploma is a manifestation of it. I find it very sad that they are not implicitly part of life in every school.

Finally, I asked Jill what being a philanthropist means to her and if she had a message to encourage others to join her:

> The fulfilment you can feel as a donor or volunteer or both is

like no other. I believe that feeling of fulfilment is an important part of being a human being and that is why it is important for us to have opportunities to give and to serve, at any age, from any background, at any point in your life. I do feel we have lost our way in excessive materialism. I would rather see more generosity of spirit. We do see this from time to time whenever there is a global catastrophe but it is not consistent.

What would I say to someone who isn't giving? That is the hardest question to answer. I simply don't understand why people don't give back, particularly when life has treated you well. Not giving is quite alien to me and I cannot comprehend it. However, if you are thinking about it but don't know where to start, my advice would be to start to think about an organisation that may have affected your life or someone you love, and give now! And offer your time. Enjoy doing it and see what a difference you can make. All the objections to giving – it is all too difficult, the money is wasted, my donation is a drop in the ocean – can be overcome by research and due diligence. There are no excuses.

What is important is to recognise what you feel passionate about, what your skill set is and what skills you want to acquire. You may be surprised by what you can learn and learn about yourself by becoming involved in a cause. The key to any kind of success must be inspiration. If you look hard enough, you will find it.

One way of persuading more people to be more generous, either with their time or with their money, is to encourage them at a formative age. The principles behind the Atlantic Diploma could be applied to all our young people at school, as early as possible. Is Mr Gove listening?

The Brooks World Poverty Institute (BWPI)
at the University of Manchester

Rory and Elizabeth Brooks

Rory Brooks is a leading evangelist for philanthropy in higher education.

When I graduated from Manchester, I didn't think I would visit either the university or Manchester again, but when Elizabeth and I went to work in the USA in our early twenties, we saw how our colleagues were giving to their colleges and communities. This had a tremendous influence upon how we felt and behaved, an influence we would not have felt in London at the end of the 1970s and 1980s. I realised that, as I had been the first in my family to go to university, it was a transforming experience that turned both of us into the people we are now.

Having returned to London and after founding MML Capital, a private equity company, Rory and Elizabeth were now in a position to make significant gifts of money and to commit their time and energy to make a difference. Rather than simply contribute to the cost of a security guard in their area to combat local crime, Elizabeth decided to try to address the causes of crime by becoming a trustee and giving financial support to a local charity working with young people growing up in difficult circumstances. Elizabeth chairs the Patrons of Tate, whose annual donations are crucial to Tate's ability to build the national collection of British art and the collection of international modern and contemporary art.

Rory initially supported a chair of enterprise at the University of Manchester Institute of Science and Technology (UMIST) and became chairman of its Alumni Society. When UMIST merged with the Victoria University of Manchester in 2004:

> We realised that this was an important moment in the history of the university and an opportunity to help build its capacity as a centre of excellence. We could also see that in future, higher education in Britain would need more investment. We wanted to fund something that was not business-related and that was not then being supported by others. We were also looking for a cause that would have impact beyond Manchester and academia. It is clear that poverty on a global basis is the most serious inequality we face and that, in the midst of so much wealth and prosperity, it is simply not right that we should have so many people on the planet who are living desperate lives.

The Brookses understood that their own personal resources could only make a limited impact on the ground so decided to establish the Brooks World Poverty Institute as a centre of research bringing together anthropologists, economists, political scientists, sociologists, architects and planners with the common goal of helping to eradicate poverty. Nobel Laureate Professor Joseph Stiglitz was the Institute's chairman.

Rory Brooks muses:

> Have we changed lives? Our money is very small in the face of a massive global problem but we can punch above our weight by promoting research which leads to better policies and better outcomes for very poor people. We are beginning to see the impact our work is having in Bangladesh and Zimbabwe, for example.

Before visiting the University of Manchester, I asked Rory what impact philanthropy has had upon the Brookses' lives and if they could recommend giving to those who have yet to commit:

> We have found that although our giving is planned, our philanthropy has taken us on an unplanned and unexpected journey which has enabled us to discover and unleash creativity in ourselves and the people we work with, and to have an experience which is so motivating, exciting, energising and thrilling. To know that we are doing what we can to make the world a better place is very motivating. It really is possible to make a difference even with limited funds. And whilst it is our aim to use our good fortune to help others, our lives have also been transformed.

❦

Huraera Jabeen, postgraduate student

When I agreed to talk to Huraera Jabeen, who is engaged in postgraduate studies with BWPI, I had not realised I was meeting a philanthropist. Passionate, eloquent and evangelical, she launched into the story of her life with such urgency that I soon understood why she should look so fulfilled on a cold, wet and grey day in Manchester:

> I was born in Bangladesh in 1971 during the war of liberation from Pakistan, at a time when there was great anticipation for change. My mother told me that whenever there was bombing, she could feel me tensing and cringing in the womb and then I would relax when the shelling stopped. Peace came when I was only six months old so that was a good time to begin life.
>
> Relatively speaking, we were privileged. I grew up in a liberal

environment, part of a very large extended family, many of whom lived in the countryside, so I knew how people lived in rural areas. From an early age, I was aware of the need to help others. Whoever you are and wherever you are, you have to give something. And the poor do give to the poor.

After graduation, Huraera started working as an architect but soon realised that her vocation was to help the poor more directly. She looked for development-related work and won a British Council scholarship to study in the Development Planning Unit in University College, London which led her to work for BRAC University (an associated institution of BRAC, formerly the Bangladesh Rehabilitation and Aid Committee), the world's largest non-governmental organisation (NGO), where she was based in Bangladesh.

My supervisor said that if you want to know how to help people who live in slums, then you have to go and see for yourself. So I went into the biggest slum in Bangladesh. I was considered a very odd person, even by my mother. Being in the slums was a revelation for me and a shock to my value system when I thought about how much I was being paid compared to their incomes. I sat on a woman's bed and she said to me: 'You should not be here. But you are here and that changes everything.' And then I thought about whether I would welcome them into my home and allow them to sit on my bed?

I realised I had a lot more to learn. Although I was engaged with the poor, I realised that I was doing what everyone else does which was labelling them as poor, rather than thinking about the causes of their poverty. Labelling was a way of keeping them at a distance. Many people just regard slum dwellers as criminals. I realised that I needed to learn from their experience if I wanted to learn about community development. I was fortunate to have been given an education and this has given me a perspective.

Knowledge is the greatest gift. So I realised that I needed to understand the reasons for inequality so that I would then be in a position to search for solutions. So I applied to undertake research into the impact of climate change on the slum dwellers in Dhaka, the capital city, and that is where I met Rory and Elizabeth Brooks. They invited me to Manchester in 2009.

Huraera's project is to research the impact of climate change on the everyday lives of men and women in the slums. Policy planners are currently focusing upon climate extremes, such as impacts of heat and intense rain on slum dwellers, rather than average weather conditions. Her research is bringing grass-roots experience to policy-makers for the first time.

I have discovered that the poor have developed their own ways of building homes that can cope with increased heat which are cost-effective and efficient. I have asked the people if they are happy with what they have made for themselves and they say it is good enough. All this is done by the people for themselves within their own social and cultural context. There is no recognition of this at the policy level. When the policy planners say we need to change the drainage system to cope with more water, they are not considering the needs of the urban poor who are 30 per cent of Dhaka's population.

What we are saying is that what the poor have achieved and built are assets and should be recognised as such. This is radical. The government does not need to create new housing from nothing. They need to adapt policy to recognise and build on the assets that already exist. There is a common misconception that the poor are always asking for something. They are realists and will be happy with small improvements. This is real sustainability.

As a result of Rory and Elizabeth's decision to invest in BWPI, everyone learns, including them. The result is that this new knowledge will have an impact upon the lives of millions of people. When they visited Bangladesh in 2009, a member of the community asked Rory what the results of our work will be. He pointed at me and said: ask her in three years' time. So I feel very responsible.

Think about wealth in the old days. We thought about gold and minerals. Nowadays, wealth is as likely to be about information, how you use it and turn it into knowledge. Knowledge is wealth. Knowledge creates opportunities. Yes, my personal life has been enriched in so many ways but the impact of all this upon others will be truly significant. Something of value has been created for millions.

❦

Dr Niki Banks, Research Associate

Niki Banks felt an emotional and intellectual tug towards development issues whilst at university. She worked for BRAC for a year and a half, working in three city slums. Her PhD was funded by the Brookses, after which she spent time in Uganda, and she is currently preparing a research proposal on urban poverty in Africa and its impact on youth. She has also been working on climate change and poverty in Bangladesh.

BWPI puts the results of our research into academic journals and we then give the information to the policy people via workshops at the local level. We have to find ways of packaging our reports in a way that will reach the right audience and be accepted.

Urban poverty is under-researched and is a relatively recent phenomenon in Bangladesh. It is also a big problem for policy planners who prefer to ignore it. There is an ongoing belief that Bangladesh is a rural society, but soon there will be more people living in cities than in the countryside. Policy-makers do not want that to happen and neither do the wealthy who have a lot of influence over the policy and who are not naturally sympathetic to the needs of the poor.

The real issue is insufficient work and very low pay. The poor are crippled by debt and it costs more to live in the city. The slum leadership is a very small circle that owns the property which the poor rent. If we want to deliver a new drainage system or latrines, these resources may be kept by the leadership and distributed to their cronies. They use aid to consolidate their power. Inequality is getting worse in the slums.

So we have to work with communities at grass-roots level, mobilising the poorest to articulate their needs and challenge the power of the leaders to weaken their influence. The importance of our research is to enable the Bangladesh authorities to understand what is happening at ground level.

I would not have been able to do a PhD without the support of Elizabeth and Rory Brooks. The whole experience of being part of such a high-quality team is so valuable. Our work has been driven higher by being part of BWPI. We would not have the same global profile without their philanthropy and we would not have been so effective without it.

Professor David Hulme, Executive Director

Not surprisingly, David Hulme ñeeds to travel and was abroad when I visited Manchester. We spoke later on the telephone and I asked for his perspective on the Brookses' philanthropy, its impact upon his work and what BWPI may expect to achieve.

Rory Brooks and I started talking in 2005. This was a time when the university was thinking boldly after its merger and Rory wanted to refocus and increase his commitment. A group of us had been working for some time on poverty issues and the university had been interested in low-income countries for sixty years.

So we were already doing a great deal of work but there was so much more to be done which we could not afford to do, mainly because what we wanted to achieve fell outside the remit of government-funded programmes. When you are funded by government, you have to fulfil their objectives.

We were able to have a very imaginative and stimulating discussion with Rory Brooks. Good philanthropists, such as Rory, are interested in pushing out the boundaries. When well executed, philanthropy can enable universities to be much more flexible in the way that they work, particularly in research. He listened and encouraged us to redefine our objectives. He has certainly and quite rightly been demanding in terms of output and objectives, but, having satisfied himself that he believed and had confidence in what we wanted to do, he has left operational matters to us. He does not micro-manage. We launched BWPI in 2006 as an international centre of excellence, established to create and share knowledge to end poverty and to shape policies that deliver real gains for people in poverty. The two main benefits are that funding from the Brookses has enabled us to attract more PhD students, thereby establishing a successor generation of academic professionals who undertake work which was previously unaffordable.

You know what we have been able to do in Bangladesh but our ability to work in Zimbabwe has been crucial, principally because the usual sponsors are not prepared to invest in what are perceived to be failing countries. The Brookses' money enables us to start research programmes into Zimbabwe and to collect previously unavailable data. This has enabled Zimbabwean academics to remain connected to the outside world and has given us access to politicians and civil servants from a research- and evidence-based point of view.

We have been able to develop an excellent relationship with the Minister of Finance, Tendai Biti of the Movement for Democratic Change. He gave a lecture at the university last year. It is crucial he understands why states fail and how they can be saved. He gave a masterclass to our students, who were riveted.

We have got to a point where the government in Zimbabwe is able to start thinking about the measures it can take to rescue the failing state; the need to invest in some welfare provision such as pensions and to underpin the financial situation with sound banking. We have been working with all the political parties in an attempt to help them understand how to build upon land reform, which has resulted in 141,000 new small landowners. We need the new landowners to understand that they have a stake in a stable government that is committed to maintaining an infrastructure and a functioning society, that they are in fact capitalists.

Having digested the irony that those who forcibly grabbed land in a country which calls itself socialist are becoming capitalists,

I am amazed at what such a – in relative terms – modest investment has been able to produce. I hope Rory and Elizabeth
Brooks' imaginative philanthropy will encourage others.
However, the point is not just what you give but how you do
it. As I am now non-executive, independent and beholden to
no one, I have no need to flatter and can say what I believe and
know to be true. This is philanthropy at its best.

❧

Dame Nancy Rothwell, President and Vice-Chancellor,
University of Manchester

From medieval through Victorian to modern times, philanthropists have been responsible for founding and funding our great
universities. Yet, only a dozen years ago, the number of academic
institutions attracting private donations was small, in contrast to
the USA and other countries. This was before the great reduction in state funding for the higher education sector.

Concerned by the squeeze on public funding and the need to
compete in the market for philanthropic donations, the Higher
Education Funding Council for England (HEFCE) commissioned a report from More Partnership which was published in
2012. Their review told a more positive story indicating a significant change in attitude and policy in the last five years.

Funds raised annually have increased from £513 million five
years ago to £693 million today. Sixteen per cent more institutions reported an overall rise of 35 per cent in funds raised
from 54 per cent more donors. We know that higher education
accounts for more million-pound gifts than any other sector.
However, over 200,000 donors gave to UK universities in
2010–11 and their gifts range from 50p to £75 million, so the

universities are being much more successful in engaging modest donors as well as billionaires.

Giving to higher education in the UK has even grown since the recession started in 2008, in contrast to North America and whilst other charitable giving has declined at home. 'Why?' I asked Dame Nancy Rothwell, President and Vice-Chancellor of Manchester University. I also asked her to explain what makes universities so appealing to major benefactors. We only had half an hour to talk over lunch but she barely paused for breath, never mind a sandwich:

> We have changed, particularly since the merger with UMIST in 2004. There has been a tremendous change in ambition, change on the campus and real change in the approach to philan-thropy. Previously we fundraised for the odd project but there were no targets, absolutely no strategy, no commitment and no engagement with alumni and donors. Fundraising is now mainstream and we have a first-rate director and team who are there not just to raise money but to nurture relationships and develop partnerships.
>
> We have been successful because Alan Gilbert, our Vice-Chancellor after the merger, came in with a very clear sense of purpose: to lift our game with a strong commitment to outstanding research, excellent education and social respon-sibility. This has changed us. We have put a lot of effort into being accessible. We are in a relatively wealthy area with a lot of deprivation close by. We are committed to producing graduates who have a strong sense of social responsibility and who have a commitment to volunteering.
>
> We are welcoming, embracing and leading change. The big challenge we face is twofold. We have lost almost all the taxpay-ers' investment in students so we have to bring that back via

fees. There is some public investment in science and if we lost that it would be problematic. Investment in research is very low compared with our international competitors. And there is no capital funding for universities, which is a very big issue.

However, we must be positive. There are great opportunities for philanthropists and we welcome them. I want our donors to see themselves as investors. If you invest well in the higher education sector, you can achieve a huge return in terms of societal and personal impact. We have a scheme for the best students from Uganda, Rwanda and Bangladesh in memory of Alan Gilbert who died so soon after his retirement. They do very well and all go back. I would argue that £10,000 or £20,000 invested in those students will be worth far more than ten times that in their own countries. A young man came from Rwanda to do project management. I asked him why and he said because he was going back to create his country's first international airport. Another student is going to restructure the public health service in Uganda. Investing in people via higher education can make a huge impact, whether in conflict resolution or research into Alzheimer's. You can see where the money is going and you can follow the student, which is very motivating for the donor.

One Kenyan student grew up in the rubbish tips of Nairobi. His father was shot by the drug barons and he says he found a prospectus for Manchester University in the rubbish! Someone in the World Health Organization helped him study and to apply to us. He won a scholarship to do a one-year master's in management studies and he passed with distinction. I think we are looking at a future leader of Kenya and all from an investment of £10,000.

The Brooks World Poverty Institute is making a real impact. One of our staff in the institute there has been doing research into supply chains between the northern and southern hemispheres. One result has been to link southern producers with northern companies and that has real impact over and above the value of academic research. We have had a great exchange of students through the BWPI.

David Hulme and BWPI have won a £6 million investment from the Department for International Development. This probably would not have happened without the reputation we have earned and that would not have been possible without the philanthropy of the Brookses.

Nancy Rothwell sees the university playing a major role in the renaissance of Manchester, working closely with the city authorities, philanthropists, the local enterprise partnership and schools. She places great emphasis on the university's commitment to social responsibility and the development of a culture of giving:

We are very keen on the idea of global citizenship. We have the Manchester Leadership Programme involving over a thousand students which I would like to see rolled out to everyone. Philanthropy and volunteering are an important part of the course. We also do a lot of voluntary work with schools. We help deprived kids with their applications to any university. This has all happened in the last ten years as a result of our decision to have social responsibility as one of our aims. That was a big decision. Appointments and promotions take this into account. We will know when we have been successful when young people apply because of our social responsibility commitment, when our donors and investors acknowledge it and finally when the local community talks about *our* university rather than *the* university and we are part of their community.

My time was up. I reflected that all universities now need their vice-chancellors to be a force of nature.

Dame Nancy said: 'The university is a very generous environment because money is not a driver. I could earn five times more elsewhere but I am not interested.'

❧

Chris Cox, Director of Development, University of Manchester

I wanted to hear from the man responsible for raising the money and to have his perspective on why philanthropists should give to universities and to Manchester in particular. Chris Cox has been Director of Development since 2005. He was appointed shortly after the merger. I know from personal experience that heads of fundraising need to be able to manage upwards, downwards and sideways simultaneously and I wondered how he had coped with a newly merged university fired up by ambition. He told me that one of the most important factors determining success was that the university was sufficiently imaginative to give him time to develop relationships with donors so that they could help shape a thematic fundraising programme. This meant that gifts were strategically aligned and also meant that the university was able to develop a sophisticated message which was more likely to appeal to donors:

> The easiest way to describe our approach is to say what we don't do. We don't play the alma mater, sense of loyalty, you-must-give-back card. We rarely refer to the university's standing. We focus much more on the issues the university is addressing beyond the campus, that we are an effective agent for change in issues that are as important to our donors as to ourselves, such as inequality in education and the need for scholarship funding.

Our feedback tells us that scholarships make a difference to our students from poorer backgrounds, whatever government might say. Scholarships help to encourage students who are worried about taking the plunge because even the possibility of debt of £30,000 is off-putting. We are the only country in the world that has gone on to full-fee system within a year. Others have phased it in. Scholarships are the most single popular cause for donors and alumni scholarship donation has gone up by 40 per cent in the last year, despite the recession.

Our programme for outstanding students from Bangladesh, Uganda and Rwanda is appealing to donors because it attracts some of our brightest students. Poverty is a key area for us, as are social cohesion, cancer research and regenerative medicine. All this enables us to talk about the university as an agent for change and progress. Our case for support is much more about the future rather than the university.

We are very clear that we are not expecting private-sector support to keep the lights on. We try to steer clear of what might be politically controversial and we were initially nervous about asking for private support for tuition fees. However, the extent of the financial crisis meant that people got over that and are giving to scholarships.

Increasingly, it is becoming impossible to do a PhD without private funding. Government funding is in short supply. The crunch point comes in 2015 when the first undergraduates who have paid fees consider the possibility of doing a postgraduate degree. How can they consider with such a high level of debt? The government is silent. This looks like a train crash in two years' time and the main casualty will be research. This is very serious for the knowledge base for the country.

People do not realise that the USA puts a higher proportion of GDP into education than we do in addition to a huge amount of philanthropy. The level of public investment in education in the US is far higher than here and US universities are not entirely dependent upon the private sector.

Supporting a postgraduate student can be a very rewarding experience. It can open a new way of life for a donor, new ways of thinking and new networks. If only more people knew what it is like to give, they would do it. Giving is such a positive thing to do. But people do need to be asked in the right way.

Unfortunately, the government doesn't have much idea. Most politicians and civil servants believe people get out of bed in the morning and think: 'Oh, I must make my charitable donation today.' That it is somehow going to be the top of their list of priorities. This is, of course, nonsense. Government has no idea what is involved, how long it takes, the importance of being asked by the right person in the right way at the right time. Government just doesn't do empathy or high-end emotional intelligence.

However, when people say that we should be entirely funded by government, we say that our turnover is more than Manchester airport and Manchester United combined. Does it ever make sense to depend upon one source of income? We need a strong philanthropic contribution to help guarantee our independence from government.

I left Manchester having concluded my investigation into the role of philanthropists in education. Inevitably, having just visited the Brooks World Poverty Institute, I found myself being led by the primary concern of many donors today: poverty and deprivation. Our next stop will be a soup kitchen in the USA.

CHAPTER 8

Dignity and respect: philanthropists and fulfilment

Who would have thought the six-year-old working-class boy serving soup to people poorer than himself in Peabody, Massachusetts in the early 1960s would one day become feted internationally as a banker and a philanthropist, receiving the Prince of Wales' Ambassador Award in recognition for his services to the homeless, a CBE for his services to the arts and to charity and be made a Knight of the Order of St Gregory by Pope John Paul II for his humanitarian work?

John Studzinski joined Morgan Stanley in 1980 and moved to London soon after, where he was instrumental in building the fortunes of the company in Britain and Europe. After three years with HSBC, John now runs Blackstone Advisory Partners and is a senior managing director of the Blackstone Group. He divides his time between London and New York but to those of us who have worked with him over the years, he is regarded as a Londoner and I suspect that is how he feels.

I came to know John when he was a trustee at Tate and saw first-hand how a committed philanthropist works and we discussed this as I was preparing for my book:

The point is that it is not about the money you give, it is not what time you get up in the morning but what you do in the day. You can sometimes accomplish more with two-thirds time and networking and one-third money. It's about the three Ts: time, talent and treasure. We need to encourage the former two, if we are to harvest the third.

The core of philanthropy is about passion. In the late nineteenth century, philanthropy was about administering to the poor and homeless, part of a Victorian mindset about looking after people. At the same time the great robber barons built their great fortunes and I love the notion that behind every great fortune there is a great crime and because a crime has been committed, there is great guilt. You had people wanting to give back great sums of money by building schools and hospitals.

John believes that philanthropy should now be more broadly defined and that we can all play a role in changing society for the better. He believes that being part of something is important:

The Brits think you cannot teach volunteering but that is rubbish. I started dishing out soup to the poor in the US at the age of six, part of my family's tradition. The poor are part of life. And I learned as a child how to make them part of mine. I came from a working-class and immigrant background. My parents are Polish and came through Ellis Island. I am first-generation American. We were brought up in a diaspora of people who helped each other, the community helping the community.

If every child over the age of ten had a few hours pushing people around in a wheelchair, their outlook on life would be transformed. There is a whole range of things people could be encouraged to do. Young people need role models. Volunteering and giving time is a way of teaching the young philanthropy, even though it is nothing to do with money. I take children from the age of ten to Lourdes, but rather than teach them Christianity I ask them to help the old and sick with their chores. You would be surprised how the children start to glow because this is the first time they can help someone else. This is the way to teach people basic human values. You cannot teach a child to give money but you can teach the value of service, the importance of respecting the old, the sick and the different.

John is concerned that the young are becoming disengaged and more isolated because information technology is limiting social interaction.

I worry about adults who have achieved extraordinary material success but who seem similarly disengaged and isolated from the rest of society, and who neither pay tax nor give charitably. I am sick and tired of all this talk about people not paying their taxes. I pay my taxes, but then all Americans have to. I am fed up with those Brits who don't pay tax by escaping to Monaco and they have titles. It is a disgrace. These knighthoods should be withdrawn.

I asked John what charities should learn from his experience as a philanthropist and how they should engage those who are not giving:

Half of the richest 10 per cent don't give. They have to be taught. It can take people who were once poor a long time to get onto the philanthropy bike and then learn to ride it. You have to get people engaged before they give, through outreach and advocacy. You have to be able to share your passion with them and to get them to respond by sharing their ideas. Don't ask for money straight away. Just asking for a cheque might work but it can be a bit of a kiss-off. They may walk away and you may never see them again.

The key to persuading people to give is to have a relationship with them. People need to get to know, like and respect the people they are dealing with. People need to feel trust and that they are going to be treated as a human being and not just as a cheque book. Look at Tate: some people have been invited to dinner for ten years before they made a gift! If you give people security and nurture their passion at their pace, the gift is more likely to come.

I asked John what advice he would give to the rich who are as yet unsure about giving:

What are you interested in? What do you want to learn about? Who do you want to meet? Who do you want to hang around? Go to a charity and ask them what do they really need and then do something really transformational for them, but which only you can do. Find someone you think you might like and get to know them really well. Find charities you really believe in and which have visionary leaders.

John was, of course, describing himself and what he has done. I asked him what principles motivate him, in life as well as philanthropy:

The need to respect and preserve human dignity. I work for the homeless to try to give their lives more structure. One in four ex-servicemen become homeless and that is shocking. We don't do enough to prepare these men for civilian life. I work for human rights and I support the arts. I created the Genesis Foundation ten years ago which supports and nurtures young artists in addition to funding them. All these causes I support come back to identity, self-worth and dignity.

For further illumination on how to be a good philanthropist and to illustrate the good giving can do, I talked to three of the charitable organisations John supports.

❦

Ken Roth, Executive Director, Human Rights Watch

Human Rights Watch has come to the fore in recent years. When I was young, Amnesty International was the major force focusing on human rights but now they share the stage, at a time when they seem to be needed more than ever. Ken Roth explained how this came about and the role John Studzinski has played as vice-chairman.

We do have a mass membership which is important to us but most of the money we raise comes from major donors. Small donors give from a core belief in our mission. Major donors share that belief as well, but they often also want to make a personal impact with their gift, to help to change the world for the better. We have to show them that through our lobbying, media coverage and efforts to prosecute abusers, we can make an important difference; that through our work made possible by the support they give, we and they are making an impact. Once they see that, donors become enthusiastic supporters.

John Studzinski has given generously, but equally impor-tant, he has recruited many influential donors from all over the world. He became involved fourteen years ago when Human Rights Watch was a quarter the size it is now. We were not a global operation then. We now operate in some ninety countries worldwide and have advocacy centres in Paris, Berlin, Geneva, London, Brussels, Washington, New York, Tokyo, Johannesburg, Beirut and Brazil. As a result, we have significantly increased the number of governments we can reach. That helps us to maximise pressure on abusive governments. For example, Zimbabwean President Robert Mugabe doesn't care about what the US and the UK think but he does care what South Africa thinks. Sri Lanka may not care about the US and Europe, but it does care about India and Japan. We now are poised to influence foreign policies of these important regional powers.

John has been one of the strongest proponents of our strategic, global development. We are now also a global brand with an international board. John has been instrumental in our growth because of his powerful international network, including donors, journalists and government officials.

Amnesty International globally is some four or five times bigger than we are and relies upon mobilising a mass membership. We don't try to replicate what they do. We complement each other, with Human Rights Watch focused on shaming abusive governments in the media and promoting the policy debates needed to enlist pressure from influential governments for abuses to stop. Our budget and staff are much smaller, but we are able to recruit first-class people who often become world experts on a particular country or issue, such as Syria. Our researchers immerse themselves in the countries where they work. Few others will have their depth of knowledge. This is our strength. We also have emergency teams of researchers without portfolio who can go into emergency situations to assist the country researcher when problems become too overwhelming for one person to handle alone.

Our fundamental core value is the dignity of every individual. We focus upon the needs and the plight of the weakest and most disadvantaged in society. We try to address inequality not through emergency aid but by drawing attention to, and ending, the structural and political causes of oppression and the poverty it produces.

Our ability to operate is entirely dependent on voluntary income. To maintain our independence, we accept no state or public funding. The leadership and generosity of John Studzinski and people like him have enabled us to be in the position we are today, able to draw attention to atrocities and human rights outrages across the world, not least currently in Syria and the Middle East, and to generate pressure for them to end.

❦

Sir Nicholas Serota, Director, Tate

I wanted to explore further the idea that philanthropists can contribute so much more than just money. John Studzinski has been exceptionally generous to Tate in a number of ways and I asked Sir Nicholas Serota what that involved:

We first encountered John in the early 1990s when he was a rising star at Morgan Stanley. With his increasing interest in the visual arts, he was attracted by our thinking about the future of Tate, our wish to renew the collection and advance the place of the visual arts in society. We were at the early stages of thinking about creating a museum of modern art in this country (which eventually became Tate Modern). His position was not simply the point of view of a serious collector but more from the perspective of enabling a better understanding of the arts and by what our plans would mean for London.

He helped us to raise money at a very early stage in the creation of Tate Modern and was amongst the first to commit a serious sum to it. He gradually became more and more involved and eventually served as a trustee for ten years. He continues to be close to us and has been crucial to stage two of Tate Modern by becoming a benefactor for the second time.

John doesn't sit on the sidelines. He doesn't just give money and play no part. There must be many causes that approach him which he doesn't support, partly because he is so busy and committed to business at an international level. He will only get involved where he can really help and where he can make a difference through his acumen, his wit and an acute sense of what needs to be done at a particular moment. He is a participant.

John is unusual in that he punches above his weight with his giving. He has given £5 million to the expansion of Tate Modern and that must represent a significant proportion of his wealth. There are plenty of rich people who don't give a fraction of that. He has this commitment to giving across a range of causes such as Human Rights Watch; he gives to a local charity (The Passage) that relieves poverty and helps people to get off the streets. He is also engaged with high culture and is able to balance those interests, regarding the arts as being as valuable to society as these socially useful causes. He believes that the arts give people opportunities, they raise aspirations, give young people the opportunity to express themselves, affording them the chance to have a much broader vision of the world. The arts are about the exchange of ideas at an international level. All this gives you a sense that the money you are putting in can make a positive difference to people and to society.

I asked Nicholas Serota why fundraising for the arts can be more challenging:

There are a number of reasons why the arts are at the bottom rather than the top of the list of charities receiving donations from individuals. The creation of the Arts Council after the Second World War was very necessary and a very good thing but it did mean that people were able to persuade themselves the arts were provided for and philanthropy was not needed. It has only been in the last twenty years that has begun to change because state funding has not increased and has been reduced in recent years. Also, arts organisations have begun to realise that plural funding from a range of sources makes their position more sustainable. There is a great deal to be said for having a body of people around you who care passionately about what you do, critical friends, rather than just addressing a government minister. The arts have, as a result, become much better about formulating reasons to give.

Over the last twenty-five years, Tate's grant from the taxpayer has declined from being 80 per cent of budget to 35 per cent, the balance being raised through earnings and support from the private sector. During this period, audiences have risen from 1.75 million to 7.75 million a year (with another 20 million visiting online) due to expansion to St Ives and to Liverpool, and the creation of Tate Modern.

Philanthropy of every kind has been crucial to enabling Tate to attract such a vast audience. Tate Modern is now the most visited museum of modern and contemporary international art in the world. Gifts of capital, corporate sponsorship and annual personal giving, not least by Tate's 104,000 members, have enabled this to happen despite a decline in public funding and recession. We would never have been able to expand Tate Modern or to renew Tate Britain without private support. Forty-two million of the £45 million we have just raised for Tate Britain is private money. We are renewing a building that is over a hundred years old, created by an act of philanthropy by Henry Tate on condition that the nation would look after it! The majority of the money donated to the renewal of the building has come from Britain and from people with family ties to Britain.

Much of the money for the creation of and now the expansion of Tate Modern has come from overseas, which is not surprising as the building is the home of our international collection. Our American donors were attracted by the idea that there would be a new museum in Europe which would engage in dialogue with their own institutions and which would present the work of American artists. And they like the idea of supporting and being involved with one of a very few museums in the world where you may be sure to see the greatest artists exhibited.

Given Tate's record in attracting both philanthropic and moral support from donors such as John Studzinski, I asked Nick Serota why the arts should continue to receive support from the taxpayer:

We are rather good at the arts in this country, we are good at film, theatre, literature, all kinds of music but perhaps the biggest change we have seen is that Britain has become a much more visually conscious nation in recent years. The visual arts have flourished, starting with Henry Moore and Barbara Hepworth after the war. British architects are now recognised all over the world. All this has been made possible by investment from the taxpayer.

The Olympics opening ceremony was a work of art, based upon the achievements of artists and creative people who were nurtured by the public sector.

The Olympics opening ceremony, almost universally acclaimed, was funded by public money and whilst we were on the thorny subject of tax, those who pay and those who don't, and as John Studzinski has expressed himself forcibly on the subject, I asked Nick for a view:

There are two kinds of non-doms. There are those British people who choose to live abroad to avoid paying British tax and who, with a very few notable exceptions, are not philanthropic. And then there are those who are not British who choose to live here but who need not pay British taxes. Some of these non-doms from other countries who live here are exceptionally generous and philanthropic. I think it is perfectly reasonable that people who live here long-term should make a contribution and many do. It was unfortunate that a move came before the recession that implied that people were not pulling their weight and were avoiding tax. This was done for political reasons and may have discouraged some from making a commitment. And I think it unfortunate that those who have come to live here and who have been exceptionally generous have not always been acknowledged or fully recognised.

The way the non-dom tax arrangement was introduced was clumsy and unhelpful to institutions that need to raise significant money from such people in the national interest and for the benefit of the public.

One of the problems we have is that politicians don't

understand people who give money. That is a big problem. The other challenge we need to overcome is to encourage governments to be consistent. Politicians find it hard to think about the long term. They should be thinking about where we want to be in ten to twenty years and how to get there. If you look back twenty-five years, the arts were in a very different place to where they are now. Look at what has happened to the Royal Opera House, the National Theatre and many smaller theatres and art centres and galleries across the country, where we have seen a remarkable flowering thanks to the National Lottery. Who would have thought that 400,000 people a year would visit an art gallery in Margate? This has happened as a result of commitment and investment from both the public and private sector and shows what can be achieved by thinking long-term.

Nick Serota welcomed the efforts of Jeremy Hunt, former Secretary of State for Culture, Media and Sport, to raise philanthropy on to the national agenda but is critical of the impression that was given that things could happen overnight. Governments have a habit of lecturing arts organisations, implying they are not very good at fundraising. Maria Miller, successor to Jeremy Hunt, said shortly after her appointment that the arts need to become better at asking than receiving. Coming soon after the tax relief row following the 2012 Budget when philanthropists were branded as tax dodgers, and ignoring the many hundreds of millions of pounds raised by the arts in recent years, not least by Tate, Miller succeeded in alienating those philanthropists who have helped to fund a remarkable flowering in the arts as well as those who have created it.

If only our government ministers had the insight, intelligence, strategic skills and commitment to the long term that are the characteristics of our most successful arts leaders. It is these attributes that philanthropists such as John Studzinski are looking for, and that is why I regard our most effective philanthropists as investors. John Studs, as he is known affectionately, has as diverse a portfolio as we are about to find out on the streets of Westminster.

※

*The Passage, Westminster, London, Mick Clarke,
CEO and Sister Ellen Flynn, Chair*

There are almost 2,000 people sleeping on the streets of London and a large proportion of these will end up in Westminster and in the care of The Passage, a Catholic charity based near Westminster Cathedral. John Studzinski is a member of the board, a volunteer and a donor. I asked Mick Clarke, chief executive, how The Passage helps the homeless and how he and his colleagues are coping with recession:

There has been a big increase in 'flow' but we do seem to be coping. We tend to get hit first by tomorrow's social exclusion problems. We have a street team out in Westminster every night of the week and every day of the year. We have about 200 people a day coming through our doors. The challenge is to see that number of people and treat everyone as an individual.

We manage because we constantly remind ourselves what our values are and these can be found in any faith or system of belief: 'Kindness is the key to hearts.' We aim to encourage and to inspire but we also challenge and encourage those who come to us to transform their lives, albeit with our help. This can be the way you say 'yes' and the way you say 'no'. The key to this is respect.

We charge for food and clothing. This is about dignity. We don't want people to feel that they are charity cases. We also offer a variety of other services, mental health work in partnership with the NHS and we also help people to find work.

We do offer shelter in this building for those who need it. However, it is not acceptable for us to say come to us and we will look after you for a few days and then you can go back onto the street. We look at the issues that have led to people going on to the street. If there are drug and alcohol issues, these need to be addressed. We are all about trying to break the cycle and referring people on to specialised services as appropriate.

The Passage, which celebrated its thirtieth anniversary in 2010, has a turnover of just over £4 million and it had to make savings in its 2011–12 budget of £500,000 because of cuts in its statutory funding and declining fundraising income, despite an increase in the number of rough sleepers in London. The Passage is having to do more with less.

Mick Clarke praises the commitment of Westminster Council but worries that the government funding the council receives is no longer ring-fenced. His fundraising target is a challenging £2 million a year. John Studzinski is a great help in this respect:

John is very generous with his money and has helped to raise a lot of money for us but he is even more generous with his time. In addition to volunteering by serving food, John puts in a lot of time as a trustee. We meet for at least an hour every month, despite his international travel schedule, when we look at 'the business of the poor'. I feel I can discuss anything with him. I am amazed he can give so much time to me and it makes a big difference.

I would like to challenge the concept of what philanthropy is. However important money is, time is crucial. It is right that the very wealthy should give but it is all relative. Anyone can be a philanthropist if they have time to give. However, that should not be an excuse for the wealthy not to give.

Once a month, we receive a letter from an elderly woman and inside is a piece of cardboard upon which is taped a pound. This is like the widow's mite. This woman is a philanthropist.

Sister Ellen Flynn is the living embodiment of The Passage's mission: 'To encourage, inspire and challenge.' Formerly chief executive of The Passage and now Chair of the Board, Sister Ellen is a Daughter of Charity. As such, she belongs to an international Roman Catholic congregation of women founded by Vincent de Paul and Louise de Marillac. Their guiding belief is that 'love embraces social justice and we commit ourselves to work for social transformation to change the unjust structures that cause poverty'.

John was at The Passage before I was. He had been involved since he arrived in the UK from the US in the 1980s. By the time I arrived in 2000, he was part of the brickwork. At that time, we only had a day centre and he helped us by raising the money to build a night shelter which transformed the organisation and our ability to support homeless people. He was there when Cardinal Hume provided night shelter in sleeping bags on the floor of the cathedral hall in the late 1990s. Just before I arrived at The Passage, John had chaired the fundraising committee and helped my predecessor, Sister Bridie Dowd, to raise the £2 million we needed. It would not have happened without John.

He likes to know exactly what is going on and what the policy implications are so that he can make high-level representations.

He is such a powerful advocate and ambassador. He is particularly good talking about the causes of homelessness.

John's mantra is all about dignity and respect. He talks about the causes of homelessness as the four legs of a chair. There are four things that hold your life up: family and friends, income, health and housing. Usually, there are a number of complex issues that make all the legs fall off a chair. For example, if you have mental health problems, suddenly all these legs become wobbly. This is a problem that has the potential to affect a number of people.

When John was running Business Action on Homelessness for Business in The Community, he would organise Seeing Is Believing visits. He brought people like John Varley of Barclays as well as other chief executives and that is how we built up many of our existing corporate relationships. He did a lot of work with Marks & Spencer, who provided over 900 jobs for people who had been homeless.

John visits Passage House as often as he can and always on Christmas Day. He likes to talk to the people who are staying there and so he gets to know what the effects of policy are first-hand. So when he advocates, he can talk about real people rather than say what a great organisation we are.

By now, I had a much clearer view of commitment, of John Studzinski's commitment to human dignity, what that entails, what it means and what it can achieve with money and, above all, with time which really means the giving of one's self. I was beginning to learn more about Sister Ellen and her commitment to the relief of poverty.

I asked Sister Ellen, who takes no prisoners in defence of the poor, to tell me more. As she explained to me the iniquity of poverty and the challenge of overcoming it, I wished her eloquent, passionate and remorselessly logical exposition could have been heard directly by those who scapegoat the poor by describing them as work-shy skivers. This is what Sister Ellen told me:

Of course poverty is relative. I am a Daughter of Charity. We are committed to people living in poverty, that is our mission and the reason for our existence. There are 17,000 of us in ninety-one countries. In the UK, we are in declining numbers but we are trying to remain at the coalface as the demands upon us increase with the recession.

The effects of current policy in this recession are to make the poor poorer. Unfortunately, the wealthier of our country are not touched by this in the same way and the result is increasing inequality. And what is happening in the name of welfare reform will only confirm this.

Whilst there may be a small number of people who play the welfare system, that is such a small minority. In Victorian times, the poor were criminalised and now they are demonised and sometimes this verges on criminalisation, even now. This is not a solution, you cannot cure a social ill by enforcement. You will never convince me that you can.

We tend to migrate between the enforcement approach and the liberal approach and neither can provide a solution to what are often complex problems. There is a solution and it is somewhere in the middle. If you treat people only with enforcement and not with dignity, you end up with full prison cells. If you treat people with compassion but with no challenge, if you say it is OK to be homeless and to sleep on the streets, because it is your choice and we will feed and clothe you, you are colluding in a social evil. Homelessness is a social evil.

The real issue is what has caused this social evil. For me, if you want to serve the homeless and help them, then we need both compassion and carrots such as food and clothing. You provide aid but in doing so you also need to provide systemic changes, both to the system that has created that homelessness and in the life of the individual. We try to inspire them and help them to find solutions that may transform their lives. We try to help people attain a life with some quality in it which is sustainable and does not require them to sleep on the street.

More social housing would certainly help but that is not going to solve people's other problems. We should be trying to regenerate communities but we will probably not succeed unless we address personal needs and engage with people to consider what would really improve their lives.

People have criticised me for laying down conditions for charity. Some believe charity is about having no conditions and not making any demands. I couldn't fundamentally disagree more. I know why people say that and why Christians say that. In almost every miracle, every cure, every interaction in the Gospel Jesus required people to take action for themselves. That is the basis of my philosophy. What we do at The Passage is to give choices back to people. We restore that to them because by becoming homeless they seem to lose choice. We say to people that their lives do not have to be like this. You can make it better if you want to. We can help but we cannot do it for you. We act as midwives accompanying new birth as people try to create a new life.

The main problem is that we live in a society that doesn't believe there is poverty in this country. At every level of society, we don't want to believe we have people who are poor. This is more insidious than dealing with poverty in developing countries where poverty is so patently obvious and everyone can believe that it is there. That makes it possible to build communities for people who can help themselves. The vast majority of people who come to The Passage are isolated. We need more acceptance and understanding of the spectrum of misfortune that leads to homelessness.

Those who might be philanthropists need, like John Studzinski, to get a grasp of the real situation. If they believe there is poverty then they can believe in a solution. They need to reflect on these matters and do some research. People need to make up their own minds based on real information, not on biased and inaccurate information or propaganda from the media.

That is why we need more money from the private sector, to enable us to do our real job. Public money is providing half our budget and this enables us to be independent. We need to be careful about government asking charities to deliver some services. They do so because it is often cheaper. There is a case for this, of course, but the charities find themselves working for the government. The primary role of welfare charities has always been to fill in the gaps. We are in danger of the voluntary sector losing its role of enhancing what government does. I believe we can provide services far superior to those provided by government.

Does it matter if we ignore poverty? Of course it matters because that says something about us as human beings. For me, that is a totally unacceptable view. Humans are nothing without each other. Right now, the rich are getting richer and the poor are getting poorer. This is a fact. Do people realise that?

Have we gained a consumer society and lost a real one? If people think we have, they should address their own personal lives and see if they are in order by asking: Are you fulfilling your personal responsibility to those who are less than fortunate than yourselves?

CHAPTER 9

The Prince's Trust and the young unemployed

When the Prince of Wales retired from the Navy in 1976, he used his severance pay of £7,500 as the initial investment in The Prince's Trust, a charity devoted to supporting the disadvantaged young by helping them into employment. Prince Charles was following in the tradition of his parents, grandparents and great-grandparents, whose commitment to charities grew as an evolving constitutional monarchy yielded political power. The trust is now working with 55,000 young people a year, about 5 per cent of the total who are unemployed, and has a turnover of £56 million.

The problems facing the young are even worse now than they were in 1976. At the end of 2012, youth unemployment was forecast to rise again to 1 million, equivalent to 20 per cent of all those aged under twenty-five. At the same time, The Prince's Trust reported that one in ten young people feel that they cannot cope with daily life. The Prince's Trust Youth Index revealed that young people not in employment, education or training are more than twice as likely to feel unable to cope as their peers. Martina Milburn, chief executive of the trust said:

A frightening number of unemployed people feel unable to

cope – and it is particularly tough for those who do not have a support network in place. We know at The Prince's Trust that it is often those from the most vulnerable backgrounds who end up furthest from the job market. Life can become a demoralising downward spiral from a challenging childhood into life as a jobless adult. But, with the right support, we can get these lives back on track.

The Prince's Trust's capacity to support young people is dependent upon its ability to attract the support of philanthropists and before I spoke to some of the trust's most generous supporters and heard from some whose lives have been transformed by its work, I talked to Martina Milburn and asked her what it means to work for the trust and about the challenges facing her and her colleagues:

The great motivation for working here is the young people. When you meet them and they are so brimming with pride and confidence, this is the best feeling in the world. We have offices in every part of the UK with 1,100 staff and 6,000 volunteers. It is this combination of staff and volunteers working at the local level that makes us so effective and binds us together. The volunteers are mostly working people and they help with mentoring and fundraising. Their commitment is extraordinary.

The demands upon us have grown considerably since the start of the recession. The most worrying trend we see is the growing number of young people who have been out of work for more than six months because that is the point where they get depressed and become most vulnerable.

We have a long-term ambition to work with 100,000 young people or 10 per cent of the current number of young unemployed. This means we have to increase our turnover from £56 million to over £100 million. We know the demand is there so we have to ensure that we grow in a planned and sustainable way.

Martina told me that the trust has to rely upon significant donations rather than the mass membership of small donors which sustain many of the major charities with household names. Research showed that The Prince's Trust cannot compete with cancer or animal charities. The trust has made a conscious decision to support young people in need and this cause does not have the same emotional appeal. The trust therefore focuses its fundraising on companies and individuals who can give at least £25,000 a year and currently has 231 patrons giving at that level and, in some cases, giving considerably more.

I asked Martina about the role of the Prince of Wales:

It is extraordinary what we are able to do for the young with a relatively modest investment. It all comes down to the vision of the Prince and I don't think he gets enough credit for it. Whilst he is not involved on a day-by-day basis, virtually all our programmes have come out of his head. He has sat down and listened to what the young people have told him about their lives, he will then form a view and will sit down with me and we will work out together what is possible and what is not. This is all his vision and the programmes come about from him really listening and understanding what he is being told. All in all, his charities are raising up to £120 million a year.

The Prince understands and we all recognise that our next big challenge is to ensure the young have the right skills in order to find employment – in science, technology, engineering and maths or, as we call it, STEM. It is vital that we get this into our DNA. This is additional activity for us but I am convinced we will be failing young people if we don't help them use technology to market their business or use 3D printers for manufacturing. We have had a great boost with a gift of £500,000 from Will.i.am, the musician and technology pioneer, who donated his fees for appearing on the television programme *The Voice*.

The majority of our young people subsequently ask if they can help us. So we have a scheme where they can become a young ambassador. We have a waiting list and they find it very hard to say goodbye when it comes to the end of the year. We still get letters from young people years after we have helped them.

Before meeting some of the trust's patrons, I looked at some of the stories of those who have been helped.

Afran Naseer, known as Naz, got involved in the wrong crowd in Bradford and was sent to prison at the age of twenty-one. Whilst in prison he decided to try and build a better future for himself and took part in The Prince's Trust programme.

Naz had a difficult childhood after his father died when he was five. He was the only child in a one-parent family and the lack of any constant and significant male role model took its toll. He joined a gang when he was a teenager and was given a nine-year prison sentence for a drug-related offence.

In prison, Naz reflected on his mistakes and began to think how he could change his life for the better. Although he was suffering from low self-esteem, his commitment to turn things round resulted in him being offered an opportunity to join The Prince's Trust team programme. He overcame his problems and supported other young people on the course.

Following his release, Naz worked for the trust for two years, initially visiting schools and educating young people about life in prison and then supporting, training and guiding young adults aspiring to become youth workers.

Naz has since set up his own social enterprise, 'Con-Sequence', which involves visiting youth centres and schools to work with vulnerable young people and deter them from a life of crime. Since the organisation started, he has helped 1,400 young people who are at risk of offending, in Bradford, Liverpool, Birmingham, Middlesbrough and Dewsbury. He currently employs five outreach workers who are all ex-offenders.

His dedication to give something back to other people and to use his experience to help others is making a real difference to the lives of young people across the north of England.

> Without The Prince's Trust, I don't know where I would be today and I cannot thank them enough. Many of the young people I work with don't have positive role models in their lives. I try and help them see an alternative path by trying to make them learn from my mistakes.

Leon White from Birmingham is twenty-four. He had been working as a self-employed musician for four years when work dried up. He struggled to find work for eighteen months and spent most of his time indoors trying to keep out of trouble.

Leon had been bottling things up since his father died when he was fourteen. He stopped going to school. 'My dad was the backbone of our family and so when he died I was of the mentality that I had been cheated out of a good start in life and really went off the rails.'

Leon left school with no qualifications, which made it even harder for him to find work. Despite applying for countless jobs, he wasn't getting anywhere and the continuous stream of rejections got him down and he felt worse and worse.

It was on a visit to the job centre in 2012 that Leon heard about The Prince's Trust and became involved with its Get into Hospitality programme. At the end of the two weeks, he was offered not one but two jobs. He is now employed full-time in a front-of-house role for a hotel. He is feeling much more positive about his future:

> My confidence has improved 100 per cent now that I am in work. I just needed to be given an opportunity. The Prince's Trust gave me a reason to get up and I cannot tell you how much I enjoy having something to get up and do. It has changed my life.

Keen to give something back, Leon is now volunteering as a Young Ambassador for the trust, helping other young people in situations similar to the one he found himself in.

Those who work with The Prince's Trust and with young people in general talk about the importance of role models. The same applies to philanthropists. I met five significant donors to The Prince's Trust and they each had a different approach to giving, very different stories to tell and each in their own way was a great role model for those wondering about taking the plunge into a life of serious giving.

❦

Nick Jenkins

In 2011, Nick Jenkins was in the press, on the verge of receiving a windfall of up to £100 million from the sale of Moonpig, the online personalised greetings card company he founded. Nick told me that he is writing a book for himself so that he could work out a strategy for his charitable foundation.

Money is only a way of keeping score. The most important thing about money for me is freedom. I can use my time as I like. This morning I was at Holloway prison looking at employment policy for re-offenders. I can choose to do that because I don't have to go to work.

Nick is in his forties. When he realised that he had a lot of money, he started to worry about what would happen to it if he died in a skiing accident. He decided to set up a charitable foundation and to devise a strategy for how the money should be used. He wanted to be sure that all the money he had made did not go to waste.

Devising a strategy for philanthropy is more complex than I had realised. And my thinking about the charity world has changed dramatically. What is the real role of charity today? Is it just about need or is it more than that? I have also realised that the need to give is just as important as the needs of charities.

To some extent, all of us have a need to participate in society whether it is sponsoring a charity run or cake bake or volunteering in a charity shop. This is a core part of humanity. If we just say that we pay our taxes and the government does everything else, then we are lesser human beings. For me, it is not so much a matter of giving but how I can help and add value. And adding more value is more important than me just feeling good.

We were to return to this theme and I was to challenge Nick's view that all of us feel we have a need to participate. There is no evidence that the majority of those with his kind of wealth are participating. People who are as generous and charitable as Nick are exceptional. I asked him about his involvement with The Prince's Trust:

I joined the Enterprise Fellowship because I can do a lot in terms of advising young people how to set up their own business. That is a really valuable thing to do and the young value hearing from someone who has set up a business and who has taken the time and trouble to talk to them. I do this quite a lot anyway, partly because I had so much advice when I was setting up business. And I am very happy to put some money into the pot to help the young set up their own businesses. A lot of the money doesn't come back but it is enjoyable.

I have been supporting the trust for three years. I think it is really important to help the young who have nowhere else to go. I have seen three good businesses get off the ground that would not have succeeded without The Prince's Trust. It is not so much that I want everyone to be able to set up really good businesses that will employ lots of people, although that is good. It is just as important to help them to become self-employed. Realistically, that is the best chance for some young people and they will probably find life much more fulfilling in that way. We mustn't set up young people to fail and to take on risk they cannot handle.

I have been talking to people at the trust about young offenders. So many companies don't have a policy and Moonpig didn't. There is just an assumption that if someone has a criminal record, you don't employ them. Working Chance is a non-profit recruitment agency that works with offenders so I decided to use them to recruit some call centre staff. The Prince's Trust can have a lot of influence by asking companies what their recruitment policy is.

Nick was keen to return to the role of charities as he wrestles with how best to use his charitable funds:

Charity has always been there. The Church used to act as a sort of welfare state and the demand became much greater in the nineteenth century. If you look at GDP figures in 1870, 90 per cent was private spend and government only accounted for 10 per cent. Government is now spending between 40 and 50 per cent, and there is a much more complex relationship between the state and charity. We spend £400 billion on health, welfare and education. Personal giving is around £10 billion. You could argue that personal giving is marginal. Is it the interaction between charity and the state that makes the difference?

Charities can sometimes be misleading. They prefer to tell fluffy stories to attract headlines rather than explain how complex their needs are, for example they will say that 40p will give someone breakfast. A charity like Centrepoint does terrific work but they are dealing with complex problems and they don't present it like that. If the problems were more straightforward, money would have solved them years ago. What we are left with is a complex residual problem that is hard to resolve. For me, it is important to understand all the issues and problems so that I can give from a knowledgeable point of view. It is a lot easier to write a big cheque when you are convinced that you really are going to make a difference.

Nick is clearly frustrated that although there is a need for his money, charities are not always presenting their case for support as effectively as they might and he suspects that government believes that people like him are going to walk in and compensate for reduced public spending in the wake of a retreating state:

Every charity is busting a gut to raise as much money as possible.

There is no more money to close the gap. Any notion that the amount of private philanthropic giving is going to expand to compensate for lower public spending on welfare is ludicrous. This is not going to happen. It infuriates me when politicians imply that it could happen.

I am happy to pay tax as this is my contribution to society but we all have a view of what is acceptable. I feel paying more than 50 per cent is ridiculous. I do give away a lot in addition. And tax incentives are important as they mean I can give away twice as much as I would spend on myself.

The state now has responsibility for welfare but this is being questioned by the concept of the Big Society. I don't know whether it is ignorance or not but some politicians are beginning to hint at the notion that the state should pull back and the Big Society should fill the gaps. This is an incredibly dangerous point of view. Taxation is a much more efficient and cost-effective way of dealing with the problem.

I left Nick without us having agreed a strategy for his charitable foundation. However, any charity that succeeds in attracting his support will have done so after rigorous analysis and can probably count upon a serious commitment. The Prince's Trust has passed the Jenkins test. So far, the government has not and we shall return to the Big Society conundrum when all the evidence has been gathered.

❦

Dr Rami Ranger MBE, FRSA

Rami Ranger was almost penniless when he arrived in Britain in 1971, before The Prince's Trust could have helped him. He started his business operating from a shed and with £2 in capital. Today, he heads up two of the UK's fastest-growing companies, Sun Mark Limited and Sea Air & Land Forwarding Limited, based in Greenford, Middlesex.

Rami is chairman of the Pakistan, India and UK Friendship Forum, chairman of the British Sikh Association, President of The Punjabi Society of The British Isles and co-founded the British Asian Conservative Link. He was appointed MBE in 2005 for services to British business and to the Asian community. His wealth was estimated to be £95 million in the *Sunday Times* Rich List for 2012.

Rami is also a patron of The Prince's Trust and so I visited him at Sun Mark's headquarters. Justifiably proud, he showed me around his expanding business premises. We greeted cleaners, office staff, people packing containers for export and the drivers of huge lorries preparing to drive overseas. Rami knows everyone by name and the response to his greetings were as enthusiastic as his. Over lunch, I asked him to tell me his story:

I come from a very humble background and lost my father before I was born. He was assassinated during the partition of India as he was against the division of the country on the basis of religion. We lost our breadwinner, our ancestral home and our country and we became refugees. We were eight siblings with a remarkable mother. She worked as a teacher in a junior school and brought us up in immense hardship. Despite our difficult times, she always had faith in human nature and found people ready to help us. We all went to school, college and university with the help and generosity of others and became well settled. We are now able to help others who are less fortunate than others. I could so easily have been a liability instead of an asset if help had not been forthcoming.

I came to the UK in 1971 to study law. Unfortunately, I could not afford to complete my studies and I had to start work as a chef. I progressed quickly and I was a district manager within two years. Eventually, I was able to set up my own freight forwarding business and in everything I did, I tried to add value by offering something that encouraged my customers to stay with me. As my business grew, I set up Sun Mark, a separate business for marketing and distribution and started representing famous brands in emerging markets. Sun Mark Ltd is the only company to have received The Queen's Award for Enterprise in International Trade for an unprecedented four consecutive years and we have won The Queen's Award for Export previously for my shipping company. This is the highest honour a business can receive and it was my proudest moment in business.

I asked Rami about his philosophy regarding charity and why he supports The Prince's Trust:

I believe a caring society is a good society. If we are caring, we will benefit from the environment we have created. The government cannot do everything for us and we should not expect this either. We must all do our best for the kind of society we want to live in. Some can give money and some can give time if we are to create a cohesive society for our children and grandchildren to live in.

By helping the needy and vulnerable, we will turn liabilities into assets. I am a living example of this. I now sustain thousands of British jobs and export British products to 108 countries. Once I had nothing and now I have everything, thanks to those caring people who helped us when we were struggling. I have also learned that by being generous one feels satisfied and has peace of mind. Giving to others actually motivates us to achieve more for ourselves. My mother used to say: 'God gives to those who give to others.' How right she was. I gave and have gained by giving.

As a patron of The Prince's Trust, I share my story with the young people who are going through difficult times and who need encouragement and support. I hope that I am able to give them hope that one does not need a rich father or an elite education to realise one's dreams. However, one needs self-respect, a good work ethic, empathy for others and, above all, total commitment to work. I tell them that the difference between success and failure is very small. Successful people help others so that they are respected; failures, on the other hand, expect it to be their divine right to be respected. That is why it is important that, to be respected in society, we should benefit others.

I was introduced to The Prince's Trust by Christoph Courth and the deciding factor for me was his enthusiasm and the trust's track record in its ability to reach large numbers of young people who need help. The people there have great ambition and are determined to try to turn liabilities into assets. Britain is a great country with a great sense of tolerance and sense of fair play. As a result, an ordinary immigrant like me could realise his ambition and can now help others. The key to success is all about outlook and attitude. Of course I understand that many who have had a tough start in life need help to get into that state of mind, just as I did, and that is why I am so delighted and so proud to be supporting The Prince's Trust because this is what they do and they do a brilliant job.

Before I left Rami, I asked him if he had any advice for those who are not charitable and who are wealthy:

'We must learn to give to make Britain a better place.

Arguably the most famous Briton, Sir Winston Churchill, said: "We make a living by what we get but we make a life by what we give."'

❧

Anonymous Donor E

Donor E has pledged £500,000 to The Prince's Trust over three years. He has had a very successful career in the City and when he sold his company in 2008, he established his charitable foundation with a personal donation of £15 million. He has a number of non-executive directorships, co-chairs a capital appeal for his Oxford college and is involved with the appeal for Canterbury Cathedral.

Donor E is a quiet, modest and unassuming man, notable traits in someone who is so good at making money. Before we talked about The Prince's Trust, I asked him why he decided to give money away when a majority of his peers do not:

I am reticent about my giving which is why I have chosen to be anonymous. This is partly because of my Anglican faith. Giving is an important part of being a Christian and we don't seek or expect recognition for what we believe in. I was brought up in a religious household. My mother was generous with her time as well and I was brought up to expect to put my pennies in the collection box. This continued at school where there was a strong sense that the world is bigger than we are. There was also a strong volunteering ethic and so giving has always been natural for me.

I converted to Anglicanism at Oxford and became much more aware of global poverty. I didn't really know what I wanted to do after university and tried advertising but that wasn't for me. I then joined an investment bank in the early 1980s and realised finance was what I wanted to do. When I had my own business, we always had a day a year when our corporate earnings and salaries were devoted to charity. I wanted charity to be part of our culture and a reminder that there is another world beyond business. I think this is really important when there is so much cynicism about making money. When I sold my business, I had far more money than I needed and established my trust. My priorities are education, the arts and Christian causes.

I asked him why he thinks more of his peers do not follow his example and what might be done to encourage others to be more charitable:

In my experience, those who I know and who are wealthy are very generous, particularly to my Oxford college. However, those who are better educated tend to have more of a social conscience. Some self-made entrepreneurs are not so well educated. They have little time for friends and for networking where they might be influenced in favour of giving by the behaviour of their peers. Some have a hard-bitten view of the world. Perhaps they need time to cool off after they have made their fortune, to think things through and get a sense of perspective. Then there might be a transformation of attitude. Tax incentives are helpful but I believe leadership by example and peer group pressure must be the most effective ways of persuading people to be more charitable.

It is not a coincidence that people in the US are more charitable and more religious, or that the Chinese have little or no religion and are not remotely charitable. They are going flat out for materialism and the poor are being left way behind. China must be one of the most unequal societies in the world.

I thought of the people I know who are generous and not religious, but I share his concern about a lack of moral compass even if our views about religion are not the same. I could feel a discussion about the Big Society coming on and neither of us could resist. Donor E told me:

> The Big Society is a well-meaning attempt to deal with our problems. We have lost social cohesion. But it is a concept rather than a reality. Some in our immigrant communities will find the concept patronising because they already have a big society and a culture of giving. Immigration has brought us new blood in terms of charitable giving. This must be as a result of religion. I worry about how much religion has been diminished in public life and how faith has been driven underground.

Donor E agrees with me that citizenship and our personal responsibility for sustaining our civil society should be taught in school:

> Many people wish to live here because of our civil society. It is always best to catch the young but education should continue throughout life. The banks, wealth management companies and the legal profession could do far more to promote philanthropy and legacies.
>
> We could be much better at acknowledging and recognising donors, despite me wishing to be anonymous! Oxbridge and some of the arts organisations are very good at this. We could be much more imaginative about giving national honours to those who are charitable. There should be separate category

for good works, volunteering and giving money within the existing system. But the media can be so sneering and cynical about people who have made money and this may deter some people from being charitable.

We have to find a way to help wealthy people understand and feel that giving to charity is something they need to do, that it becomes something they value. Charity then becomes as important if not more important than a new Bentley. I know how difficult it is to persuade the rich to give from my work with the church. Our poorer dioceses in the north have a much higher per capita record of donation than wealthy areas in Surrey. Why? I suppose the poor are not saddled with mortgages and school fees but I am not going to let the middle classes off the hook. As for people in my position, it is absolutely inexcusable not to give. I have far more than I need.

I failed in my attempt to persuade Donor E to reveal the names of the meanest parishes in southern England and we moved onto his support for The Prince's Trust:

I belong to the trust's Enterprise Fellowship Programme which supports the young employed who might be budding entrepreneurs. We try to get them back to work through mentoring. I talk about my business and how it was established. I find these young entrepreneurs very inspiring but sometimes we tell some that they should not be entrepreneurs if they are temperamentally unsuited. I find working with the trust very enjoyable, not least the networking with my peers. Entrepreneurs often lead lonely lives and this kind of collective charitable activity is very motivating for us.

Every cause or appeal stands or falls according to the quality of its leadership. I have been involved with The Prince's Trust for more than two years. I suppose this is because of the Prince of Wales who I find a most interesting and inspiring man. I think what he has done for the young is extraordinary.

There may be some truth in the criticism that some who support The Prince's Trust are attracted by the prospect of being showered with royal stardust although why that should matter is a mystery to me. However, I could not think of a less likely candidate than Donor E who seemed far too serious, centred and focused to be distracted by anything so trivial.

The interview had to end because of Donor E's appointment with his osteopath. Such is his modesty, he cycled to Kentish Town. As I left his apartment, admiring his collection of contemporary art and an enviable view, he told me that the previous owner had been Tom Jones, the singer well known for being showered on stage by the underwear of his adoring fans. The incongruity was striking.

✣

Ian Mukherjee, Amiya Capital

Many of the people appearing in this book were new to me. I was looking for signs of the philanthropic whim and indulgence alluded to by Polly Toynbee, but there had been none so far. I have met some very different people and all of them could be role models for those contemplating philanthropy. I had not yet met anyone to whom I could not relate and I had been struck by the enthusiasm of those I had interviewed for the cause of philanthropy and their wish to persuade others to follow their example. Ian Mukherjee is an enthusiast. A friendly man in his early fifties, he met me with a warm and broad smile. I knew I was meeting someone who enjoys life and that the omens for the interview were good.

Ian has been a partner with Goldman Sachs and after he left he set up Amiya Capital. Now notably philanthropic and a patron of The Prince's Trust, I asked him when he started giving and why:

Philanthropy has been in my mind since childhood. My Dad was a doctor, originally from India. He met my mum at Doncaster Royal Infirmary where she worked. They were both very caring people. I was brought up in the north-east of England and was very impressed how my dad helped people and how he made people's lives better in our community.

I was interested in finance from an early age but the idea of helping people was always there. I worked for Goldman Sachs for nearly fifteen years. A lot of the senior people there are very philanthropic. Philanthropy and public service are in the culture and this left a strong impression on me.

I set up my own company in 2005. I was aware time was passing, my kids were growing and I realised I had been very fortunate. I come from a normal background. My dad was from a poor family in India and my maternal grandfather was a coal miner from Yorkshire. My dad was always a Tory and my grandfather was a staunch Labour and union man. I understood both perspectives, that we need wealth creation and growth but I also understand that we need a fair society.

My wife and I are not extravagant. She is also from the north of England, went to the local comprehensive and we met at university. We realised that we had more money than we could spend and we didn't want to spend it. So we set up a charitable trust. And we feel we are only at the beginning of a philanthropic journey which we intend to last a lifetime.

The passing of wealth to children can be a burden and a curse. There is equal dysfunction in rich families as there is in poor families. How can I persuade my children to study, to work and to achieve if they have no incentive to do so? I don't intend to leave a fortune to my kids although of course I will give them help. However, I hope they will learn to be generous and philanthropic because, all being well, they will inherit the foundation. The best I can give them is their education. I want them to have a normal life.

I asked Ian how he became attracted to and involved with The Prince's Trust. He had started to send cheques to charities as soon he began to earn a lot of money. He became involved with Get Kids Going, a sports charity for disabled children and ran half-marathons for them but was looking for something more tangible as he found writing cheques boring. He needed to be convinced that the charities he was supporting were effective and that he could believe in what they were doing:

I came across The Prince's Trust about seven years ago. What I liked about it was its industrial scale. There are 160,000 registered charities, probably too many, but The Prince's Trust is tried, tested and trusted. It has both form and reach.

I met a young woman at one of their lunches and she told me a heartbreaking story. I thought I was so lucky my mum was not a drug addict, she didn't leave me on my own for twenty-four hours a day to fend for myself in a council flat when I was four years old. I realised how hard it must be to get through to the other side. It was relatively easy for me because my parents gave me all the values, the education and all the help I needed. This young woman had spent time in prison and her life has been transformed with the help of The Prince's Trust. That is how I became involved.

I get invited to events that these young people also attend.

I took my twelve-year-old daughter on one occasion. She was quite shocked because she had not come across such poverty and deprivation before or met people from such different backgrounds. The trust is helping tens of thousands of young people so I decide to give my support. I am now part of the Investing in People programme and a gold patron. I am very impressed with the quality of what the trust does. Government couldn't and shouldn't do this.

In addition to his financial support for The Prince's Trust, he does what is called 'motivational speaking': 'I tell them that if they want to be in business, they mustn't give up, they must expect bad things to happen, there will always be problems, relish the thought of solving them, try to be positive and to think outside of the box.'

Ian supports a number of other causes including the Mayor of London's Magic Breakfast Programme, Shine, Help For Heroes, a charity in India that does educational work in the world's biggest slum in Mumbai and a school in Tanzania. I asked him what might be the key to persuading more to follow his example:

Giving has to be a personal journey. Nobody told me to do it. I knew I was on this journey from an early age but that is not the case with everyone as we are all shaped in different ways. Getting people to understand charities is a challenge. There is not much research that will tell you who you should give to but in the end you have to work it out for yourself. How do we get more people on the road to giving? We have to educate and motivate. More recognition would help. If the motivation is not internal, then you need to find ways of encouraging people that will show them how advantageous giving can be as a route to the recognition they may be looking for. We should adopt a tax system that positively encourages philanthropy, as in America.

Schools have a big responsibility in making children aware of the needs of others. I was ten when I did my first charitable thing. We did something for Oxfam where we wore the same clothes, ate less, slept on the floor, weren't allowed to shower or bathe for a week and were sponsored to raise money for famine in Africa. It made a big impact upon me and was great fun.

As I left, Ian said: 'Do let me know if I can be of any more help in trying to persuade others that giving is good for you.'

I shall certainly accept Ian's generous offer. Meanwhile, it was time to return to the north.

❧

Terry and Liz Bramall

I have always been impressed by the modesty of some of our most generous philanthropists. Terry Bramall gave £100 million to the charitable trust he founded with his wife Liz when he sold his housing business, Keepmoat PLC, in 2007. They live in a handsome, elegant but not remotely grand villa in Harrogate. They have clearly thought through how to make the best use of their wealth. Terry told me: 'We hope we have kept our feet on the ground. People think that having a load of money is a panacea. It isn't, that is rubbish. Wealth provides no long-term satisfaction at all.'

I asked Terry and Liz to tell me their story. Terry:

We were brought up as churchgoers so we were minded to be charitable but we were not able to do much when we were young. My father played the organ in church and he gave of himself freely. He would do anything for anyone and I observed how generous he was.

We became serious about giving when we endowed our foundation. It was a good decision because we were forced to make it at this transformational moment in our lives when we sold the business. The money is not ours any more and we have learned how to be professional about how we give it away.

We decided that we did not want the foundation to be a big operation with a chief executive and an office. Having run a large organisation, I found the prospect of running another one unappealing. I thought it more efficient to run the foundation as simply as possible. We knew there were plenty of organisations out there who just needed the money and who were very skilled at what they were doing and they were delivering what we wanted and they were being very effective. And that meant we could be active straight away.

The Bramalls' first task was to define the objects of the foundation, which they agreed with their daughters so that they could make a family decision: Church of England; young people; health, education, music and charities in the localities where the money was made. Amongst their first gifts were donations to the Sing Up campaign in Bradford which led on to support for music at the cathedral and in the community as well as funding for the buildings. They also gave financial support for children attending the cathedral school in Ripon.

I asked Terry and Liz why they had decided to be so exceptionally generous to The Prince's Trust.

Terry:

We knew early on that we wanted to support the disadvantaged young and we realised that The Prince's Trust was doing an excellent job in Yorkshire and Humberside. We give £1 million a year to the local office of The Prince's Trust and leave it to them to decide how to spend it.

We started off giving £250,000 a year but after a year or so, we were so impressed with what they were doing, we increased it to a million a year. I knew they were doing a strategy day so I thought the sooner they know the better. So I rang them up as I thought it might make a little bit of difference!

Liz:

Yes, we are happy and we are enjoying it. We have had some wonderful times with The Prince's Trust. We went to a prize-giving in Leeds last week and were amazed by some of the young people who had been so low that they had contemplated suicide. And now they are starting their own businesses in their early twenties. These young people now have real charisma and are so inspiring.

Terry:

I put myself into their position and think I just couldn't do it. They get so low and then they come up, are so successful and then become ambassadors for the trust and are giving in return. They haven't all been on drugs although many are and some have been ill. We met one girl who suffered badly from ME and she is now busy and successful with her own confectionery business. It is sometimes difficult for the young to find employ-ment and often better for them to be self-employed.

There was one young woman we met who has been to twenty-two schools in a short period because her mum kept moving and she was becoming very disruptive at school. She went on to The Prince's Trust programme and was transformed, she was almost a new person. The trust says its success rate is 75 per cent. It is supporting about 5,000 young people in Yorkshire. The challenge is that there are 100,000 young people in the area who need their help. There is a long way to go but by helping 5,000 so successfully shows that something can be done.

I asked Terry and Liz about the other charities and causes they support. Liz used to be a nurse working in hospices so they have supported local hospices as they receive very little public funding. The biggest single donation they have made was to the university Terry had attended, to fund a new music building:

Liz: 'Usually we don't want our name on projects. However, as a result, some other people saw the building and what we had done and that inspired them to give which was terrific.'

Terry:

At Birmingham, the music facilities were terrible and now they have an iconic building. Now we are going on to support some of the work within the department. There is a five-year programme to support both teaching posts and some students.

Supporting education is important to us and we started with the school in Ripon where we helped students who wouldn't have otherwise been able to afford to go. We have just started a programme at Leeds University to help those who wouldn't go otherwise. These are disadvantaged young people within a ten-mile radius of the University who show real promise. They have been chosen by their teachers during their last two years at school. This is a terrific programme to which we are committed for ten years. They don't have to go to Leeds, they can go to any university. These kids are just fantastic. Helping them is a marvellous thing to do.

I asked Terry and Liz to reflect on what they have learned from their philanthropy so far and whether they had any advice to give to other people who are financially independent but not being charitable.

Terry:

When we were brought up in South Yorkshire, things were not valued unless the government provided it. We are now in a different era. It is now more acceptable to give, the means are there and so is the need.

Our foundation is very efficient, far more efficient than government could be. We like working with local government and other private funds. That is very appealing. I like the idea that we put a pound in and it helps to generate another pound from someone else.

We do get a lot of satisfaction from giving money and we also really enjoy the people we have met. Some of these people are amazing. At Birmingham, everyone is so welcoming and makes us feel we are right at the heart of the university and that makes us feel very privileged. It is really thrilling to feel that we are making a difference.

Liz:

The pleasure we get from this is extraordinary. Most people who give will make their biggest gift when they die. We are lucky enough to have all this money and can give it now. What I would say to those who are not yet giving is this: 'You will not understand the pleasure you will get from giving until you do it. So do it!' Giving is a two-way experience. If you give, you receive.

Terry: 'We have also learned that you can do a lot with a

relatively small amount of money. And we know we help by talking to people and giving our time.'

Liz:

It is important to plan and know that you have a set amount each year to give and you give regularly. That is the way to do it well, an important lesson we have learned. The young should be brought up to give and thinking about giving if only to share. That should start in the family but then continue in education. Some people find it impossible to share, it is just take, take. Perhaps they would find it easier if they were taught.

Terry:

Some people are mean with themselves. It is true, some people are selfish. I think it is a massive challenge trying to change such people. Our own children were brought up differently. Our two daughters are our fellow trustees and we did educate them to be charitable. I hope Liz and I have always put something back. If people are only interested in themselves and only concerned about making as much money as possible for themselves, then that is their loss.

Terry and Liz Bramall clearly enjoy sharing their good fortune and embody the concept that giving is good for you. They were glowing as I left, heading back into the wind and rain to catch the train back to London to meet a young man who had been helped by The Prince's Trust and who I hoped would be as charismatic and inspiring as the young people Terry and Liz had met in Leeds.

Duane Jackson, founder and CEO, KashFlow

Duane is almost half my age but at thirty-four has probably already seen more of life than I have. Duane is one of many of those rescued and re-launched by The Prince's Trust. I met him in Bermondsey, in the offices of KashFlow, his highly successful business. KashFlow is 'accounting software without all the hassle'.

Giving as a kid would never have occurred to me. I grew up in the East End of London and was in children's homes from the age of ten. You move around and never get settled anywhere. I moved in with a foster family at the age of fourteen and had a strong impression that they were only in it for the money. Being a foster parent is relatively well paid. They get allowances for things like bedding and when I was leaving care and moving into my first flat, they tried to stop me taking my bedclothes. I was only able to take them after my social worker intervened. They did give me a stable environment but there was no love. There was no consistency and no one who was there just for me.

Being in children's homes is an interesting way to grow up. I got involved in a minor fight in which no one was hurt but there was broken glass. The social workers sent me to a secure unit and then they tried to terrify me what would happen to me if I had to stay there. That was quite challenging.

The one good thing about my childhood is that it taught me to be self-sufficient. But many of the people I grew up with in care are now drug addicts, living a life of crime or in prison.

At the age of sixteen, social services arranged a council flat for me in Stratford and I managed to get myself a job as an office junior in a travel agents. I must have been one of the very few in my block who had a job because the noise all night and every night was absolutely ridiculous. So I did one of the stupidest things I could have done and gave up the council flat and moved into a private flat and so my costs went up.

I had always been interested in IT. When I was in the children's home aged fifteen, I was kicked out of school and then taught myself how to program so I had these skills from an early age. I started to do all the IT stuff at the travel agents but they couldn't afford to keep me on. They did help me write a CV in which I was described as an IT manager, and they helped me get a job.

I soon found myself in contract jobs earning £45 an hour which was good money then. Afterwards there was a gap between jobs and I turned down a few that paid a lower hourly rate than I had been used to. Money was running out, I had a girlfriend in New York I wanted to see. When I was over there, I bumped into a friend and he told me he was involved in drug trafficking. In those days, there was no issue at customs at JFK and so I decided that trafficking drugs was the solution to my financial problems.

I didn't know that the gang I was getting involved with was under surveillance. On an important trip to Atlanta, the courier pulled out and I said I would cover for him. And I got done arriving in Atlanta with 6,500 ecstasy tablets. They then gave me a choice: either I went ahead with the delivery of the drugs to New York or I went to prison immediately. I was unable to communicate with London and thought it was in my best in interest to go to prison, even though I was told I could be sentenced to twenty-five years or life. I thought my life was over.

Then someone I worked with in UK heard about my problem and came over to the States to see me. He offered to pay bail of $50,000 which let me out of jail for up to a year. I was able to return to the UK and he gave me a job. I was amazingly lucky. And during this time, in 1999, a deal was done between the US and UK authorities that I could be tried here. I was tried at Southwark Crown Court in July 2000 along with eight others, and was told to expect twelve to sixteen years. I was really lucky to get only five years, which meant half that with parole. I started at Brixton, which is not a nice place, then Camp Hill on the Isle of Wight where I started teaching IT, and finally Ford Open Prison.

My first girlfriend at the age of eleven was Nadia but she moved away from the area when we were fourteen. She heard about my situation from a mutual friend and wrote to me at Ford. She came to see me when I had six months left of my sentence. As part of the resettlement process I was allowed out for a few hours at weekends and by the time I was free, Nadia was three months pregnant. I suspect lots of people thought the baby wasn't mine but they didn't know I had been allowed out before my sentence ended!

So I had a baby on the way and a girlfriend to support with £1,000 I saved whilst working in prison. And no prospect of getting a job. And I had seen guys in prison with pictures of their kids on the wall and decided that was not for me. There was a lot of pressure on me to return to crime, mainly from the people I had been involved with before but, fortunately for me, the guy who was the main threat and wanted to kill me because I had slept with his girlfriend whilst he had been inside died unexpectedly of a brain tumour.

The Prince's Trust had visited Ford and I realised that my only hope of going straight and seeing my daughter growing up would be to start my own business as an IT programmer and web developer. So I applied for a loan and a grant, amounting to £4,000 of which £1,500 was a grant. I had to prepare a business plan and I thought that would be it. I soon realised I needed to do more such as market research, and the trust people were brilliant in mentoring and coaching me during three months' work on my business plan.

The grant and loan I got from the trust paid for a desk and a computer and I operated from our one-bedroom flat with a newborn baby. So I was literally squatting on the living room floor. The trust continued to mentor me and offered a support network which was incredibly useful. And I had three years in which to repay the loan. I was making enough money to survive.

I continued to attend Prince's Trust workshops and these gave me an opportunity to step back and think. I began to realise how difficult I found it to work the software I used for my accounts. So I started to think about designing something for my own use. So it was through attending the trust's workshops that I realised two things: if I wanted to be successful and make money, I needed to sell a product, not just a service, and that I am the kind of a guy who is much better behind a computer rather than managing people. I also realised that there was a demand for the kind of solution to these accounting problems which I had designed myself, a solution that doesn't speak jargon and that is easy to use.

So that is where KashFlow came from. I started the company in 2005. It was very much market-led. I was independent by then but I still went to the trust's networking events because I found them so useful and that is how I found my first twenty clients.

Remember, there was no one in my family or social circle who had started a business or who knew anything about that sort of thing. Those who do set up businesses tend to come from a completely different social background. So joining The Prince's Trust support network changed my life and changed my outlook so that I was able to get the kind of peer support I could never have hoped to encounter in my former life.

There is a charity called the London Youth Support Trust and Lord Young (David) was its chairman. They set up an incubator business hub in Hackney. They asked The Prince's Trust if they had someone who could do the computer stuff and I blagged my way in. Lord Young was chairing it and at the opening we were on the platform together and also had an opportunity to talk. And he said that if I needed investment, I should let him know. And so I got back in touch and he became my chairman and has been a mentor ever since.

Our turnover will be over two million this year. I have just bought a house in Hove for almost a million in cash. And we have some money left over to do it up. Nadia and I come from very similar backgrounds and it's great that we were each other's first loves.

Because I am a success story for the trust, I do go to small dinners and cultivation events for the trust to talk to potential donors. So I am giving a lot of time. I was at a dinner in the private room of Mosimann's, I passed the Duke of Edinburgh having his dinner in the public area. At the end of the event, one of the guests made a donation of £100,000 which was great. I went to another dinner at the top of the Gherkin and I was sat next to a guy who ran a big investment company and he called to say he wanted to see me and he offered me a million to buy the business. All as a result of me giving time to help the trust raise some money. But I turned him down as it wasn't enough.

This is what I would say to someone who doesn't give or is unsure. My life has been transformed but it isn't just my life. Four lives have been transformed, my wife's and our two daughters. And then there are all the jobs we have created, including jobs for ex-offenders. We are currently employing thirty-five people. Then think of all the tax we pay and that is a very good return on a cash investment of £4,000. Of course, the trust has had to spend much more than that in terms of the time devoted to me but the outcomes are surely worth it. This is a great investment in both financial and social terms.

And as we are doing so much business with the companies set up with the trust's help on the trust's recommendation, this will become formal next year and we will give 35 per cent of the top-line revenue resulting from these recommendations straight back to the trust. So the new business gets a discounted rate, we get a new customer, and The Prince's Trust has more money to help establish yet another business. I suppose this is enlightened self-interest.

I am now thirty-four and not yet ready to give personally because of family commitments but I am aware because of the people around me that this is something I should be doing if and when I sell the company. I was on the stage with Will.i.am when he gave half a million to The Prince's Trust. So my plan is that I will give when I next have a dollop of cash.

I have also been helping the trust by giving advice to some of the kids who were caught up in the riots in 2011. I talked to a group in Tottenham. I was able to relate to them because we came from the same background. There is Generation X and Generation Y and I want to see Generation DIY. I think there are opportunities for young people if they are prepared to seek help to help themselves. It is incredibly easy to start a business. All that matters is: are you good at what you do? It is a bad time to find a job but it is a good time to start a business.

I am now a member of the Worshipful Company of Information Technologists, the newest Livery Company, and of course our purpose is charitable. So I am starting to give back and look forward to doing more in the future. It feels very good to have a future.

CHAPTER 10

Families: commitments and communities

Many of Britain's most generous philanthropists have established foundations, such as the Wolfson, Clore and Hamlyn Foundations and the Sainsbury family trusts. I decided to investigate three smaller foundations where the family is responsible for taking decisions rather than a large body of trustees.

As an introduction, I must include Trevor Pears who chairs Pears Foundation. Trevor is the quiet man of British philanthropy and that is how he likes it. Behind the scenes, Trevor is an active campaigner for more philanthropy and chairs the Give More campaign.†

The William Pears Group is a privately owned property company. Pears Foundation began in 1992 but became much more active when Trevor started to give more of his time to its affairs. The family company is now run by his two brothers and Trevor devotes all his time to running Pears Foundation and promoting philanthropy. Under Trevor's leadership, Pears Foundation is giving in excess of £8 million a year to a range of projects supporting initiatives around identity, community and citizenship in Britain, campaigns against genocide and

---

† www.givemore.org.uk

crimes against humanity, and exploring the potential for philanthropy. The foundation is also supporting the Pears Business Schools Partnership, a collaboration between the London Business School, Cranfield School of Management and Said Business School at the University of Oxford.

Trevor told me that his experience of taking over the family foundation has made him realise that the more you focus on giving, the more you give away. He disagreed with me when I said there is no culture of giving in Britain and told me we should focus on what is being done and celebrate it. Trevor is, of course, quite right that there are cultures of giving here, but they tend to be faith-based and I continue to maintain there is no national culture of giving.

Trevor is, however, highly motivated to encourage more people to give more: 'Where are the great philanthropists of the twentieth and twenty-first centuries? Apart from Bill Gates and a few others, the über-wealthy of today are not great role models.'

We are back on common ground. I asked Trevor to tell me about the ethos behind the Give More Campaign:

Give More is a very simple idea. In response to increasing need, the campaign seeks to encourage everyone who can to do a little bit more, whether it is in terms of time, energy or money. Philanthropy is about caring not just about giving. Philanthropy is not just about the rich. Everyone should feel that they are contributing by caring, giving time or even a little money. And we need to learn how to talk about this. Being philanthropic should help you to identify what kind of person you are or aspire to be. Do you want to be part of society or apart from it?

The families you are about to meet decided long ago where they stand.

Sir Alec Reed

Sir Alec Reed is best known for founding REED at the age of twenty-six, one of the largest employment agencies in Britain as well as a number of other businesses including Medicare, which is now part of Superdrug. Now in his late seventies, Alec is as energetic as ever, spending most of his time tending The Reed Foundation, which he established in 1985. Alec is a serial philanthropist and, in addition to the family foundation, he also founded Academy of Enterprise, Womankind Worldwide, Ethiopiaid, Reed Restart at Holloway Prison, Women At Risk and the West London Academy School. If that were not enough, he also founded the Reed Business School and The Big Give. He is also a keen supporter of The Prince's Trust.

Alec is clearly a man with prodigious energy but he is also notably imaginative and empathetic. Like many successful entrepreneurs, he has little time for convention, moving from no religion to Christianity to humanism, and from centre-right to centre-left politics. When I met Alec, I had the feeling that his views are still as changeable and his enquiring mind is still as lively as ever. I asked him why he is so philanthropic:

My mother had a very strong sense of fairness and those of us who have made a lot of money have had a lot of luck, to give us money making ideas, to give us energy and a sense of purpose and to find the right people at the right moment.

We need entrepreneurs and everyone should benefit from the wealth, jobs and tax revenue that follows from their initiative. However, there comes a point when what I call financial obesity sets in and that is bad for everyone. Being financially obese is very bad for anyone's emotional health and many seriously rich people are seriously unhappy.

Alec's solution was to give away some of his excess pounds. His awareness of the neediness of others began at Drayton Grammar School when one of his best friends got into trouble and ended up in Borstal: 'We were similar in so many ways and some psychologists say there is not much difference between the minds of entrepreneurs and criminals! His experience reminded me how fortunate I was to have supportive parents. Since then, I have always been conscious of those who slip through the net.'

Alec became aware of growing social problems in the 1960s related to homelessness and drugs. He read a series of articles in *The Observer* which also listed relevant charities and their contact details. He would go on to adapt that idea to the age of the internet when he started The Big Give.

I read in *The Observer* that there was a centre for drug addicts close to my Bond Street office. I became a volunteer for one evening a week. All I had to do was talk to them and keep them there and out of trouble for a few hours. The problem was that there was nowhere for them to go after 11 p.m.

Alec was frustrated that he could not offer more practical help. Thinking about this, he realised that although the first priority for an addict will always be for heroin, the second priority will be work, if only to earn enough to pay for the habit. In the early 1970s he started ARC (The Addicts Rehabilitation Charity), then AREC (Area Addicts Rehabilitation Employment Agency). Later, Alec bought a farm in Cornwall where addicts could recover and he would occasionally take his children there. I asked Alec how he came to set up The Reed Foundation:

I had set up a small charity in Windsor in 1972 which supported local causes. When I made £5 million from the sale of Medicare in the 1980s, I put it into what had been called the Reed Charity and renamed it The Reed Foundation and then we were off!

I wanted to be even more philanthropic than I had been before, and I was feeling grateful having come through serious cancer, but let us be clear that there are tremendous tax advantages in setting up a charitable foundation. I was avoiding paying both capital gains and inheritance tax. However, I was motivated by a strong desire to use the money to help others.

The Reed Foundation has a very simple mission statement which gives it total flexibility. It is up to me and my three children to decide how we spend the money. We employ no staff and all the administration is carried out by my personal assistant. I put the money into a foundation because I believe in separating decisions about how much you give and what you give it to.

I try to apply the same innovative and creative skills as I do in business. And I have learned that philanthropy and working with charities can be as complicated as business.

Setting up Ethiopiaid was very difficult because of cultural differences relating to expectations and ways of working. But it was worth it. The poverty in Ethiopia in the 1980s had to be seen to be believed. The experience of our first project there helped us to learn how plans can unravel when there is no common language and mutual misunderstanding.

I like to support projects run by those I trust. Women who have difficult births in Ethiopia can have a horrible bladder condition which makes them incontinent and then they are outcast by their husbands. There are an estimated 40,000 women with this condition living isolated lives and scratching a living. In the past twenty years, Ethiopiaid has donated three million to the Addis Ababa Fistula hospital which provides surgery, allowing the women to start a new life.

Alec is really a feminist although he denies it. He certainly appreciates and respects women and is well aware that Reed's early success had been founded on the women in his work-force. It occurred to him towards the end of the 1980s that as there was already an international charity for the old, there should be one for women in developing countries who need help. Developing this idea and being aware that women are more charitable than men and give more time to volunteering, he decided he should establish a new charity that gave money directly to women to spend. Alec invested £1 million in estab-lishing Womankind Worldwide, the philosophy being that women are best equipped to solve many of the problems they encounter. The charity is working to counter some oppressive cultural practices such as female circumcision. Womankind has now merged with Women At Risk, a charity Alec started a few years later to help women in the UK suffering physical and also mental abuse.

Alec's most recent big idea is The Big Give, the website he launched in 2007 to help wealthy donors find and donate to causes close to their hearts:

I wanted to find a more intelligent way of giving money to char-ity. Initially, I wanted to attract online donations of £100,000 or more but I was persuaded by charities that this was aiming too high. So we hit on the idea of matching funds donated online so that a gift of £5,000 becomes £10,000 and running the offer over a few days. This proved to be a winner and The Big Give Christmas Challenge in 2012 raised over £10 million for 355 charities.

The Big Give Christmas Challenge is a unique matched-funding initiative, which Alec launched in 2008. During the challenge, his funds – and funds from a number of external corporations and foundations – join with pledges from charities' own major donors to double online donations from the public. In the past five years, the challenge has doubled over 50,000 donations and raised over £40 million: 'The benefits of matched funding are well known – however, the challenge adds a little extra "spice". Donations are matched on a first-come, first-served basis which creates a real buzz and excitement – and the challenge is so popular that funds often run out in minutes!'

Alongside the challenge, The Big Give also helps charities to find trustees, hosts exclusive events and runs a Philanthropy in Schools programme to teach the next generation the impor-tance – and joy – of intelligent giving.

Alec was knighted for services to business and charity in 2011. Never content with the status quo, he is looking for the next big idea. Whatever that turns out to be, he has set high standards for the future of The Reed Foundation and for his children to follow.

Sir John Mactaggart and Fiona Mactaggart MP

The Mactaggart family's philanthropy began more than 100 years ago but has been reinvented by the current generation. The Mactaggarts and their investments now embrace two continents and five countries and they appear in the *Sunday Times* Rich List as one of Scotland's wealthiest and most charitable families. Sir John Mactaggart heads the British branch of the family and I asked him how the family's giving developed:

My great-grandfather, the first Sir John who founded the family property company, had a very strong sense of charitable obligation and devoted much energy and some of his personal wealth to helping his fellow men and women. But there were no memorable 'touch-papers' in my youth to light up my interest in being a benefactor. Our parents instilled into us a basic sense of decency. Our mother was very involved with the RNLI but probably for what her engagement with the charity meant to her rather than the cause itself.

My father and his brothers set up a charitable trust in the late 1960s with initial capital of £25,000 donated by the family company but it was completely inactive for the first ten years. However, some successful investment decisions in the 1970s have transformed our charitable assets into a fund worth £11 million today and we gave away over £450,000 in 2011.

One of the interesting things about a family charity, as opposed to a foundation established by an individual benefactor, is that it needs to be a pretty broad church. For example, even two generations of Mactaggarts include elected representatives of the Labour, Conservative and Liberal Democrat parties but these differences, far from driving us apart, actually make us stronger.

The trustees have to approve all donations even if they might have personally preferred another cause. On one occasion, the auditors listed one of the recipients as being the 'World Peasant Association', much to the surprise of the more left-wing Mactaggarts who had never come across that august organisation. In fact, the donation had been made to the World Pheasant Association which is concerned with the survival of the species.

It seems clear that it is this current generation of Mactaggart baby boomers who have revived the family's philanthropic traditions and I asked John Mactaggart if the younger generation is involved:

Many family members are not particularly interested in the 'business'. But some of them have very adventurous ideas about charitable initiatives so we have set up a system of family trustees which allows the younger generation to participate and to learn. When they do become involved as family trustees, the younger generation discover that giving money away is actually very much more difficult than they had first envisaged. Good decisions on giving require time and effort.

At our Annual General Meeting we have introduced a new concept, the 'Charity Presentation Initiative'. Any teenagers who attend are given a fifteen-minute slot before a panel to 'pitch' for a pot with a first prize of around £3,000 on behalf of any charitable cause that has captured their imagination.

I asked John how the family allocates donations to more substantial projects:

It is extremely important that any foundation becomes involved with some ground-breaking initiatives to effect change. The trustees provide a platform for ideas. Every year, we vote for a special project which will receive a grant of up to £100,000. The decision is highly dependent on the initiative and energy of the individual sponsor and that is how it should be in a family foundation. Previous special projects have included Maggie's Highlands Caring Centre, Battersea Arts Centre, Defeating Deafness and the Exumas Land and Sea Park.

I asked another family member for her perspective. Fiona

Mactaggart has been Labour MP for Slough since 1997 and is John Mactaggart's sister:

> I realised in my early twenties that I did not want to work in the family business and that there was no role for me. But I was very interested in charity and I believed there was a role for me in developing the family's philanthropy. We were being generous but our approach was very old-fashioned in the way we made decisions and in the causes we supported. Now the younger generation is involved in making proposals for our foundation to support the causes they passionately believe in.

The Mactaggart family has had a home in the Hebridean island of Islay since the 1930s and owns an estate which includes farming and holiday rentals which provide work in an area once blighted by high unemployment and alcoholism. The family is committed to investing in Islay and in the welfare of the most vulnerable there, particularly the young. In addition to funding for the island's only swimming pool, the family bought and transformed a property that became the CyberCafe where the young can access the internet and socialise. There are also plans to convert a property to provide social housing with disabled access for the young islanders who would otherwise have little hope of a home of their own.

Their great-grandfather was a successful property developer who made much of his fortune developing low-cost housing in Glasgow. Inspired by his example, the family has also set up Commonweal, a charity devoted to the specific purpose of providing researched and proven solutions to housing needs. This initiative carries forward the family mission to achieve social justice through housing. Commonweal is chaired by Fiona Mactaggart, and John Mactaggart is her fellow trustee.

Fiona Mactaggart explains what Commonweal is doing in north London:

> We are, for example, helping to provide homes for mothers who have been in prison and who need to be reunited with their children. We are examining the possibility of helping people whose lives have been damaged by miscarriages of justice. We don't run these projects ourselves. We find partners to do that. We provide investment and seek investment partners. We have created a social investment fund in which we invite charities to invest. They get a share of capital receipts when properties are sold and we offer a 4 per cent return on their investment. The same applies to any investor. This method is actually cheaper than paying expensive rents in the private sector where the main beneficiaries are commercial landlords.

Social enterprises and venture philanthropy are controversial: some argue that money that would otherwise be given to charity is being diverted towards investments which pay a return on capital. There is a strong counter-argument that charities need to invest and that social investment may be the most effective means of bringing more money and much-needed capital into the voluntary sector.

❧

Michael Oglesby CBE, Manchester and the Hallé Orchestra

I returned to Manchester to consider a third family foundation and to compile a final portrait of a philanthropist.

Manchester features significantly in this review of philanthropy, partly because of its history and partly because of its current renaissance. Moreover, the arts have so far been under-represented given an inevitable focus upon poverty and deprivation, yet they have played a significant role in the history of Manchester. There is another reason. I was born and brought up only thirty miles away. I remember how dingy and depressing Manchester was in the 1950s and 1960s when I was growing up; the city is now vibrating with energy despite obvious signs that the recession has stalled some property developments and continuing poverty associated with high unemployment in the area.

In the nineteenth century, Manchester was the second wealthiest city in Britain and one of the wealthiest in Europe. However, the majority of its population belonged to the industrial working class and lived in circumstances that would be unimaginable today. However, there were early signs that those who became rich through the textile industry, manufacturing and trade understood that a healthy and contented workforce was better for business. By the 1850s, Manchester had an appalling reputation for ill health and for what was deemed 'immorality'. A strong partnership began to build between local government leaders and the private sector with a determination to improve the quality of life in the city, and so Manchester developed a reputation for both radicalism and enterprise. One of the first manifestations of this was the opening in the 1840s of the first public park in a British city.

In 1850 the ratepayers of Manchester voted 4,000 to 40 in favour of funding a public library. Manchester became one of the first cities to build a university where opportunity to study was not preceded by a test of religious opinion. This was unprecedented and was supported by the wealthy who gave generously to the university.

There was also an acknowledgement of the needs of the

working classes and a belief in the link between a healthy, contented, educated and entertained workforce became evident in Manchester's growing reputation as a city of culture. Local politicians and business leaders shared a view of what they wanted the city to be and this view also supported the long-term objectives of philanthropists. In 1857 this resulted in the first exhibition in Britain of art from private collections. The Great Exhibition in Manchester was supported by the Prince Consort and private philanthropists who believed that it would stimulate industry, 'elevate taste' and offer 'educational direction'. The Exhibition was visited by Queen Victoria and Prince Albert and attracted an astonishing 1.3 million people.

Here was the visible truth the cotton magnates were looking for, that the transformation of Manchester into a centre for culture was good for business. The Great Exhibition of 1857 led directly to the formation of the Hallé Orchestra and we will return to its story shortly.

Manchester has suffered in the intervening years, from the decline of the textile industry and global depression before the Second World War, from the collapse of empire and lack of competitiveness after the war. However, the explosion of the huge IRA bomb in Manchester in 1996 and the Commonwealth Games in 2002 reignited local determination to invest in the city's future and to follow the example of its forefathers. Greater Manchester continues to appreciate the benefits of strong links between the public and private sectors and between culture and business and is continuing to invest in culture. Manchester is now the second most visited city in Britain. Manchester City Council is building a new arts centre for the Library Theatre and the Hallé Orchestra is regenerating a local landmark by transforming St Peter's Church in Ancoats into an education and performance space. Manchester University is thriving and

extending its links with the city and the region as well as internationally. None of this would be possible without philanthropy.

Michael Oglesby's property company, Bruntwood, has
its headquarters in Manchester. The company has a portfolio of more than one hundred buildings in four cities. The
Bruntwood brochure illustrates the company's commitment to
the cities and communities where it invests under the heading 'Making A Difference'. The company spends 10 per cent
of its annual profits on charitable activity, amounting to more
than £1 million a year, and the family is giving away a further
million a year through its charitable foundation. The company
supports sustainability, community and cultural projects
including West Yorkshire Playhouse, the Hallé Orchestra,
Birmingham Repertory Theatre and Manchester Art Gallery.
The company also supports the Bruntwood Academy, a partnership between the Octagon Theatre in Bolton and a local youth
club with the aim of helping disadvantaged young people to
develop through theatre and creative writing. The company
also supports the Royal Exchange Theatre, notably through
its sponsorship of a national initiative, the Bruntwood Prize
for Playwriting.

In addition, the Oglesby Trust supports research and conser-
vation at Chester Zoo, a major capital project at Chetham's
School of Music, education workshops with Feelgood Theatre,
leadership and mentoring projects for the young with the
Reclaim Project, the Eden River Trust, the Mango Tree, an HIV
charity in Africa, the Royal Northern College of Music and the
Hallé Youth Orchestra.

All of this activity suggests serious commitment, consideration and planning by someone who combines all the skills
of an entrepreneur with an acute social conscience. I wondered
if all this had been in Michael Oglesby's mind when he was

considering establishing a charitable foundation. Recovering from dental surgery and gamely sipping a little soup, Michael told me what happened:

The decision to become significantly philanthropic began at midnight over a bottle of wine on a boat off the coast of Turkey. At that point in my life, aged fifty, I realised that I would have measurable wealth rather than just being well off, and that I needed to think about my children in relation to this wealth.

I was absolutely clear what I did not want to do: that was to put any pressure on my children to come into the business and I didn't want them to have an expectation of coming into wealth that could have been life changing and in which they had no part in creating. So I decided that a large proportion of my wealth should be given to charity and so I set up the charitable trust.

The original objectives were very wide and still are. We could support almost anything, the arts, medical research, improving people's lives. But I began to feel I wanted to do more with the money I was able to give away and to shape both the process and direction of spending. This coincided with my worries about the effect of wealth upon my children receding. One of the drivers for setting up the trust was gone but we knew after ten years that we had made the right decision. Our giving began to grow from £100,000 a year to its current level of around a million.

Aged sixty, I began to think about how the funds might be used after I am no longer around. I didn't like the idea of the money being managed by people who didn't have the enthusiasm and drive of the people who had made it. So I started to spend more time on philanthropy, my wife became involved and then my daughter and other family members, including my granddaughter who is twelve. And now I am in my seventies, I am thinking how I can make maximum use of the funds whilst I am alive.

I asked Michael if this would involve spending more money and, if so, on what. He is planning to spend more but these plans were initially somewhat thwarted by falling markets. He is not contemplating 'spending down' the foundation's investments and hopes that the next generation will create new wealth to add to the foundation. As for priorities now:

> I have been thinking more about addressing some of the social issues that are so prominent now and with a view to changing the focus from cure to prevention, and really looking at the causes of the problems we face. For example, we have funded research into the problems facing children who are brought up in foster homes and, although some of these are successful, we will focus our funds on encouraging more adoption.
>
> We are now spending one-third (and growing) of our funds on social issues. We are in discussion with the University of Manchester about some work in maternal health. Some young unmarried mothers don't take their medication and their children are undersized. A medical problem becomes a social problem. We are becoming involved in the disparities in health between different parts of society. For example, I live in an affluent area of south Manchester but two miles away from me is one of the largest council estates in Europe where life expectancy is eight years lower. This is shocking.

Mindful of Polly Toynbee's criticism of philanthropists who exert too much power and influence over charities, I asked Michael how he sees his role:

I believe philanthropists have a role to play provided charities are prepared to work with us. Increasingly, the problems we face need to bring together a range of organisations and people from the public and private sectors who have totally different cultures and who have their own agendas. I am in a position to bridge the gap and to say things that others cannot, for example the Pakistani sex ring in north Manchester which many people knew about but few people were initially prepared to talk about it.

'We have so many lessons to learn from the Victorians. This is how they behaved: they saw an issue and charged in on a white horse, no doubt trampling on a few people on the way. People like me are able to do this. For a start, no one is paying us. Everyone else round the table is being paid and has a vested interest. I am not beholden to anybody. I can bring ideas to the table that others cannot and I think this is liberating. I can be as rude as I like to the Arts Council or to the Secretary of State. People don't have to accept what I say, or agree with my views or take my money. I do try to be consensual but everyone approaches everything from an angle. I don't have a problem with people criticising what I do. And I don't mind if they don't take any notice but I do object if I come up with irrefutable facts and people ignore them.

I asked Michael where responsibility should lie.

We have huge, sometimes seemingly intractable problems. We cannot ignore them and we must address the causes. Who should be responsible? The state has a role but I believe it should be commissioning rather than doing even though it doesn't seem to be very good at it. I am a great believer in volunteers.

For me, volunteers are the Big Society. There is a huge amount
of volunteering going on in Britain but we need much more.
Not everyone can be a philanthropist with money but everyone
can be a philanthropist by giving time. The media sneer at all
this but look at the NHS. Volunteers have a huge role to play by
putting their arms around people when nurses have do not have
the time, inclination or skills to look after patients properly.

Society has to change because we are not managing our
problems well. I believe there is a pendulum swing now
and attitudes are changing towards a much greater realism and
acceptance that the debt culture is wrong and we need to face
up to austerity.

I asked Michael for his views on those who are not charitable
and what should be done to encourage more people to give:

There is something in the notion that the uncharitable are both
mean and unimaginative. People who not give? That staggers
me. We need to find ways of engaging those who are selling
their businesses and making a fortune. There they are, a new
yacht here and a gin palace there and I think, for heaven's sake,
philanthropy is much more rewarding and important and so
much more fun.

Charities need to find ways to get people fired up, to find
ways of stimulating people so that they want to get involved.
Too many of the small charities are not prepared to spend
enough on fundraising and invest in good people. My children are involved with an outstanding group of youth clubs.
They found business people in local towns and persuaded
them to give. The results are outstanding, five new youth clubs
costing five million each. Many of these people had no previous experience with philanthropy but now they can identify

with their success and the benefits these clubs are bringing to the young people. That is the way to motivate potential philanthropists.

I asked Michael why he believes the arts should be supported by philanthropy:

The arts have a problem in terms of fundraising because they have to compete with causes that pull at the heart strings. We have to get people to understand the role the arts play in society. A society without the arts is dead and has no soul. Creativity is so important in respect of everything we do. And looking at it from a commercial perspective, if we stop educating and training people in the arts, the nation will lose its ability to compete. Here in Manchester, we see the arts playing a very important role in the future of the city and the part they play in creating wealth and jobs. The arts have always needed patrons and they always will. I think it is slightly unfortunate that the state has provided so much. I don't think so much public patronage has helped them justify their role in society. The arts have to be much more savvy about how they run themselves. Some of the big ones have been very successful in diversifying their funding and have used that to grow sustainably but the smaller ones don't yet get it.

You have to be ambitious to get the big money. The money won't get out of bed for small things. You have to have a big idea, so I persuaded Chetham's School of Music, that had never raised £1 million before, to embark upon a £50 million scheme and we have raised over £30 million to date. I am a supporter of and a great admirer of the Hallé and I encourage them to be adventurous and to set their sights high. Mark Elder is ambitious for the Hallé and I admire that. There was always a danger that it might become a civic orchestra rather than a citizen's orchestra for the people of Manchester. It constantly needs to be adventurous, stimulating, inclusive and educational. I hope that what we give is helping them to be ambitious. Recently, if some of us had not pushed and persisted, it is doubtful if they would have gone ahead with one of the most exciting new ventures in Manchester for some time, the conversion of a beautiful church, St Peters in Ancoats, into a public space for rehearsal, education and outreach.

Michael Oglesby is a contemporary example of those Victorian philanthropists who did so much for cities because they were ambitious, challenging, imaginative and took the long view.

❦

Sir Mark Elder, Music Director, Hallé Orchestra

I talked to Sir Mark Elder, music director of the Hallé Orchestra since 2000. Mark is a former music director of English National Opera and a conductor of symphony orchestras and opera companies around the world. His appointment to the Hallé has been acclaimed as a turning point in the fortunes of a distinguished orchestra which was almost forced to close in the 1990s because of a financial crisis. The Hallé was saved by special funding from the Arts Council but that would not have been forthcoming without a public campaign and donations from the people of Manchester exceeding £1 million. Before telling us why he accepted the invitation to become music director at such a difficult time for the Hallé, I asked Mark why the orchestra matters to Manchester:

Everyone knows that the Hallé is an integral part of Manchester's character. Even people who do not come to our concerts know that Manchester would be much poorer without the Hallé because it stands for something staunch, northern and passionate. In the days before Christmas, we do five sold-out carol concerts and a performance of *Messiah*. Some of those attending don't come to anything else but for them, it is an annual ritual that they celebrate at this time of the year. There is a sense of ownership and recognition throughout north-west England, although many people do not know why we are called the Hallé and that the man who founded us was a German.

Karl Hallé was a great pianist who fled the revolutions in Germany and France and found himself being invited to Manchester. He was amazed that such a great and wealthy city had no musical life. This was a man with a great social conscience and a great sense of ambition who realised that he could give something to the people of Manchester that all the great German cities had traditionally had. There were people living in the city who longed for music.

Hallé had never formed an orchestra before, he did not speak English and he had never conducted anything! However, he was a great pianist, the first to perform a complete cycle of the Beethoven piano sonatas. I believe that what Hallé did was a gift to Manchester. He was invited to form an orchestra to play every morning as part of the Great Exhibition of 1857. He was such a charming man and he had so many friend-ships, from his past career, that he was able to do what he had never done before; including forming, running and conduct-ing an orchestra. This was quite an extraordinary achievement. When the exhibition finished, the musical community decided the orchestra should not be allowed to fade away and so the

Hallé orchestra was born and it performed an annual series of concerts. This was Hallé's gift, undoubtedly made possible by local philanthropy. 'Hallé was a pioneer through ambition and social conscience. He felt the people needed more cultural life and he made it happen. What he did was thrilling and is a great inspiration to me.

I asked Mark why he accepted the invitation to become the Hallé's music director when a conductor of such international renown must have had other tempting offers:

I have been in Manchester for thirteen years. I always take the long view and I believe that whatever happens must be the right thing. I had the opportunity to be music director of an opera company in America and the idea was so attractive that I nearly took it. But my guts were telling me that I should go to Manchester. The Hallé was in desperate need of new focus and new leadership, the finances were dire, the orchestra nearly died and Manchester had to make a choice as to whether it should be supported or shut down.

The timing was right for me. I felt I had something to give. And I had such overwhelming support from the people of Manchester, a feeling from so many people of a great love for the Hallé and what it has always stood for. The position of an orchestra in a community has interested me for years, and joining the Hallé gave me an opportunity to work with people I can relate to, to make music with and for, and enhance the power of music in the widest possible sense.

Manchester's sense of identity and what its people wanted it to be was already evolving. The city had strong leadership from Sir Richard Leese, the Labour leader of Manchester City Council, and its chief executive, Sir Howard Bernstein. I talked

to them before I became music director, and was impressed with
their dynamism. They have both given so much to Manchester
in their determination that it should be a city that people want
to work in and live in, a city that reflects the twenty-first century
and that is also a European city. John Summers, the Hallé's chief
executive, and I both wanted the same things: that Manchester
should be a city that relates to the rest of Europe. We must get
away from the notion that everything happens in London. That
played a large part in my decision to come to Manchester.

Above all, of course, it was my belief that I could make
wonderful music with the orchestra. The Hallé has always been
full of fine players and this first decade of our new century has
seen many talented young players joining the orchestra, and
indeed, I believe we were the first to have an equal division of
the sexes.

That is why I decided to come to Manchester and to be the
Hallé's music director. I would not be here if I did not believe
that both the public and private sector had confidence in us.
In creative work, conviction is an essential element and that is
what people respond to. I receive so much from music. I have
a constant sense of renewal, and I guess that is the same for
people who come to concerts and for whom music is important.
I feel very fortunate and I am acutely conscious that I could
not do what I do and give what I can give, without what I have
been given.

I left Manchester with a greater appreciation of the meaning
and power of giving and of what philanthropy can achieve.

CHAPTER 11

Charities: a view from the front line

This is a book about philanthropy and how to persuade more people to become donors. So far, our journey has been viewed primarily, if not exclusively, from the perspective of philanthropists. As we approach our destination, a consideration of the relationship between the voluntary sector and the government (and of whether the Big Society has any meaning) will be unavoidable if we are to understand how we might become more charitable and persuade those who are not yet giving to dig deep into their pockets. First, we should hear from those who run charities or who have responsibility for raising their funds and look at what philanthropy may achieve. By doing so, it should become clear how much we need charities.

There are 162,000 charities in Britain and twenty new charities register with the Charity Commission every day. Accordingly, I am not going to attempt to present the views of the entire sector. Instead, I talked to seven very different charities to find out what challenges they are facing.

Most of the largest and best-known charities depend upon a very broad base of support and do not engage in what is known as major gift fundraising. There are exceptions, such as the NSPCC, which was conspicuously successful with its

£250 million Full Stop campaign chaired by the Duke of York. Some charities are almost entirely dependent on public funding.

☙

Esther Rantzen, ChildLine and The Silver Line

One of the many excuses offered by those who do not give is that they do not believe they can make a difference. I realised that I needed to talk to someone who has made a difference. Esther Rantzen has been a campaigner all her life and is perhaps best known for creating ChildLine, the charity for abused children. Her most recent project is The Silver Line, a charity for the lonely. I wanted to know what lies behind Esther's achievements, what motivates her, how she motivates others and what she has learned about giving. From one perspective, Esther is an entrepreneur. She has created successful businesses because, in a limited sense, that is what charities are. I am hoping that by the end of our conversation, we will have learned enough to persuade entrepreneurs and anyone else who is sitting on their money or spending it on things that bring only transitory satisfaction that by using it creatively and by being generous, they may also make a difference.

Esther set up her first charity when she was a teenager and it is still going. The Out and Abouts charity is attached to a synagogue in north London and involves providing transport for disabled people, so they can enjoy an afternoon of singing and bingo. I asked Esther what makes her want to spring into action:

I start with the cause. My involvement and commitment usually starts with a story about an individual and a personal experience which illuminates an injustice or source of distress. I was horrified that so many of the disabled people in St John's Wood spent most of their lives imprisoned in their homes.

When I became the producer and presenter of *That's Life!*, the TV consumer show, we told the story of Ben Hardwick, a little boy who was dying of liver disease and who became the youngest person to have a liver transplant. I became aware of Ben when his mother Debbie rang to tell us that he would die in a matter of weeks without a transplant. One week later he had his transplant because TV has a unique power to tell a powerful story that reaches a huge number of people and makes them care.

Like many people, I find it hard to be moved by an abstract issue like the Child Poverty Action Group, Oxfam or Save the Children. But if you show me their work in action and show me a child who has benefited from their work or is in need of help, then I am more likely to be seized emotionally. I have to be touched emotionally if I am to be involved.

The idea of ChildLine came to me as a result of the deeply tragic case of a toddler who had died and I realised that we were finding vulnerable children far too late to save them. And we needed to find a way of reaching them in time to have a chance of protecting them and transforming their lives. So we made a television programme called *Childwatch*. It was based on a survey of adults who had suffered cruelty as children. We wanted to see what lessons they might teach us about protecting children in the future. Whilst we were preparing the programme, we opened a helpline after a *That's Life!* programme and the one hundred children who rang were disclosing abuse which they had not been able to talk about to anyone else or to seek help in any other way. I realised that talking about their suffering had helped to empower the children and enabled them to realise that it wasn't their fault.

When I realised the impact of that helpline which had only been open for forty-eight hours, I got completely hooked on the idea. I remember walking into the *That's Life!* production office the next day and meeting the social workers who had taken the calls. That was my 'on the road to Damascus' moment. I suddenly realised that this was more important than anything I had ever done, being able to help children from avoidable pain. When we opened ChildLine some months later, we were deluged with phone calls, 50,000 on that first night in 1986.

ChildLine continues to operate and is now a part of the NSPCC. More than 2.7 million children have been helped and the charity is needed more than ever given the revelations about Jimmy Savile. Meanwhile, Esther's work continues:

The new project is The Silver Line for lonely, isolated older people. Because I experienced loneliness myself following the death of my husband and I am living on my own for the first time at the age of seventy-one, I wrote about it and had the most amazing response. People wrote to say how brave I had been to be so honest. Loneliness carries such a profound stigma in this country. I was asked to speak at a conference by the Campaign to End Loneliness and I had an incredible sense of déjà vu. Twenty-five years earlier, I was talking about another stigma, child abuse, and the answer had been to create a special helpline for children. So I asked if there should be a helpline for the old and the lonely. And the experts said: 'Yes, do it!'

So we are just starting The Silver Line although I suppose it is a crazy time in the recession. We have a pilot programme in the north-west of England and we are already seeing results. I know there is a real need. Age UK put me in touch with a woman called Barbara who said she spent last Christmas Day pressing the voicemail message on her phone so she could hear a human voice saying, 'you have no new messages'. This Christmas, The Silver Line spoke to sixty people, some of whom told us we were the only people they had spoken to all day. It's wonderful how a phone call can offer hope and companionship.

I asked Esther how she found the money to launch ChildLine:

I firmly believe that if you get the right message to the public in the right way, they will respond and they did. When we launched ChildLine, we did get some state money. Norman Fowler was Secretary of State for Health and he gave us £25,000 – a lot in those days. I told him the story of one young woman who had taken part in our Childwatch survey. She had said: 'As a child, I was never frightened of being mugged or raped coming home in the dark because what was waiting for me at home was far worse than that could ever be.'

Esther secured a donation from the Variety Club of Great Britain to match the grant from the government and offices were donated by BT. However, a philanthropist made a dona-tion at a crucial moment and secured the future for ChildLine:

We had a wonderful philanthropist called Ian Skipper who gave with his heart. He asked me what it would cost to underwrite ChildLine for a year and I said 'half a million' which turned out to be an underestimate. Ian became a trustee and continued to donate which meant we could create a team that could meet the huge demand from vulnerable children who had nowhere else to turn. I don't know how we could have launched ChildLine without Ian. We had to hire staff and train volunteers and we could not have done that without him. Ian's gift changed thousands of lives for the better.

Once we were operational, money came in by the ton. One widow sent us her wedding ring. She wrote: 'I haven't any money, this is all I have, so please have it.'

I asked Esther about the funding for The Silver Line and if philanthropists are responding:

The Department of Health has given a grant of £50,000. That allowed us to hire a CEO. Our treasurer has contacted some of his business colleagues and they became founding supporters by giving £25,000 each. Those early gifts from generous people have been crucial in enabling us to start The Silver Line. BT has given us free phone calls and equipment, the offices have been 'donated', a big insurance company has promised us £150,000. Comic Relief has funded the pilot and we have £150,000 in the bank. However, the early signs are that we could need £3 million in our first year. In which case, we will need several philanthropists like Ian Skipper who, alas, is no longer with us.

The Silver Line pilot will help Esther and trustees to determine exactly how the new service should be promoted and to whom and this will have an impact on funding:

We have to learn how to create a service that older people will use. That generation is notorious for having too much pride to accept help. And if I am right and there is a stigma attached to loneliness, we cannot call The Silver Line a loneliness helpline. It can take time to earn someone's trust to get to the bottom of a problem. We learned this at ChildLine. If old people are being abused or neglected, it may take time for them to talk about it.

However, if our pilot shows that people are prepared to admit that they are lonely, then this is a much easier ask than providing a more general service for older people. At the moment we say, 'No question too big, no problem too small, no need to be alone.' Simply by offering friendship, 'No Need To Be Alone' will be an easier mission to fulfil.

Esther and I then discussed what is most likely to motivate donors:

I want our donors to feel as passionate as I do about what we are doing. Some people may say that they are paying their taxes and that is enough, but there is a difference between paying tax and giving to charity. I am committed to paying tax but I am not emotional about it. That is the difference between being a good citizen and giving to a cause about which you feel passionate. I want my donors to feel passionate because this will help them to feel connected to our work, be more generous and, as a result, they will feel more fulfilled.

Look at what happens on the documentary series *The Secret Millionaire*. It features people who have focused on their business all their lives. Most of them are workaholic and their families retreat to the fringes of their lives. On the programme, they meet people who have nothing and yet devote their lives to other people. This is a life-changing moment for the millionaires and changes their values. It reminds them who they are, what their skills are, the value even small amounts of money may have. They find they are not only giving money but time and a part of themselves.

Donors often gain self-esteem from their giving. At some point in life, most of us will find ourselves asking: Who am I? Do I want to be this person? Are there things I am curious about and need to know more? Do I want to change my life and do I want to make a difference? Giving is a way of answering these questions.

Thanking is fundamentally important. And I think what matters even more is to tell donors that they have made a difference. We should be taught about making a difference when we are children. If we are teaching children citizenship, I believe an hour a week should be devoted helping others, shopping for old people perhaps, or taking disabled people on outings. I have seen the effect on prisoners working with extremely disabled children. They came back inspired by what they had seen, by the dedication of the staff and by what they had been able to achieve by helping kids and their parents who were facing even worse challenges than they were. They felt good because they were able to do something that made a difference.

It is too easy for people to think they cannot make a difference. I love this story I was told by Ray Barnett, the man who created The African Children's Choir. A man is walking along a beach in California. He walks around a headland to the next bay where a huge wave has thrown up a vast number of starfish on to the sand. There they are, dying under the baking sun. In the distance, he sees a man who is picking up the starfish one by one and dropping them into the sea. So he goes up to him and says: 'Excuse me, don't you see there are a million starfish on this beach and you cannot possibly make a difference to them. There they all are dying in the sun.' The other man said: 'You are quite right. I cannot make a difference to them all but I can make a difference to this one, and this one, and this one…'

I have written a book to find out what difference ChildLine has made to some of the children who used us over the past twenty-five years. What difference does ringing an anonymous telephone line make to them? They said it transformed their lives because for the very first time, they had hope. They spoke to someone who said: 'This is not your fault. We can change things for the better.' So I met young adults who had rung ChildLine and some told me that without our help, they would not be here.

And I realised that I was talking to a teacher, a social worker, someone who created a charity, someone who worked with disabled children, another working with prisoners and a nurse. These children had never forgotten the help they were given, and now they are giving back. Because they were given hope. And we couldn't have done that without the generosity of so many thousands of people who gave money and their skills to ChildLine. They made it possible.

Esther Rantzen and her colleagues have offered hope to millions of unhappy children. She would not have been able to so without the generosity of Ian Skipper, the philanthropist, who gave ChildLine a generous donation at a crucial moment and gave it financial viability. Esther is now trying to help isolated older people via The Silver Line and she needs someone to be as generous as Ian Skipper was. Whoever steps forward need have no doubt that they will be making a difference.

❦

Lucy Sargent, Head of Major Gifts, Marie Curie Cancer Care

Marie Curie Cancer Care provides high-quality nursing, totally free, to give people with any terminal illness the choice of dying at home. It is also the largest hospice provider outside of the NHS. It supports more than 35,000 terminally ill people every year. The charity has invested less than other comparably sized charities on advertising hitherto, partly because management was commendably concerned that the highest possible percentage of its funds should be spent on care. More recently there has, however, been a shift in favour of investing more in marketing and fundraising. I asked Lucy Sargent about this, the challenges facing the charity and the importance of recruiting more major donors.

A significant issue facing us all is that as the baby boomer generation ages, there will be a significant increase in the number of people dying each year, as much as 17 per cent more over the next few decades. At the same time, the NHS is struggling to find £20 billion in efficiency savings and is in some parts of the country closing hospitals, yet this is still the place where most people die. We have been concerned about this for some time saying that we must plan for the increasing need for end-of-life care.

We anticipate more demand for our services so we need to invest in more marketing, as that will be key to generating more revenue. There is no doubt that spending more on marketing in recent years has helped us to tap into the massive amount of empathy the public has with our work. This has been shown through the growth of our Great Daffodil Appeal. As a national charity, we have a very broad base of supporters and our strength has always been in community fundraising. It is the man on the street who gives so generously to Marie Curie. In twenty years of fundraising for other charities, I have never before experienced people crossing a railway station to empty their purse into the collection box because we had been there for a member of the family when they were dying. People who have very little to give will empty their wallets because we were there for their families.

Marie Curie Cancer Care's income in 2011/12 was £117.25 million, of which more than half came from private-sector fundraising, including legacies. Public funding via the NHS totalled £36.5 million.

> Our public funding from the NHS has not yet been cut but we are increasingly concerned about competition from the private sector, who are interested in providing health care to an ageing population. Our strength is accumulated knowledge and a strong track record. The changes to the NHS in England do leave us with a huge amount of uncertainty.
>
> The big issue is to find better and more cost-effective ways of caring for people at the end of life. We know that when someone is cared for at home by Marie Curie, it saves the NHS an average of £1,140 in hospital costs. With so much pressure on funding, the sensible thing is to invest in community care, which is what we do. This is a good time for us to be seeking philanthropic support but also a challenging time, as our funding from the NHS is uncertain and because we must grow in order to support more people.

Marie Curie Cancer Care's investment in major gifts is beginning to pay off and there is now greater emphasis upon building relationships with major donors across the charity. Five years ago, the charity had only nine gifts of more than £20,000 in a turnover of £100 million. Income from major gifts is currently £4.2 million a year and is projected to reach £9 million within three years. I asked Lucy how this would be achieved:

> We are changing the way we relate to and work with our volunteers. For example, we are setting up regional fundraising

groups, relying on volunteers to take on much more fundraising. Our fundraising staff will manage these local groups and will have clear targets.

We are also creating volunteer boards around every hospice and investing in a county patron network. Our hope is that the volunteers will become a powerful group of ambassadors. Each patron will have a formal remit akin to a job description and a target of £10,000. We will offer them a range of ways they can help and will also monitor their progress in terms of the influence they have had – doors opened as well as the money raised. We will also expect them to give within their own means, or through a legacy.

Marie Curie Cancer Care has a strong case for support and is seeking funding for a range of projects, including sponsoring a nurse for three years at £20,000 a year. Donors are also invited to fund research programmes such as understanding more about the needs of young adults with terminal illnesses. The fundraising team at Marie Curie is leading the way in the use of volunteers to raise funds. I asked Lucy what challenges she sees in the future:

This part of our fundraising strategy is shifting as we work with more and more influential and senior volunteers. It requires a confident fundraiser with the ability to manage and support this articulate and sometimes challenging (in a good way) group. It's all about relationship building, which makes it challenging when the fundraiser moves on too quickly. Keeping staff over longer periods can be a big challenge for charities.

Also, there should be more publicity over tax-effective giving as donors still aren't aware of how they can give tax effectively.

It would be wonderful to see the government consult more with charities and donors over the impact of tax changes upon philanthropy. We need consistency and stability and to create a forum for discussion.

The figures prove that Marie Curie Cancer has been successful so far in its strategy to engage with philanthropists. The charity holds a trump card at a time when standards of nursing in both the public and private sectors are being questioned following revelations of lack of care and abuse. I asked Trevor Pears why the Pears Foundation has made a seven-figure gift:

I could tell you that we are supporting Marie Curie Cancer Care because we believe that they perform a vital role in society, offering care and assistance at a time of enormous vulnerability. Also, I could say that the organisation is well run and research-led; this would all be true and important. However, the core reason why we support and value their work can be answered very simply: the Marie Curie nurses. Anyone who has the pleasure and privilege of meeting one of them and hearing what they say, think and do will also want to support them.

As I left, Lucy said: 'There is a real opportunity to make more of the joy of giving.' She is right. Fundraisers must be able to reflect the sense of fulfilment that all committed donors experience, in order to convince the stony hearted. As public funding via the NHS is likely to decline in real terms, the need for more philanthropy is obvious if Marie Curie Cancer Care is to meet the inevitable growth in demand.

Lord Deighton, donor, The Dame Kelly Holmes Trust

Paul Deighton, formerly a Goldman Sachs partner, is now a Treasury minister in the coalition government and a member of the House of Lords, but when I visited him at his Canary Wharf office in October 2012 he was enjoying his last few weeks as the chief executive officer of the London Olympic Games Organising Committee (LOCOG). He looks like a man who relishes a challenge. He talked enthusiastically about his new job in government, which is to help deliver infrastructure as part of a strategy for economic growth. 'No pressure, then,' he quipped. I wanted to talk to him about philanthropy and sport, but we began by talking about the success of the London Olympics and the extraordinary effort by volunteers or 'games-makers':

I wasn't surprised by the volunteering response. We knew people wanted to join in. The demand for tickets was huge, and a quarter of a million people applied to be volunteers. We were able to accept 70,000. We were always very realistic about the job. People might be stuck in a car park all day. They understood that and didn't mind at all.

People wanted to be involved in something in which they could take pride, something which showed that our country excels. They gave their heart and soul. There is a strong tradition of volunteering in Britain but, excluding war, it has never had to deal with something the size of the Olympics. But we need to be cautious about expecting that we may have unleashed a new generation of volunteers who are going to look after the old, for example.

Three things struck the International Olympic Committee as exceptional about the London Games. Firstly, that we had a vision to inspire and encourage young people to take up sport. Secondly, public engagement was exceptional and every-one went crazy. Thirdly, we had a big programme for schools, in addition to the volunteer programme, and a project called Inspire that encouraged local projects. It was all very British: initial scepticism, then a feeling that the Games might not be an embarrassment and, finally, euphoria.

Paul Deighton made a lot of money whilst he was a Goldman Sachs partner and as a result of its flotation. I asked him about his approach to philanthropy:

When I came to work here for LOCOG, there was a bonus scheme to encourage the new CEO. I announced I was giving my bonus to charity, not because I am particularly generous but I have been very lucky in life and I thought it was the right thing to do, particularly as this is a public position. It is very difficult to persuade those who are not giving. They need to find out for themselves how great it feels. They have to try it to see if they like it.

My philosophy for those of us in banking is this. Our timing was lucky and we were smart enough to spot the potential for making a lot of money. It was clear to me that my skill was in spotting a market anomaly. I don't mind giving some of it away because I was lucky to get it. A lot of people in bank-ing, perhaps too many, think they are making so much money because they are smarter than everyone else. There are lots of equally smart people who are doing things which don't generate so much money. I don't feel I really deserve all the money I have but I wouldn't go so far as to call that guilt. It seems the right thing to do and I am surprised and a bit disappointed that more people do not feel the same. If you have been really lucky then you should share your luck. In some respects, you can turn your philanthropy into a business and your return takes a different form and can be equally if not more satisfying.

My wife and I support a range of charities. These include Women for Women, an international charity working in countries devastated by war. We helped women setting up businesses in Nigeria. We support the arts, including the new Tate Tanks at Tate Modern, and we are planning a programme for young artists. We have also given to Kelly Holmes's charity. Her main focus is young people who need to find their way, probably not on traditional paths. Sport is a big driver for social change. You could describe sport as one of the most effective social workers we have.

Paul Deighton is a modest man, considering the achievement of his Olympics team. We must all wish him luck at the Treasury, not the most popular institution with most of the people I have interviewed. However, it seems he was also being modest about the role he and his wife, Alison, have played in the success of the Dame Kelly Holmes Trust, as I was to find out.

※

Julie Whelan, Chief Executive Officer,
Dame Kelly Holmes Legacy Trust

Dame Kelly Holmes is one of Britain's greatest middle-distance athletes, winning gold medals for both the 800 metres and 1,500 metres at the Athens Olympics. She retired from athletics in 2005 and established the Dame Kelly Holmes Legacy Trust in 2008. Dame Kelly's goal is 'that young people and our athlete community are healthy, confident and able to determine and achieve their own aspirations'.

I asked Julie Whelan about her role in the DKH Legacy Trust, the challenge of establishing a new charity during a recession and the role philanthropy has played in its success:

Kelly founded the charity and I set it up for her. We are both campaigners. We started just as the recession hit and it turned out to be for the best, because it forced us to think differently about the partnerships and relationships we needed, what different sources of income we should have, the importance of a mixed economy and not relying on government funding. This helped us to be creative and innovative.

We also had to decide exactly what our focus should be. There were two things Kelly wanted to do. She wants to support young people because that is a priority for her, but she also wants to help her peers who have retired from sport. And we had to decide if we wanted to support kids with sporting talent or kids who are disadvantaged. We experimented in our first eighteen months and we were quite open about this, which I think was the bravest thing we did.

Our mission is now clear. We help retired athletes use their world-class experience to engage, enable and empower disadvantaged young people to lead more positive lives.

And our focus will remain on those young people (16- to 25-year-olds) who are marginalised and vulnerable, including those in care, unemployed and disabled. We are using sport as a catalyst for social good. We help the young to make positive decisions about their lives, in terms of both attitude and behaviour. And we measure that in terms of their commitment to making a habit of sport and to volunteering and to then moving into education. We do this with the help of Kelly's peers who are also in a state of transition. We help them to network and to think about their aspirations. When their sporting career ends, it is hard for them to think about what comes next. This is an example of Kelly giving back to her own community.

The DKH Legacy Trust helped 15,000 young people in its first three years and this number had grown to over 36,000 in one year during 2011–12. I asked Julie how this was made possible:

When you are new and without any evidence of the impact you have made, you have to look forward, promote a vision for the future and hope that people will buy into it. We have our diamond in the sky and that is Kelly. As she is known for running, we started community fundraising by asking people to participate in local events and runs. This first grass-roots level fundraising and activity is absolutely crucial. This encourages people to go on to make a financial commitment because they see something happening in their own area and they like to give back to their local community.

As people felt recognised and valued for the help they were giving us, they became volunteers and, in some cases, donors were offering gifts of between £1,000 and £5,000. We started to tell them more about our aspirations and plans and we learned that you cannot rush these kinds of conversations. This was how it was with Paul and Alison Deighton.

Kelly talked to Paul at a time when she was thinking about setting up her own charity whilst she was actively support-ing fifty others. But then that is Kelly, she is such a giver. Paul suggested that Kelly should talk to Alison and that was very good for us because Alison is tough and tenacious. She is very generous but insists upon knowing what our impact will be. We were a very small charity at that point in 2010 and this was our first professional dialogue with a professional donor at that level.

We wanted to apply for the London Mayor's Sports Fund.

We needed some matched funding and secured some from UBS. We started a negotiation with Alison. She helped us by testing and honing our bid, making us accountable from a donor's perspective. We learned so much from this relationship and the Deightons' donation of £30,000 was successful in helping us to secure a donation from the London Mayor's Fund. The end result is that, after scrutiny by the Lottery and Sport England, we have a grant of just under £7 million over four years to expand our Get On Track programme in England, a great return on Paul and Alison's investment.

The DKH Legacy Trust has also enjoyed great success with corporate sponsors and on the basis of the achievements of its first four years is looking to the future with confidence. Encouraged by all the backing and financial support it has been given, DKH Legacy Trust has set itself a target of reaching 200,000 young people by 2016.

The Lottery has given us such a boost just at the right time because we now have the evidence to prove that our work and the people we work with – donors, mentors, volunteers – are making a real difference. The local authorities we work with are really impressed with what we are able to do with young people because we are getting different results, and this must be because we are working with professional sports people as mentors. Our model is also influencing local charities and we will use some of this money to invest with them. These are our new partners in the future.

We have transformed our board to ensure Kelly has the right team around her so we can build on these achievements, with a particular emphasis on fundraising from individuals as well as corporates. We have a target to increase unrestricted income by over 80 per cent over the next four years and individual giving will be crucial in helping us to achieve this.

Julie Whelan and her team are clearly inspired by their founder. Dame Kelly Holmes has a well-documented history of overcoming adversity, including being in care as a child and suffering depression and serious physical injuries. The team is buoyed up by the support of donors such as Paul and Alison Deighton and has learned that success in Britain today is often dependent upon building partnerships. Philanthropists are keen on partnerships. They like to see their money making more impact. It was pleasing to hear that DKH Legacy Trust is working with a major benefactor we have already met:

> We are about motivating young people who may not have it to start with but we try to inspire them to find their own motivation within themselves. We believe that we are giving them social capital. They often do not get that at home so that is where we step in. This is the basis of our Get On Track programme and I was thrilled when I visited Reading recently to see some of the young people we have worked with. They had developed such confidence, an inner strength they draw upon in adversity and this is what matters to Kelly because this is what she had to do in her sporting career.

> We worked with the John Madejski Academy and Sir John has been a great supporter. He is a classic. He was keen to be a real partner and he and Kelly got on really well. There are lots of young people in Reading who are leaving school at sixteen in a vulnerable state, so we involved them in Get On Track. What John Madejski and his team at JMA have done is to make the people who live there proud. He has done an awesome job there and has been really good to us.

I asked Julie to send me a report of a young person from Reading who has been through the Get On Track Programme. Andy Lunnon was mentored by Adam Whitehead, an Olympian. Bullying at school shattered Andy's confidence. He stayed at home for weeks on end and gained a lot of weight. On the first day of mentoring, Andy was so uncomfortable he was on the point of leaving, but Adam noticed his discomfort and persevered. Andy lost three stone in six months, put in the work to become a personal trainer and now volunteers with a local NHS charity to promote healthy eating and tackle obesity. Andy has gone on to coach youth football. The DKH Legacy Trust's links with the FA has allowed Andy to work with Reading Football Club to polish his coaching skills. According to Andy: 'Get On Track changed my life. I feel I have made great strides and still have more dreams and ambitions. I am confident that I can overcome anything on my journey to achieving them.'

☙

Jon Snow, Chairman of the New Horizon Youth Centre (NHYC), London

Jon Snow is best known to the public as a broadcaster and particularly for fronting the evening news on Channel 4. However, he is also known to many as a trustee of charities. In north London, Jon is known to hundreds of young people because he is chairman of the New Horizon Youth Centre, a day centre set up by Lord Longford for homeless and vulnerable teenagers. I asked Jon how he had become involved:

I was employed there as director forty years ago and I have been chairman since 1986. My charity, the Homeless Network, is part of a 'hub' with The Passage. NHYC deals with young people who are on the streets. They are very vulnerable, often have mental health problems; they are unemployed and often disconnected from their families, and many of them have been abused. In fundraising terms, they are not a very attractive group because too many people think they have brought it upon themselves.

Inequality is currently appalling and poverty is becoming worse. When the poor are branded as work-shy, the blame game is becoming as bad as it was in Dickens's time.

We really have to justify ourselves. However, I have been surprised and gratified by the response of companies and trusts during this recession and our fundraising income is going up in response to growing hardship and poverty. However, they are becoming much more selective about whom they support and they are much more inclined to give to those who have a track record. Corporate support is increasing, particularly from the banks that are taking corporate social responsibility more seriously.

I asked Jon how much the charity depends upon public funding:

Sixty per cent of our budget used to come from public funds but this has been reduced to 30 per cent, so we have to raise two-thirds of what we need from the private sector. Actually, we do not want the state wagging this dog's tail. The trouble with the state providing a majority of funding for some social charities to deliver some public services is that you fulfil government objectives rather than those of your charity. You find yourself doing all sorts of things you should not be doing or don't want to do. State funds come with all sorts of risks and we must be careful not to be seduced by it.

A majority of philanthropists I know and have spoken to are wary about picking up what the state is dropping in its charge to reduce public expenditure. I asked Jon what arguments he would use to persuade donors:

The state is in retreat and there is an argument to be made for philanthropists to step in. We have to raise a million a year for our charity. In answer to the question: 'Why should I make up the public funding you have lost?' I say that we think we are doing something better than the state could. We are much smaller, much more efficient, we are targeting a small niche, we believe that we can provide these much-needed services much more economically.

The state is not the answer. You, the donor, know that big government is not working. It is much better to have diversity of provision. What your money enables us to do are the things that you also believe in and believe will work. You have a say in this because if you don't like what we are doing, then don't fund us. If the government does things you don't like, you cannot withdraw your taxes. You have no say but you do if you give us your money. This is what capitalism and philanthropy have in common.

Jon acknowledged that the public funding via the National Lottery has made a fundamental difference to many good causes, including NHYC: 'The Big Lottery has enabled us to rebuild so instead of being a slum, we have a modern building which is uplifting to visit and it has transformed the work we do. So the state did that, through the Lottery, but in accordance with our needs.'

Jon does not agree that philanthropists are dictating what charities do:

Of course we have to fit other people's criteria but the people we deal with are imaginative and we work well together. I work as a trustee of a grant-giving foundation and I see exactly how it works from the other side.

People who don't give are missing a dimension from their lives which can give enormous pleasure and with that comes fulfilment through enabling others to have at least a bit of a life they would not otherwise have had. That is what it does for me. Millions of people, probably a majority, are giving to charity. So in an age when most people are philanthropists, the question must be: 'Most people are giving. Are you?'

❦

Professor Iain Hutchison, The Facial Surgery Research Foundation – Saving Faces

Iain Hutchison fixes faces. He does not do facelifts. He is a consultant surgeon at the Centre for Oral and Maxillofacial Surgery at St Bartholomew's (Barts) Hospital in London. Iain looks after people who have terrible cancers or whose faces have been all but destroyed in accidents.

Iain is also the founder and chief executive of the Facial Surgery Research Foundation – Saving Faces. He was keen to remind me that surgeons are a million miles from the popular conception amongst the middle-aged and elderly that they are all as ruthless, impatient and dictatorial as the actor James Robertson Justice in those Ealing comedy films made fifty years ago. However, despite his warmth, charm and passion, it is obvious that Iain needs to be tough. Setting up a charity like his is not for shrinking violets. Saving Faces was set up to do clinical research to determine best practice. Iain told me about the challenges he has had to overcome, including raising money:

I founded Saving Faces in 2000. I soon realised that a charity is a business that has to have a market and make money. But we don't sell goods, we offer something less tangible. We do research with every surgeon in the UK to find out the best treatment for all disorders and injuries affecting the face and mouth.

All surgery is relatively successful but some treatments for the same condition are more successful than others. Accurate comprehensive UK-wide data collection on every patient could tell us which treatment works best and in what situation. Unfortunately, until now no country in the world has collected data of this quality.

Also, no surgeon has the time or resources to chase up patients after the first post-operative appointments. For example, the patient's problem may recur many years later when the surgeon has retired or the patient has moved and is treated elsewhere.

Then, surgery is totally different to medicine. You can change a drug treatment if it's not working, but surgery is an irreversible act. Surgeons need to be confident that the operation they choose gives the best result. We're not talking big differences here – one treatment may be 90 per cent successful and the other 95 per cent successful. These odds sound pretty good until you realise that with cancer, that means five out of a hundred patients will die if they have the 90 per cent chance of cure. It can be even more complex than that. If the 95 per cent treatment conveys significant disability, patients may opt for the slightly lower chance of cure with a better quality of life after treatment. So these questions are vital but as yet, nobody has the answers. Saving Faces was set up to solve this problem.

It took Iain twelve years to achieve his objective, during which he learned a lot about human nature and how to raise money:

Our first donation was the fee my wife earned from a speaking engagement. Patients and friends have been vital in fundraising. A lawyer injured in a car crash funded the legal costs of setting up the charity.

Even the poorest of my patients have been keen to help. With very wealthy patients, they are often pursued by much higher-profile causes which offer opportunities to put their names in lights. We are only a very small charity. Also, some people can't understand why the NHS is not paying for this research. In order to do this clinical research, we need people on the phone following up patients long after their treatment. Maintaining knowledge about our patients and tracking them when they move is a big enterprise.

Iain's ambition to establish a national research project examining different treatments for early mouth cancer took longer than expected, not just because all good fundraising takes time but because there's so much competition for funds, and national research bodies don't trust surgeons to complete large-scale research projects. Iain was eventually successful in getting the first ever surgical study on mouth cancer funded by a Cancer Research UK grant of £100,000 a year for ten years, and then persuaded a former patient to match this funding.

This donor, who has his name on a number of charitable projects, suggested that I ask my professional colleagues to give money to Saving Faces. This seemed a good idea – I could show my colleagues that I donate a four-figure sum every year to Saving Faces, don't get paid or claim expenses, and give about 20 per cent of my time to the charity.

But I have to say that it's been extremely difficult to get my colleagues to donate money. My experience of medicine is that only a minority give money to charities. I guess many of the doctors feel they give more time than they are paid for to the NHS and this is their contribution to society. We are not educated to give, it is not part of our culture.

Some people enjoy giving: one wealthy family donated £500,000 in one go. But some clearly do not. I look at some of the wealthy people I know who, despite having facial problems, do not wish to donate to a cause that affects them. They judge each other on how big their houses or yachts are in various parts of the world. They may be very wealthy but if they have less than their competitors, they feel poor. They have lost a sense of proportion.

Twelve years on, Saving Faces is raising £400,000 a year, of which £200,000 comes from Cancer Research UK and the former patient's donation. The remainder comes from events and general donations. The charity has minimal staff and nine full-time researchers. There are a further 250 students and forty surgeons on the books. The students receive minimal payment, and the surgeons do it for nothing.

We also do other things, like our patient-response helpline. This is a 'buddy support' system where former patients talk new patients through treatment. This alleviates the new patients' fears. For example, a young woman who had undergone recon-struction two years earlier after she lost an eye in a terrible accident was able to help another woman who had lost an eye a few days earlier in a glass accident.

We've also set up a service for dentists and doctors to speed up the referral of cancer patients to exactly the right surgeons in their area. They fill in a form online and send some photos. A surgeon, who is not paid for this, examines the form and responds in two working days, advising the doctor or dentist of the diagnosis and putting them directly in touch with the best surgeon in the area. This reduces a lot of patient anxiety and can help save lives.

Saving Faces charges the practice £3 a week for this service (about the cost of their milk bill) and all this money funds the charity so they can donate charitably or as a practice expense. There are many advantages for the practices and patients when they sign up. Yet many dentists and doctors are unwilling to give this amount.

I asked Iain about the long-term impact of the work and whether it has implications for other areas of medicine:

Saving Faces have finally set up the National Facial and Oral Research Centre with UK surgical speciality associations. We can now systematically record the treatment outcome for everyone in the UK who has facial surgery. This means that the UK will determine best treatment practice worldwide. All the funding comes from Saving Faces. At first this will cost us an extra half a million a year to run, rising to £3 million a year in five years.

Soon we will have the records of hundreds of thousands of patients. Researchers from around the world will study this data to find out how best to treat or prevent conditions as diverse as cancer and domestic violence.

I hope this National Study Centre will succeed. I recognised a problem which causes uncertainty to patients and surgeons and set up a charity that could fund and organise its solution. I believe one of the keys to the charity's success has been that I am unpaid, which shows potential donors that their money's not being used for administration costs but devoted to research work. We would never have been able to establish the reserves we need to establish and run the centre for its first few years if I had been employed. I have enjoyed the challenges despite the frustration of others often being slow to understand what we are trying to do.

Iain's career has been devoted to a part of life which is too close to death for most of us to want to think about it for more than a moment. Without his charisma and visionary leadership, there would be no Saving Faces. Iain could have given his time to private practice and become wealthy. Instead, he became a philanthropist.

✽

Helen Dent CBE, Chief Executive, Family Action

Family Action operates 'on the front line', often far from London and obvious sources of funding, and in trenches so deep most of us are unaware of their existence. Almost entirely funded by the public sector, Family Action is at the centre of debate about the role of the voluntary sector today, the independence of charities and the challenge of raising private-sector funding in a severe recession. I met Helen Dent, Family Action's indefatigable chief executive, in her sparse offices on Kingsland Road in Dalston, east London. I asked her about the origins of the charity:

Our charity was started by Octavia Hill in 1869. She was an extraordinary woman who also founded the National Trust in the same year. We provided financial help to poor families to try and keep them from being split up and put in the workhouse. She didn't support the drunk and feckless but people who had fallen on hard times either through illness or losing their jobs. She was initially bankrolled by John Ruskin until she gathered local philanthropists together to fund and set up local committees to distribute funds.

Quickly we developed the first labour exchange to match people looking for work with potential employers. Then we brought in environmental health officers to tackle private landlords. Next came family visiting services, as money was not always enough. We campaigned for twenty-five years for a state pension to keep old people out of the workhouse and that was achieved in 1908. Then we turned to income support, debt advice and eventually helped set up Citizens Advice as an independent charity to steer their development nationally. We were very influential in the 1940s helping the government set up the welfare state and children's departments; charities such as Family Action, Barnardo's and Action for Children have delivered services and influenced public policy for over a hundred years.

Overnight, virtually all of the charity's direct services became a statutory responsibility and, having achieved much of what Octavia Hill and her successors had been fighting for over fifty years, the Charity Organisation, as it was then known, could have closed. However, Helen's predecessors turned their attention to new services and new ways of working. I asked Helen what Family Action is doing now.

We are still following the social casework model Octavia Hill set up in the 1870s with our particular blend of financial, practical and therapeutic help, often in the family home, but the demands on us are now very different. Family Action works with deeply troubled families who have complex needs, often associated with parents' own difficulties such as mental illness or learning difficulties. Many of our parents are not accessing mainstream services, perhaps because their lives are so chaotic or their mental health problems so severe – so we go to them in their homes.

We do work that no one else does. Our philosophy is that if we can sort the parents out, they will be more able to take care of the children. Whilst we help the parents with their own difficulties, we focus on the importance of parenting their children well, to recognise and meet the needs of their children, to get them to school and to keep them safe.

People think families from hell are only on TV. What TV viewers do not understand is how families get themselves into this position. We see untidy, dirty homes, children out of control and out of school, no one eating properly, with parents in such a state they cannot manage themselves and their children are running rings round them. We go in and help parents to create a strategy for managing their children and setting boundaries and routines by first of all addressing their problems. If the parents have mental health problems, there is no point in setting the alarm for 8 a.m. if the children have to be off to school soon after. We suggest they get up at 6 a.m. in order to take their drugs with a cup of tea and watch some breakfast TV for quiet time, because when their drugs kick in they will be better able to cope with their children's behaviour. You help people to learn how to manage their own conditions and set priorities. Children have to go to school, be fed, be clean. We help them develop routines; we work alongside them seven days a week

7 a.m.–10 p.m. if necessary, until they become more confident. We face up to the chaos and help them break the spiral of decline. As our parents often say, 'Everyone tells me I have to improve, but no one until you has helped me to do it.' It costs £5,000 per family for this service. It's a bargain and keeps families together.

Helen Dent is retiring in 2013 after sixteen years as chief executive, during which time Family Action's budget had grown from £3 million to £23 million before the coalition government's reductions in public expenditure in 2010, when she had to make 150 staff redundant and cut services. Now Family Action is back to £20 million. By at least one measure, an expanding budget must demonstrate that the charity is highly regarded by those who fund it. I asked Helen what lies behind the figures.

Ninety per cent of our income comes from public and statutory sources. We lost £3 million overnight in July 2010 with the Chancellor's first Budget and cuts to local authority expenditure. Our income reduced from £22 million to £18.5 million in 2012. There is an expectation that we can do more with less but we have had to stop running a lot of preventive services – like many other charities in the sector – but we are growing again and our budget will be £20 million in 2013/14. We are now taking over local authority contracts. This is a lot riskier for us than establishing services from new. Once again the voluntary sector is changing and adapting.

The previous government invested hugely in services to support children and families in need, and this government is committed to our sector. But the problem is that the money is no longer ring-fenced and local government can do what it likes with its funding – including moving it from expenditure on children and families to potholes or elderly people. And the cuts continue, and whilst Family Action is winning tenders, many organisations are not, especially the smaller ones.

I worry for families in need: not only do we have less money spent on services, but the benefits paid to those we are supporting have been cut, creating a perfect storm of poverty. And there are more welfare cuts to come. Some of our families already have less than £3 per person per day after paying their household bills, to pay for food, clothes, Christmas etc. The rhetoric of the government and media doesn't help with talk of scroungers living off taxpayers. The situation is toxic and it is children who pay the price.

And is there a role for the private sector, and any prospect of it making up shortfalls in public spending?

Ten per cent of our budget is fundraised income and it plays a crucial role. If we are providing a statutory service then we believe local authorities should pay and they do. But there are things they will not pay for which we know are good for families and children. If we are working with people in their homes, we help to build their confidence and self-esteem by organising days out, running holiday clubs and homework clubs or swimming lessons etc. We also use voluntary income to fund research and pioneer new models of working.

Our scope for increasing fundraised income is limited. We have a low brand profile which makes cause-related marketing a challenge and our funding from the business sector is limited and is restricted to support services. Hopefully that is changing as public awareness becomes more attuned to growing poverty. Eight per cent of our voluntary income comes from trusts and foundations and most is restricted to specific projects. We run a very tight ship in terms of central costs – we have to. Most unrestricted funds which fund central costs come from individual and major gift fundraising, which needs upfront and expensive investment. Thank goodness for our loyal and imaginative donors: some have helped us through the cuts by helping us to invest in our business development. We would not have grown without them.

I asked Helen if private-sector income is more secure than public funding:

No. Low interest rates mean everyone has less to give. This has led to a review of funding priorities by donors and we have lost out to those who are smaller and even more vulnerable than we are. However, this a problem for every charity so we are trying to make the best possible use of voluntary funds.

In Family Action, we believe it is part of the role of a charity to identify and move best practice forward. We have used a combination of Big Lottery money and funds from the Tudor and Monument trusts to fund a three-year trial working with volunteers to support women who have post-natal depression. Most afflicted women are not getting the help they need. This service would not have been piloted by a statutory service because of the risks involved in working with volunteers. We have used these funds to research perinatal services, hold conferences and publish papers, and worked with specialists to help promote the need for the service which we expect to be funded by public money. We demonstrate to government and to many other organisations what works and how, backed up by the evidence. The private sector or fundraised income is crucial to our ability to play a pioneering role, which is exactly what charities should be doing and indeed have been doing for hundreds of years.

There are those who are critical of charities that are more than 50 per cent funded by the public sector, the argument being that they are working for the government, they are not charities and should not be entitled to tax relief. I asked Helen why the government and local authorities are funding charities, knowing perfectly well that the reason must be cost, but I also wanted to know if being almost entirely publicly funded effectively neutered charities like Family Action:

We are cheaper because we are more efficient and cost-effective. Our management charge is 10 per cent and, like for like, theirs is about 25 per cent. Our pension costs are lower and so are our salaries. However, there are other reasons why. Many of our services are funded by a variety of sources: health, local government, school budgets, GP funding. As a voluntary organisation, we can lever in all those funds to make our service viable. Accordingly, we can reach some very vulnerable families that the statutory authorities cannot reach – often families falling through the cracks.

Publicly funded charities like Family Action are necessarily vulnerable to cuts in public spending, but national and local government must be aware that private-sector income may fall if they cut too deep. Donors are often deterred by the withdrawal of other sources of funding, particularly public funding. I asked Helen if the staff of Family Action feel that they are agents of the state:

They do not. Many of our staff work in the statutory sector and they come to us on lower salaries because they like the responsibility for running services and they tell us they can be more creative and flexible. They enjoy a lot of delegated responsibility.

We have thought about services it is not appropriate for us to run and are better run by the public services. And we simply do not tender for services that are not adequately funded or where we do not like the proposed model of delivery.

But we have more to offer than just being cheaper and I think many public funders appreciate this of the voluntary sector. We are a national organisation and have far more experience of running more services than a local authority. Some of our service users will engage better with us than with the statutory sector.

One of the great things about Britain is that we have a vibrant charitable sector. It has been a fundamental part of our civic society for hundreds of years – as Dahrendorf said – a thousand flowers blooming. We do not rely on either charities or the state to provide services. One influences the other. My main concern is that many of the small and medium-sized charities will disappear in the current economic climate with a loss of services; a loss of people and their contribution to society. We are the 'Big Society' in action.

Is the government listening?

PART 3

How we might give more

'The man who dies rich, dies disgraced.'
– Andrew Carnegie

CHAPTER 12

Giving when we die

Death might seem an odd starting point for persuading people to be more generous, but I am following the lead of our government. In 2012, the Department for Culture, Media and Sport (DCMS) commissioned a report, 'Removing Barriers to Legacy-Giving (in the cultural sector)', which was published by Legacy 10, an independent campaign to encourage more people to leave money to charity in their will.

A colleague and I were asked to undertake research and advise the Legacy 10 team. I interviewed a number of philanthropists. Many of their views are reflected in the report's recommendations to DCMS and have helped me to form my own views as to how we might become a more charitable nation. Most of the interviews were conducted in the summer and early autumn of 2012, when memories of the Budget debacle over capping charity tax relief were raw. A great deal of anger and frustration was expressed, but I believe something positive could come out of a tide of negative emotion, as we shall see.

Those I interviewed were unanimous in acknowledging that the coalition government should be given credit for raising the profile of philanthropy despite all the inconsistency and confusion generated by the Budget. Moreover, many in the charity sector, irrespective of their personal politics, praised Jeremy Hunt, former Secretary of State at the DCMS, for his

leadership in promoting the importance and relevance of philanthropy. Jeremy Hunt commissioned the Legacy 10 report to
investigate how more people may be persuaded to leave legacies
to the cultural sector. I asked Roland Rudd, its chairman, about
the report and why he had started the Legacy 10 campaign.

The idea for the Legacy 10 campaign began with a conversation I had with Jeremy Hunt, who was frustrated that although
the government was doing something big and bold in favour of
charitable giving by reducing the rate of inheritance tax applying to estates where at least 10 per cent is left to charity, there
was little evidence of anything happening. I said a campaign was
needed to raise public awareness.

We recognised that this should be an independent campaign
and I was prepared to lead it. The maths is very compelling.
If you take an estate of £1 million with a 10 per cent legacy
to charity, net off tax relief and the charity could benefit by
£64,000 at a cost of only £17,000 to the heirs. For a relatively
small cost, you can make a substantial gift to charities.

We need to get this message out. Up to 70 per cent give to
charity during their lifetime, but out of the 40 per cent who
make a will, less than 7 per cent pledge a legacy. Recent polling
suggests that when people were made aware of the tax change,
they would do something about it. Within six months of the
launch, an opinion poll conducted by Populus showed that
awareness of the change amongst the over-65s had increased
from 21 per cent to 34 per cent.

Roland has form and strong views on charitable giving. I asked
him about his own philanthropy:

My mother had a very simple philosophy. If you are privileged, you must think of others and help to leave the world a better place that when you entered it. We had causes we were interested in from an early age. One of the first I supported was Amnesty International and I remain a supporter.

I have always been involved with children's charities. I was a patron at the NSPCC and I am now supporting research into rare diseases at Great Ormond Street Hospital. I am also involved with PACES, which helps Palestinian kids play sport and has an important impact on their lives, given they are so ground down by the West Bank occupation.

I have always been involved with the arts. I went to my first Wagner opera when I was very young. I very much enjoy supporting the Royal Opera House, which has the interesting challenge of being open and accessible whilst offering privileged access to its most generous patrons. We make sure a third of our seats are £30 or less. I chair the Tate Corporate Advisory Board. This is a very exciting time for Brand Britain, greater than it has ever been in recent memory. The Olympics were such a triumph. Tate is way ahead, even of MOMA (the Museum of Modern Art) in New York, in terms of visitor numbers and the way it engages with its audience.

I asked Roland for his take on the state of philanthropy in Britain and what more might be done in addition to his Legacy 10 initiative:

Only a minority of the wealthy are being generous and it is doubly frustrating that some of the wealthiest are not only not giving, but also are not paying their tax. This is an extraordinary indictment of people who have no shame about opting out of society. I don't think anybody should be a non-dom if you are British. The US has a very strong ethos that you pay your tax and you give. We must try to move in that direction. I sense some progress on the tax front but giving is going to take longer. It is becoming more accepted that you cannot sit on a charity board and not give. This point of view is not yet universally accepted but things are better than they were. You must contribute according to your means.

We do need people to be more open about their giving. It is commendable and admirable that some wish to be discreet but it is only by being public about our giving that we encourage others and, where appropriate, shame those who do not.

We need to nurture the young at an early age and get them to think and act charitably as part of their education. That should be a requirement. I went to Millfield in the 1970s and we learned nothing about charity. My son is at Wellington and it is very different now. I don't believe that public schools and private education has a God-given right to tax relief unless they are undertaking meaningful charitable work. Government should be tougher on public benefit.

We need much more coordinated thinking and action in government. We have to persuade ministers that philanthropy and charity really are important and should be a priority.

This is, of course, one of the unstated objectives of the Legacy 10 report and why I was so keen to be involved.[†] I have yet to be persuaded that the majority of politicians understand what philanthropy is and why it is important, and this doubt means it is difficult to take the government's commitment to encouraging more charitable giving seriously.

As only 7 per cent of us leave money to charity in our wills, it is self-evidently a good thing to encourage more of us to do

---

† www.legacy10.com

so. The government should be congratulated for introducing an incentive to help us feel more inclined to leave legacies, and many influential people are supporting the Legacy 10 campaign to promote awareness. However, whilst everyone I interviewed was in favour in principle, there were doubts about whether the reduction in inheritance tax would have the desired effect, and serious concern about the motives, trustworthiness and competence of government.

I don't think it is possible to overstate the anger felt by philanthropists, as well as charities, at the government's proposals to limit tax relief on charitable donations in the 2012 Budget, inflamed by inappropriate language suggesting that the prime motivation for giving was personal gain. Fortunately, common sense prevailed and the government backed down, for the time being.

This episode is important because it goes to the heart of the argument. We will not succeed in persuading people, and the wealthy in particular, to give unless we understand what motivates them. We know from everyone who has appeared in these pages that all of them are motivated to do the right thing, to share their good fortune, and that they are prepared to be even more generous if they are encouraged by, and become engaged with, the charities they support and are thanked by them. Donors want to know that they have made a difference and that they are appreciated. Moreover, I know from personal experience as well as a mass of evidence that tax incentives encourage people to give and to give more, whatever some donors might say.

Donors also need to be confident that government policy will remain consistent. There is a debate to be had about how much income government should forgo in the form of tax reliefs, particularly in difficult times, but if ministers are serious about encouraging philanthropy, it is madness to reduce incentives and to insult those they wish to be charitable.

'Exasperation' is the word that best sums up the mood of almost everyone I interviewed for the Legacy 10 report and this continued as I spoke to donors during the course of interviews for this book. We need to listen to what they have to say if we are to persuade others to be charitable.

I learned that a reduction to inheritance tax is unlikely to make any difference to the very rich as it adds a further complication to already complex estates where ownership of assets may not be straightforward. 'Another twig in the thicket' was how one philanthropist put it. Aside from that, everyone could see the potential for encouraging those who leave less complex estates worth between £1 million and £5 million, as well as all those liable for inheritance tax.

Otherwise, philanthropists could not understand why one relatively small part of the government had commissioned a review of policies to promote legacies to the cultural sector only, whereas their charitable interests embrace education, health and the relief of poverty. Those who give a lot tend to have a broad portfolio of causes they support. Every discussion I had moved swiftly on to the state of philanthropy today and what could be done to encourage more. The interviewees were unanimous that philanthropy should be removed from day-to-day politics and that all parties should sign up to a long-term strategy for charitable giving in order to encourage long-term commitments from donors. Tax incentives should be simplified and extended to a wider range of assets. The government should be encouraging lifetime planned giving (lifetime legacies) as well as legacies on death. Government does not understand people who give money and does not listen to them. The left hand of government doesn't know what its right hand is doing. Most were scathing about the honours system and the abuse of political patronage and said far more could be done to recognise and encourage those who are charitable. Everyone said more could be done to encourage volunteering and interest in charities amongst children at school.

The interviews unleashed a torrent of feeling and some shrewd analysis. Whilst anger was often expressed, by far the most dominant emotion was a passionate commitment to philanthropy and an acute frustration that the government doesn't understand it, and is not doing enough to promote and encourage it. Despite the negative tone, the government would be well advised to listen to those who are making such a positive contribution to society. That is, if the government is seriously interested in encouraging more philanthropy. As the Treasury has only earmarked £25 million a year for implementing Legacy 10 tax relief for inheritance tax, we are entitled to have our doubts.

Those interviewed for the Legacy 10 review included some of Britain's leading philanthropists and captains of industry and I have selected a few quotations:
'Cynical people will say that this is the way for the government to get other people to pay its bills.'

'Philanthropy should be depoliticised, partly because people do not trust politicians on account of their addiction to short-termism for political advantage. Good philanthropy is about the long term. Philanthropy will not thrive if it becomes a political football. The country's needs and the role philanthropists can play in trying to solve them are too big and too important.'

'My perception is that the government cannot be relied upon to provide the continuity of legislation to ensure provisions affecting donations are not changed. To put it bluntly, many donors, including me, think governments are untrustworthy and ignorant.'

'Governments don't honour their own agreements. Given the way all governments have behaved over a number of years, I wouldn't leave a legacy even if I was dying.'

'Government should be putting more effort into persuading people to give now rather than when they are dead.'

'There is no incentive for the Treasury to support tax relief to incentivise charitable giving. The problem is that the Treasury is out of control and thinks it should run the government, another reason why philanthropy should be taken out of party politics. The Treasury should be told what it has to do.'

'The lack of consistency in government policy will not encourage private-sector giving, particularly when the arts are being starved of public funds, told they have to increase private-sector support and are then penalised further when they are successful. Even more insulting is when the Treasury tells arts organisations that they cannot spend reserves which have been donated by the private sector. Philanthropists think that the public sector is ducking its responsibilities, imposing rules that mitigate against good management, and government is insulting donors by the language it uses in relation to the use of tax relief. This is not a good context for encouraging more charitable giving. There is not enough trust in the intentions and integrity of government, part of a much bigger problem facing all politicians.'

'The government cannot hope to increase legacies or philanthropy in general unless there is a change of culture. Jewish people have a culture of giving and gratitude which is part of the education of Jewish children. People have a sense of responsibility towards others. Philanthropy thrives in such a culture. The evidence is there. The government should take note and give a lead by example in the way it conducts itself. And by reforming education so that young people are taught about the importance of commitment to others.'

'The Treasury is so distrustful of philanthropists. They are so negative and it is they who are running things. The Treasury should stop worrying about the wealthy setting up charitable trusts, which they see as tax dodging. These trusts are important because, with tax-free growth, they have the potential to do a lot of good. This money, which might have been spent on a yacht, becomes social rather than financial capital.'

'We must be careful not to tell people what to do with their money, that they should give and to what. Philanthropy will always be about choice. We pay our taxes to the government for it to take responsibility for funding public services.'

'Yes, we need more philanthropy but how much more can we expect government to forgo in terms of lost revenue? Society has to make a choice where priorities lie. Many people, donors included, believe a strong public sector is a good thing and very much needed, particularly now when there is so much poverty and hardship.'

If I were reading this book as a non-donor, I might be wondering why the government wants to encourage me and others to leave legacies, and to the cultural sector in particular. Don't the arts need my money now? After all, Tate has seen its public funding reduced from 80 per cent of budget to 35 per cent, in common with many others. Surely I should be making an annual dona-tion, and then consider a legacy later if I feel my experience of giving now proves satisfactory?

It is government policy for the arts to diversify their sources of funding and many of the more well-established arts organisa-tions embraced this policy long before the coalition government came to power. Government also has a perfectly sensible policy, up to a point, of encouraging arts organisations to build up reserves and endowments so that they become less dependent upon subsidy and think about investing in their future. Donors could be persuaded to believe they are investors rather than donors. This is sensible, but you can see where we are heading.

Government has been told countless times that raising money for endowments is challenging. Most philanthropists do not want to support endowments as they believe they can manage their capital better than a charity might. The most effective way of building endowments is via legacies and these necessarily take time to come to fruition, so legacy fundraising is time-consuming and expensive for charities, although undoubtedly a very good thing.

What is not good is that the government is putting pressure on the arts via matched-funding incentive schemes to put their limited resources into raising endowments *now* and to mount legacy campaigns when their annual revenue funding is being cut, and looks like being cut further.

As a potential donor, I would not be convinced that this is the correct policy for current circumstances, even if I could be persuaded of its value in the long term. What I want to know is this. Is it the government's intention that philanthropists should pick up the tab for the arts so that the government is able to reduce its commitment even further?

And why is it that, as a top-rate taxpayer, I shall enjoy a 5 per cent tax cut in 2013, worth many thousands of pounds, whilst someone who is unemployed through no fault of their own is given a below-inflation 1 per cent increase in Job Seeker's Allowance, worth 71 pence a week?

Giving more to the rich and less to the poor, enhancing inequality – is this what we mean by the Big Society?

CHAPTER 13

The Big Society is dead

Under the front-page headline 'The Big Society is dead, charities tell Cameron', the main story in *The Times* on 7 January 2013 reported that Sir Stephen Bubb, head of the Association of Chief Executives of Voluntary Organisations, had written to the Prime Minister saying that the Big Society is 'effectively dead'. Sir Stephen was reported as telling David Cameron:

As Prime Minister, you described building a Big Society as your 'great passion' and 'central to my vision for our country'. You spoke eloquently of your desire to reform public services, with a significantly greater role for charities ... The mood music across Whitehall has been that reform is off the agenda. The reality many charities now face is crippling spending cuts.

Referring to the Budget of 2012, Sir Stephen told *The Times*: 'The ensuing public statements, portraying philanthropists as tax dodgers and some charities as dodgy, sent out a terrible message about the government's commitment to charitable activity in this country.'

In 1885, *The Times* reported that the income of all charities in London exceeded the budgets of many European states. Did we have a Big Society in Victorian times and is it the wish of this government, as it was of Margaret Thatcher, that we should return to Victorian values?

What is one to make of the Big Society? How would we know if we lived in one and, to misquote Sir Winston Churchill, if it has died, how could we tell?

I suspect everyone is in favour of the general idea of a Big Society but we find it more difficult to agree what it should look like. It is all too easy to be cynical and I shall try to resist the temptation because I am serious about the need to create a good or better society by motivating and mobilising more of us, including the very rich, to support our civil society. I am serious because I believe the maintenance of our civil society depends upon all of us engaging with it, as voters, taxpayers, volunteers and donors.

There does need to be general agreement and acceptance of our role as citizens if we are to convince our sceptical potential donor and to persuade him or her that, by making an additional financial commitment to society by being philanthropic, they will be welcomed, acknowledged and thanked, and find personal fulfilment. The current concept of the Big Society is far too vague to motivate anyone. We return to a recurrent theme about motivation. What is the government's motivation and what is its commitment to the Big Society?

Let us try to get to grips with what the Big Society is supposed to be. In 2010, David Cameron said that the Big Society would enable 'the biggest, most dramatic transfer of power from elites in Whitehall to the man and woman in the street … The success of the Big Society will depend upon the daily decisions of millions of people.'

In 2011, the government's White Paper on giving said: 'We believe that everyone can make a difference. So we want to empower and encourage more people to get involved, support each other and create the change they want to see.'

What does this mean? What will be the difference 'everyone' will be making? Who will be supporting whom and what change will 'we' be bringing about?

Are we to assume that the Big Society is about empowering localism, fostering local communities through volunteering, charities and social enterprises? We are, at the time of writing, more than halfway through the coalition government's five-year term and there is little evidence that any of this has happened. Britain has a flourishing voluntary sector and a long tradition of volunteering that continues in the face of adversity. There has, however, been no transformation. Confused, I turned to others for enlightenment. Speaking at a conference on the Big Society at Christ Church College, Oxford in 2011, Frank Prochaska said:[†]

On the face of it, the Big Society described by Cameron has much to recommend it. Insofar as it enlivens local communities and reduces the burdensome regulations on charities it will be of social benefit. Charitable partnerships with local government have advantages in spreading participation and educating the central state about the pressing issues that matter to people on the periphery. But we should not assume that they will reduce the role of government or encourage volunteering or voluntary donations. What we may be undergoing is a further stage in the perfection of the state monolith under the guise of partnership ... Paradoxically the Big Society may result in more government than less.

Prochaska worries about the independence of the 35,000 charities that receive public funding, arguing that the essence

---

† Frank Prochaska, 'Is the Big Society Collectivism In Disguise?', Voluntary History Society blog: http://www.vahs.org.uk/2012/big-society-prochaska

of voluntarism is its independence and autonomy. In the 1980s, 10 per cent of overall charitable revenue came from government and that figure is now approaching 50 per cent, as government increasingly commissions charities to undertake work in its stead:

> It is telling that the first thing the government did when it said that it wanted to 'roll the back the state' was to expand the ministry that deals with the voluntary sector, in this case the Ministry for Civil Society ... What is Nick Hurd doing as Britain's minister for the voluntary sector? Well, he is spending taxpayer money on more government administration and doling out public funds to co-opted, client charities, which he will regulate and control, if only because of the need for government accountability.

Helen Dent has told us that although Family Action receives 90 per cent of its budget from public funding, she believes her charity maintains its independence because it chooses which services to seek funding for, calculates how much funding is required for quality of services and decides how to allocate its own fundraised income. She says Family Action never subsidises the public sector but uses their fundraised income to extend services or fund services, often innovative services, that the public sector will not perform. She makes a robust case and argues that it is Family Action's independence that enables it to raise funding from a variety of sources. Indeed, Helen claims that Family Action is the Big Society in action, having plural funding, working in communities and using nearly as many volunteers as paid staff, doing real, meaningful work in their local communities. However, she concedes that a high percentage of public funding can be a challenge to explain to the private sector. As Frank Prochaska points out: 'We may be reaching a tipping point, when individuals will assume that charities are essentially government agencies paid for by taxation, and consequently no longer feel the need to contribute – a problem the universities have had for decades.'

Charities such as Family Action may also face another threat as there are calls from some for charities in receipt of more than 50 per cent public funding to lose their charitable status. William Shawcross, chairman of the Charity Commission, whilst careful to stress that he was expressing a personal opinion, and making no reference to charitable status, said the following in a recent speech:

Charities should not become junior partners in the welfare state, whether or not they provide services funded by government, they must remain independent and focused on their mission. My personal view is that some charities have become dependent on the state. And I think most of the public, when asked, would say a charity is an organisation funded from private donations, not public funds.

Helen Dent also confirms that a primary reason the government is keen for charities to undertake delivery of public services is that they can do so at a lower cost. If so, that may be a sensible and pragmatic policy but it hardly chimes with the Prime Minister's Big Society rhetoric. Indeed, we may be entitled to suspect that the Big Society is about saving money and reducing the deficit. Moreover, many people, not least philanthropists, also suspect that the government's motive in encouraging more charitable giving is that the private sector will bear more of the burden as the state retreats from the public sector.

Helen doubts this will happen. In her experience, both

philanthropists and trust funders want to be assured that they are not subsiding the state, and want assurance that they will spend the money on funding activities that are good for children and families and that the state will not fund. Most philanthropists are unlikely to make a substantial commitment to funding a service long-term – or to pick up the funding of a service where funding has been cut.

I do not believe that this is an enticing prospect for our potential donor, not least because most of those who are being philanthropic do not like the idea of paying the government's bills in addition to the tax they pay.

People are cynical because they see no sign whatsoever that the government is seriously interested in devolving power. Neither has the government been in meaningful dialogue with Britain's wealthiest philanthropists in order to secure their commitment to the Big Society. Ministers appear to have no understanding of what motivates donors, or of the fact that people who give money do not belong to a single category of people but have many different interests and reasons for giving. Those philanthropists who have spoken to ministers about measures that might be taken to stimulate charitable giving, and who were initially encouraged to do so, report a lack of interest from ministers, with one or two notable exceptions, and hostility from the Treasury. It is true that some welcome measures have been introduced relating to inheritance tax and legacies and to gifts of art in lieu of tax. However, if the Big Society is to be about more than a cheaper way of delivering social services and reducing the national debt, laudable though these may be, and if its true purpose is the revival of civic democracy, greater self-determination and personal engagement with society, why is the government not prepared to give people the instruments and incentives to encourage more charitable giving?

In 2011, a group representing philanthropists and charities were encouraged by senior members of government and those who advise them at the highest levels in Downing Street to produce 'The Philanthropy Review', which contained many excellent proposals to boost charitable giving. Within months of its publication, the Budget of 2012 proposed to cap tax relief on charitable gifts, thus fatally undermining the principle that tax is not paid on money that is given away. As one philanthropist put it: 'I would not expect to be taxed on a salary that I did not take, so I don't see why I should pay tax on money that I give away.' Another of those who was involved and who believed, wrongly, that 'The Philanthropy Review' enjoyed the support of George Osborne, Chancellor of the Exchequer, said he felt betrayed. The government appears to be committed neither to the Big Society nor to more philanthropy, given the evidence so far. However, we must continue to make the case for philanthropy. Perhaps ministers will have a better understanding having heard from so many good philanthropists on these pages, and will be able to accept their constructive criticism of government, which, although often harshly expressed, is well meant. We must be encouraged that ministers saw sense and withdrew the proposals to cap tax relief following a campaign that united philanthropists, charities and those from across the political spectrum. We must, however, remain vigilant as there are those, particularly in the Treasury, who believe that people give their money away solely to avoid tax, and who are unwilling to recognise that those of us who are charitable are making a contribution to society.

The government's Big Society agenda is fatally undermined by its failure to understand a much larger constituency than just philanthropists: it has failed to understand the 66 per cent of the population are estimated to be volunteers. One in sixty of us is a charity trustee. The British are amongst the most likely in the world to volunteer, with higher levels of volunteering and a larger and longer-established charitable sector than most European countries.[†] The authors of the Demos report 'A Place for Pride' say:

> The Big Society should be a great British political success story. After all, volunteering is ingrained in British culture and our qualitative work shows high levels of pride in social and community action. The Big Society aims to promote engage-ment in local societies – something much needed in a country where only 44 per cent of people say they are proud of their communities – and to facilitate volunteering, something people say they want. But the Big Society has failed to ignite mass appeal: nearly two-thirds of British people feel they do not have a clear idea or understanding of what the Big Society is and a two-thirds majority believe that 'the Big Society probably won't work'.

The Demos report tells us that negative feelings are strongest amongst those who are supposed to be the bedrock of the Big Society – volunteers:

> Sometimes when they [politicians] talk about volunteering and all that, it sounds like they think they invented it or something. I don't volunteer because the government tells me to, I volunteer because I want to – I enjoy it and I think it is important, when you get to my age, to give something back.
>
> Honestly, I hate the Tories. And I feel angry that they have taken something I am most proud of in my community – the

---

† Demos, A Place For Pride, 2011

way we pull together and organise to keep the street tidy and safe – and they have said it is a Conservative thing. It's not a Conservative thing. It is a British thing.

Polling conducted for Demos shows that volunteering is intricately connected in British people's minds with both British identity and pride. Their focus groups suggested that volunteering is perceived as part of what makes Britain unique, and people resent it being used for political reasons. According to the Demos report:

> There is a danger that the Big Society agenda – as used by the Conservative Party and opposed and mocked by the Labour Party – risks politicising a core British value. The lack of consensus built around it as a concept has led to a feeling that the debate itself in some way sullies a source of everyday pride for British people ... a real effort to avoid this is demanded of politicians from both main parties ... and in doing so they can help to reinforce and support a key component of British pride ... in order to achieve this, government must reframe its approach to the Big Society, deliberately disassociating it from more politically disputable issues such as deficit reduction, and returning the agenda to its original principles; that promoting social networks are good things.

I believe the Big Society brand is now toxic because it has been politicised, and it was not helped by a Hansard Society poll showing that only 20 per cent of the British public believe that Members of Parliament tell the truth. However, I do believe that we should be striving towards a Better Society, by building upon a long and well-established tradition of volunteering and charitable giving. We should take the advice of all the philanthropists I have spoken to who believe this is too important to be left to disputatious political parties.

This will require cultural change. How the heart sinks when we hear that phrase, whether in respect of the banks, homophobic and racist football fans, or the National Health Service. However, Britain needs a culture of giving and gratitude, and I believe its roots are already there. It is all too easy to evoke the Olympics but it is worth reflecting on what we learned about ourselves in the summer of 2012. There will have been many amongst the hundreds and thousands who applied to be volunteers who were attracted simply by the glamour of being involved, but the behaviour of the 70,000 games-makers was exemplary and inspiring. Most people found the opening ceremony surprising. We saw a reflection of where we have come from and who we are now, and we liked it. We felt proud to be part of a country that is so enterprising, energetic, creative, imaginative, humorous and tolerant. These, along with our history and sense of tradition, are the essential ingredients of our new culture.

The people are ahead of the politicians. However, whilst so many of those I interviewed said government should keep out of the way, I believe politicians have an important role to play in supporting a new culture by ensuring that as children we are educated to understand what we can all do, and as adults we are given the fiscal instruments to encourage us to be charitable.

Rather than speculating about a nebulous 'Big Society', we should concentrate on defining what a better society might be, and how it will be supported and nourished by a culture of giving and gratitude. But before we can be specific, we need to be clear about what should happen in our schools.

CHAPTER 14

Young philanthropists: building a culture of giving and gratitude

'We have to learn what it means to be a member of the human race.'
– Sir John Madejski, 2012

For too many people, life is too difficult and our problems are too big for them to feel they can make a difference. We need to make it easier to understand how problems can be solved and needs met. We need to develop a stronger national conscience and an understanding of the importance and the role of the voluntary sector. We need to be aware of what difference we can make as citizens, not just in the money we give but also in the time and skills we bring to address the needs of others. Giving in its widest sense then becomes a natural thing to do.

The diagnosis is easy, but what is the cure? How do you change a culture and build a new one? We must start with the young. Sir John Madejski agrees:

We have to learn what it means to be a member of the human race. We must teach empathy. Part of our problem today is that people, institutions, businesses and government lack empathy and this is reflected in a weakened sense of community and social obligation. By encouraging young people to think of others, they will find that they will become empowered themselves. They will learn to understand what they can do for others, whatever their circumstances. You don't necessarily need money to care about someone else.

Every person I spoke to whilst preparing for this book agreed we need to capture the imagination of children at an early age if they are to be 'hardwired' with a sense of awareness of and commitment to others. We have seen that some philanthropists, such John Nash at Pimlico Academy and John Madejski at his academy in Reading, are encouraging the young to participate in charitable activities. Trevor Pears and the Pears Foundation are funding the Youth and Philanthropy Initiative (YPI).

The YPI was first developed in Canada and it is delivered in England by the Institute for Philanthropy. YPI describes itself as a curriculum-based education that engages young people in secondary schools, developing their understanding of citizenship and charities. Young people work in small groups to research and to visit local, grass-roots, social service charities. I met Tim Pare, YPI's director to find out more. He had taken up his new position only weeks before and I asked what had encouraged him to apply:

I was attracted because YPI is about youth empowerment and convincing the young that they can be agents of change by making them take responsibility for bringing it about, rather than waiting for someone else to do something.

I had been working for a charity I set up in Sri Lanka and I was aware before I went there that there was something wrong in Britain, a sense of expectation amongst some people who were on benefits and whose parents were also on benefits, an expectation that they deserved help but also a seeming unwillingness to look for work. I am a socialist and very proud of the welfare state but it isn't working properly. The system is actually doing damage because it has created a culture of expectation in some and does not sufficiently address the needs of others. I was in Sri Lanka, where 80 per cent of the kids live on less than a dollar a day and there is no welfare system. The people have to cope with huge increases in the price of food and life is really tough. Despite great adversity, these people are really resourceful. In west London, I would be working with people to whom I was able to offer a number of options for work or training with financial support and they would tell me they didn't want to work and ask me why they should.

What is so great about YPI is that this is early intervention. We get kids thinking about themselves, their families, their place in the community and the challenges outside it.

Tim told me that he has a different attitude to life after his experience in Sri Lanka and that his work with YPI has convinced him that teaching children at school to be resourceful and creative by helping to overcome other people's problems must be the way forward. Young people learn that they can make a difference. I asked Tim how the YPI programme works:

We are a small charity, working in ninety schools in England and Northern Ireland, and 16,200 young people will take part in the ten-week course this year. These are young people usually from years 9 and 10. We start with an assembly and presentation when we ask the kids to think about philanthropy. They think it is all about money and we explain that personal talent, resources and time are just as valuable as money. They will identify social issues they think are relevant and then form into small groups. They identify the problem before they identify the charity, which has to be close to their locality. Then they must think strategically and realistically about how the problem might be addressed, bearing in mind, for example, that Bill Gates is not trying to kill every mosquito in his war against malaria!

The kids visit the charity without their teachers and perform their own 'due diligence' by evaluating its effectiveness and finances and then they develop a case into a presentation for class heats. The winning group from each class will go to a final event which might involve the local MP.

Tim told me that there are many benefits for the school. YPI improves the children's ability to listen as well as to present. Teamwork becomes more enjoyable and highly valued, as does decision making. They also learn about leadership. Tim told me:

The greatest benefit of YPI is that it inspires young people to become engaged with their local community in a different way, not as dependent children. What makes YPI stand apart from other youth initiatives is that we do not ask the young to fundraise. This is about encouraging them to discover their own qualities and talents and to find a way to bring them together to make a difference. The problems of the world seem so huge and so complex, particularly to teenagers, and this project enables them to put things into perspective. If Comic Relief and Children in Need is your only exposure then that is good fun and entertaining, but it is not channelling their motivation creatively, releasing the inner goodness and idealism of the young and enabling them to experience fulfilment.

There is a quote on the wall in our project in Sri Lanka which reads: 'If you want to feel better about yourself, help someone else.' That is exactly what YPI is about. There must be something in our genetic make-up that makes us feel like that.

I was impressed by YPI and my conversation with Tim made me reflect upon my own experience at Giggleswick, a public school in Yorkshire, in the 1950s and 1960s. Our society might be in better shape now if our generation had learned how to be more empathetic. I spent the best part of eight years living in a rural community without learning anything about it. Apart from a small number of 'day boys', we had no contact at all with the locals, about whom we were snooty and patronising, and we regarded the 'lunatics' in the asylum down the road as a bunch of 'spastics' to be laughed at. But that was another age. Perhaps things are getting better. YPI would suggest so but, whilst admirable, the number of young people involved is small and I had to find out what is happening more widely. Trevor Pears introduced me to Andy Thornton, CEO of the Citizenship Foundation, to whom I spoke before Michael Gove, Secretary for State for Education, announced his interim proposals for the reform of higher education in February 2013.

The Citizenship Foundation was founded over twenty years ago by a lawyer and two teachers who were conscious that there was very little teaching about the law in schools. They recognised that each new generation is required to know the law but there was no provision in education to make young people aware, and ignorance is no excuse. The law is made through the democratic process, so they embraced the concept and launched 'The Democracy and Law in Education Project'. During the 1990s, the concept of 'citizenship' gained currency and so the project evolved into the Citizenship Foundation. I asked Andy Thornton about the foundation's role and activities:

In the 1990s, there was non-statuary guidance to schools, and then David Blunkett introduced citizenship as a statutory subject in 2002. This made it more explicit and many schools were devoting fifty minutes a week to citizenship. We helped to develop content, materials and do some community work. We are also lobbying the coalition government during its review of the curriculum. We have met Michael Gove and his officials to work out how the teaching of citizenship can be accommodated in his view of what the curriculum should be in the future.

It is worth considering the massive changes that are coming. There is a lot of emphasis now upon attainment, learning baseline academic knowledge in a small core of subjects.

Andy worries what will happen to initiatives in schools to encourage young people to think about their role as citizens:

I started a project ten years ago called Giving Nation. It was designed to take the school-based charity experience of teenagers and enrich that with activities to enable them to become more engaged with their communities and local charities. That project then proliferated into primary schools, and 30,000 teachers subscribe to it, involving a third of primary schools in England. Citizenship is currently statutory in secondary schools but not in primary schools, yet primary school teachers see its value.

Andy told me that 93 per cent of schools are estimated to be engaged in some kind of fundraising for charities, although that includes Comic Relief and Children in Need. There are 600 schools involved in the Giving Nation Challenge programme, in which they try to change the experience children have of being involved with charities, by moving away from teachers prompting the young to respond to charities to encouraging them to do research and pursue their own initiatives. I told Andy about the Atlantic College Diploma (see Chapter 7) espoused by Jill Longson, which I believe could be a model to be rolled out in all secondary schools.

> The idea of the Atlantic Diploma for commitment to voluntary service is not going to be taken up by Michael Gove for the under-sixteens. His vision is that schools should regard the mandatory curriculum as only one aspect of what they do. He intends to shrink the curriculum to perhaps 70 per cent of school life. The remaining 30 per cent will be decided by schools. It is his vision that market forces will decide what schools do, as parents will choose the best ones and their standards will proliferate. He believes in liberating schools from simply devoting 100 per cent of their time to a formal curriculum, a state of affairs he believes has robbed teachers of their motivation, initiative and skill. He believes choice will enable the best schools to rise to the surface. This is a bold, liberal, market-driven vision. There is a belief amongst some specialists that there is a very high risk that this may result in great schools and sink schools. The theory is that failing schools will be rescued by successful schools.
>
> Gove appears to be saying that education from the age of sixteen could have a voluntary service dimension by going through the National Citizen Service and then a possible follow-through in education, but nothing is yet clear.

I am sure the National Citizen Service is excellent. It offers young people aged sixteen to seventeen a two-week outdoor experience where they learn a variety of skills and are given a certificate signed by the Prime Minister. However, it cannot compare with the Atlantic College Diploma, which combines intellectual enquiry with commitment based upon a distinct set of values over a period of two years.

There may be much to admire in Michael Gove's reforms if they succeed in driving up academic standards. The government tells us that it is committed to raising standards, but we do not know what values our children will be taught. Surely, if the government is committed to stimulating more philanthropy, we need education to be value-based, as well as emphasising attainment, with a formal programme of engagement with the voluntary sector in the curriculum, preferably starting in primary schools. We should teach children what it means to belong to a civil society and what role is expected of them as citizens. We should expect our children to commit to a programme of volunteering and community service whilst they are at school. This would need to be a part of the curriculum, not an optional extra. Those who excel would be awarded a National Diploma (modelled on the Atlantic College Diploma in Chapter 7), a demonstration of engagement and commitment that could be required by universities and colleges and, later, by employers, as evidence of commitment, seriousness of purpose, and awareness and ability to work with others as a member of a team.

The National Diploma would also be awarded to students in the private sector. It is particularly important that the children of the privileged should be aware of their responsibilities. Gradually, generations of more enlightened and humane people will change attitudes, possibly to such an extent that there will be sufficient political pressure on the Treasury to acknowledge that a majority of voters demand favourable treatment for the voluntary sector. It could become harder for politicians to resist demands from a society that aspires to be charitable.

As John Madejski has reminded us, we have to learn what it means to be a member of the human race, and the sooner we start, the better. Whether we refer to the Big Society, the Good Society or the Better Society, whatever we aspire to is meaningless unless it is based upon values expressing humanity.

CHAPTER 15

The call to action: the need for a new social contract

Creating a culture of giving and gratitude will take time. What should we be doing now to boost philanthropy?

'The Philanthropy Review' of 2010 and the recommendations it published in June 2011 provide some of the answers. The review is the result of an initiative involving philanthropists, business and charitable-sector leaders who came together to identify what needed to be done to encourage more people to give and to give more.

Under the heading 'A Call to Action', the authors made the following points and recommendations which, if implemented, could increase annual charitable income by £2 billion by 2015 (from almost £11 billion as recorded in 2009/10 by NCVO and CAF).

The review has three goals. Firstly, giving should be made easier. Every bank or building society account holder should have the option to hold a charity account. Every chief executive must champion payroll-giving in the workplace and lead by example.

Secondly, to encourage giving, tax incentives should be simplified and applied equally to all assets, including cash. Living legacies must be introduced to make significant gifts, with tax incentives, during a donor's lifetime, not solely through their wills.

Thirdly, in order to help giving become a social norm, 'giving' education must be provided in every school and planned giving (living legacies) should be championed by professional advisers.

The authors of 'The Philanthropy Review' make the following case for philanthropy under the heading: 'What Will Success Look Like?'[†]

When an individual gives £100 to charity, society benefits from the full value of that gift, whereas when someone pays tax and does not give, society benefits only from the tax paid.

But the impact of philanthropy is far greater than its pure monetary value. The multiplier effect of millions of people making the same choice to give can – and will – lead to dramatic improvements in society.

The hospice movement came about from a desire of many to provide care for the dying and to give to this cause; the mapping of the human genome was supported by the Wellcome Trust; and organisations such as Comic Relief are the embodiment of the generosity and concern of people combining to drive social change. These are just some of the examples of the UK's greatest contributions to society since 1900.

As more people give, and people give more, we will be better placed to face challenges such as long-term unemploy-ment, increasing homelessness, an ageing population, rising demand for the care of the dying as death rates increase, improving education, sustaining the arts and the many other issues to which charities can provide solutions and much-needed support. Moreover, each act of philanthropy acts like a

---

† Details of the recommendations in 'The Philanthropy Review' may be found at www.philanthropyreview.co.uk

thread that, woven together, binds us into a richer and more vibrant society.

Bravo! However, what is the bill for what is described above and who pays it? Have we agreed the roles of the state and the voluntary sector? How much more will philanthropy be expected to contribute? What will be the cost to the government of additional tax relief to implement the recommendations of 'The Philanthropy Review'? Are we satisfied that public benefit is sufficient to justify tax relief to the wealthy? Can we evaluate a pound spent in the voluntary sector and compare with one spent in the public sector? Do charities have the skills and resources to engage with philanthropists?

I talked to Matthew Bowcock, chairman of the Community Foundation Network, a philanthropist and a member of the Philanthropy Review Board who sees opportunities in the aftermath of the 'Charity Tax' Budget row that might help advance the case for philanthropy and resolve at least some outstanding issues. Matthew believes that the row about capping tax relief threatened to unsettle the balance between government, business and civil society established in the previous century by undermining the principle that you should not pay tax on what you give away. In opposing the proposal, the 'third sector' has asserted its independence and presented for the first time a united front to challenge government. In view of the erosion of the charitable sector's independence over the past fifty years, the campaign could represent a line in the sand, leading to greater independence of the voluntary sector and a stronger voice in future. As a result, he sees growing interest in philanthropy:

Philanthropy is becoming topical. I sense that the ground is beginning to move. We have had more of a free market economy here since the Thatcher government, but no sense of obligation on behalf of the rich as there is in the US. Partly because of the welfare state and high taxation after the war, there has been a culture in which the rich believed that the state would pick up the bill. In the US, there is a social contract between the individual and society. Government plays a minimal role but provides the instruments of giving, enabling the individual to support civil society through tax breaks.

We need a social contract here. Both the state and the market economy have hit the buffers. Belief in the free market has been shattered and there is disillusion. The limitations of the state and the constraints upon it are there for us all to see. There is a moral and ethical vacuum. There is an opportunity here and the wealthy could help to fill the vacuum by showing leadership.

A social contract in Britain will be different, because the state will have to be involved to agree reforms to tax to encourage more charitable giving. This will be a challenge because there is widespread ignorance in the government and the civil service, with notable exceptions, and serious, unfounded doubts about the motives of donors. I was once asked by a civil servant: 'Why would you spend your money on what we are here to do?'

Matthew confirmed that the absence of data about who gives what and about the additional cost to government of more tax relief was a problem for 'The Philanthropy Review'. We know that 7 per cent of donors contribute almost half of all annual charitable giving in Britain but we need data from HMRC to confirm who they are in terms of the income that they give away. All the information that is available suggests that much of the money being donated annually is given by a small proportion of the population and that most of the top 5 per cent are not giving in any meaningful way.

The philanthropic cause is also hampered because there is no data that enables us to compare the value of spending in the public and voluntary sectors. According to Matthew:

> Philanthropists should expect that they will come under increasing scrutiny and pressure to justify the public benefits that their giving delivers in return for tax reliefs. In any future debate, philanthropy must find better ways to argue its value by presenting the benefits it brings to society and correcting public understanding. Evidence needs to go beyond quantifying the amount given, which is a crude 'input' measure, and include the economic and quantifiable social value delivered by philanthropic investment in projects, as well as the substantial benefit of time, talent and other non-financial resources that major donors often commit to the charities they support. Only then will the true value of independent philanthropy be appreciated and its role established in our culture.

Looking to the future and how to recruit more donors:

> We must also learn how to speak to those who are not charitably minded. Those who care tend to be self-selecting. We need to be smarter about embracing the majority that does not have a moral conscience. This generation of baby boomers is radical, healthy, independently minded, starting to retire and looking for things to do. This is a tremendous opportunity for charities, as is the inevitable rise in the death rate.

Matthew also sees great opportunities for the Community Foundation Network, of which he is chairman, given that there are currently 8 million people classified as mass 'affluents' because they have liquid assets of between £50,000 and £5 million.

The Community Foundation Network now has 3,000 donor funds worth an average £90,000. These endowment funds we manage for philanthropists are worth more than £280 million. The number of major donors who work with us is growing steadily, up from 1,400 in 2008. This gives me hope that although the overall amount of charitable giving nationally appears to be falling, some of the more wealthy are becoming more committed. Our numbers are going up.

The Community Foundation Network is now giving 22,000 grants a year to local projects, worth £63 million in 2011. Almost 80 per cent of that sum came from private philanthropy. Our focus is upon philanthropists and connecting them to communities. Community foundations should be seen as a natural part of the infrastructure of civil society and everyone should know that they have one.

So far, we may conclude that our current circumstances are propitious for more philanthropy and although the moral case is strong, we lack the data to convince government of the financial value of investment in the voluntary sector via tax relief for donors. However, although we also lack data that confirms who gives what, we are entitled to deduce from what evidence there is that not only do the poor give proportionately far more to charitable causes than the rich, the wealthiest are giving only a tiny proportion of their growing wealth.

Assuming that we find a way of defining a new social contract between the individual and society, that we commit ourselves to creating a culture of giving and gratitude supported by a government equally committed to providing the necessary incentives, are charities equipped with the resources and skills needed to raise money from the very wealthy?

Some charities such as Family Action rely mainly upon public funding, many others depend upon large volumes of small donations, and some charities such as universities, medical research, arts institutions and community foundations need the support of a small number of major benefactors in addition to their alumni, patrons and other regular supporters.

Most charities will need to find more major donors (giving more than £1,000) if they are to flourish in this harsh climate. Many charities have a successful record of major gift fundraising but it is widely acknowledged that there is a dearth of effective fundraisers and too many charities are underperforming.

What should charities be doing if they are to attract our sceptical potential philanthropist? I asked Theresa Lloyd for her views. Following a career in international banking, Theresa set up the corporate fundraising department at Save the Children, became UK director of Action Aid and was the founder director of Philanthropy UK. She is currently a leading consultant in strategic planning, fundraising and governance for the non-profit sector. She has also advised philanthropists on the development of their giving strategies. Theresa has written *Why Rich People Give* (2004) and *Cultural Giving* (2006). Ten years after the research for *Why Rich People Give*, Theresa is collaborating with Dr Beth Breeze (author of the 'Million Pound Donor' reports) on an update to this work, to be published in autumn 2013. Theresa is also a donor. She and her husband set up a family charitable trust in 1992. It is a 'flow-through' trust: in other words it is not endowed but they channel regular payments out of their joint annual income through the trust. I asked Theresa if there is a magic formula for successful fundraising and how would she approach someone who has yet to be convinced that philanthropy is worthwhile:

I believe profoundly that institutions cannot be successful in fundraising without an institutional culture of engagement. Everyone in a charitable organisation needs to share in the excitement of plans for the future and be able to articulate why their cause matters, the difference that a donation will make to people's lives, and share their passion and professional knowledge as appropriate.

Whether it is Tate or a local hospice or homeless shelter, we see what can be achieved by following these principles – and what happens when they are ignored.

Major donors see their gift as an investment in people, leadership and a project. Sometimes, donors will feel they are investing in a start-up. The idea that you sign a cheque, walk away and get a standard report a year later is way out of date. What donors *enjoy* about giving is the importance of a sense of partnership with the organisations and causes they support, and they put a value on learning, whether it is how to conserve a painting or deliver water in very poor countries.

When I worked for Action Aid, I learned how to deal with potential donors. I realised that it is hopeless to put people into categories and silos. Donors must be treated as individuals rather than as the positions they have or the roles they fulfil. Nobody wants to be treated as a cheque book. I also understood the importance of networks that have nothing to do with job titles. And I learned that fundraisers need to be persistent, passionate and committed as well as being focused and strategic. And the more major the donor, the more that they want to deal directly with those who deliver the mission, not the fundraisers.

I asked Theresa about her experience of working with charities from her perspective as a donor:

It is interesting to see how some charities approach us as trustees of a charitable trust, and to compare that with the approach to us as individual donors. Although we are a couple making decisions as two individuals, and using a trust as a mechanism like a Charities Aid Foundation account, we are more often than not contacted in a completely impersonal manner by a 'Trust and Foundation Executive' or some such. We decided to review part of our distribution policy and wrote to a number of charities we have been supporting, saying that we wanted to rationalise our giving, so as to be more focused and strategic with the limited resources we have, so please let us know what your needs are – in other words, make a case for us to continue our support. Some charities ignored the letter, others wrote inadequate letters that didn't address our questions or didn't write to us as if we are real people. Too few wrote a letter that really explained the difference our continuing and possibly increased giving could make. This was very disappointing, especially given the long-term nature of the support we had been giving to some of the charities.

In addition, most charities are not ambitious enough in terms of what they ask for, and are not willing to invest in developing really long-term relationships. Even then, if donors are inclined to give they will usually give no more than the sum requested. This is a personal view based on experience rather than detailed research but I believe that it is still the case that for many leaders of very sizeable organisations, where the budget and plans would indicate a case and need for very significant gifts, the idea of asking for £1 million, let alone £10 million, is beyond their imagination and capacity.

I think some wealthy people don't give because they are not asked properly and they are cultivated by the wrong people. There are several routes to success in fundraising, but the culture of engagement is crucial. I have little time for people who say, 'We hired someone part-time for three years and she hardly raised anything so we know we cannot fundraise.' This is a combination of naivety and arrogance. They expected a relatively junior person to do it all. Too few charities, with the exception of some arts, higher education, hospitals and house-hold-name charities, have learned these lessons. Of course there are exceptions, but too many don't ask properly; they don't offer partnership and engagement with those who lead the institution and deliver the programmes; they don't show appreciation. They are often completely naive about why people would want to support them, and at the same time do not take advantage of the substantial body of knowledge about fundraising that now exists in the UK, much of it freely available. They don't bother to get to know people, to understand their interests and motivations. They use a mass-marketing approach. They seem to be unaware that donors will usually prefer to continue supporting a charity if the experience proves worthwhile – that is, rewarding, giving an opportunity to learn about some aspect of the work, to meet extraordinary people, have fun and feel appreciated – and, most importantly, knowing that they are making a real difference. And how are they to know? By being told properly about the impact of their donation in a way that makes them confident that their generosity has added value. They want to go to interesting events where the aid worker has come straight off the plane with dirty fingernails, or the conservator can show the sixteenth-century painting on which they have been working, and where they can engage in real conversations with people at the cutting edge of the work, and others who share their passions, rather than have to plough through some impenetrable jargon too often found in impersonal routine letters from a fundraiser.

This has big implications for charity trustees, both because they too should be involved in relationships with donors and because a culture of engagement implies investment and cost. I know when a trustee tells me – usually with pride – they are spending less than 10 per cent on their fundraising that they are almost certainly not raising as much as they could.

Finally, I asked Theresa if she had any advice to offer to government and the Treasury:

The most important thing is to create a favourable tax environment, do what is necessary to encourage volunteering and 'giving' education in schools. We need a long-term and coherent policy framework and a consistently supportive message from the government that charitable giving results in public benefit, and that they recognise that the vast majority of donors are well-motivated people who contribute to society. And many major donors also raise funds for the causes they support.

We must introduce lifetime legacies whereby people can gift capital to charities in their lifetimes and enjoy the benefit now rather than when it is too late. Also, it would be a very good thing if every MP used payroll-giving because then they might take an interest in philanthropy.

And it would help if government departments talked to each other. DCMS appears to welcome and encourage philanthropy, and is investing in a programme to support arts and heritage organisations to develop their fundraising capacity and expertise, and provide incentives to donors by matching their funding. This follows a successful matched-funding scheme to encourage investment in fundraising in higher education. Meanwhile everyone I have met in the Treasury behaves in this extraordinary way as if somehow by giving one can end up being better off by claiming tax relief. They talk as though they think that all philanthropists are just out to screw us and they will somehow end up being better off by giving to charity than if they don't give. As we saw with the proposal to put a cap on tax relief for charitable giving, donors are seen as dodgy people giving to dodgy charities. Treasury people appear not to understand motivation, nor to wish to. They are part of a spectrum of cynicism about motivation, too often reflected in the media, whereby they seem to think that giving is all about tax evasion or getting a knighthood or plaudits. The idea that giving may be a humanitarian response to the needs of other people, or a wish to put something back into society, or a desire to open up the joy of the arts or sports to young people who might otherwise not have the opportunity, never seems to occur to them.

If charities are to survive and prosper by responding to growing needs, many will have to invest more in fundraising. This will be a challenge. During a conversation with an anonymous donor about the need to match the private interests of philanthropists with public need, he told me:

Many charities which are providing public services are having their funding cut and I am depressed by the reaction of some grant-giving foundations. I believe trusts and foundations should support capacity-building in charities, principally fundraising capacity. They think, almost unanimously, that charity CEOs should be spending their time revisiting their business model and reviewing their long-term strategy. I think that these people are living on another planet. Charities are closing whilst the public need is growing as poverty continues to increase. It is successful fundraising that is most likely to mitigate against closure.

I know of a charity for the homeless in London that faces losing 90 per cent of its statutory funding so I am funding their fundraising. We need to persuade more philanthropists that by helping to build capacity, they can help welfare charities maintain public services.

Donor F is the final witness in my testimonial to the value of philanthropy and my mission to encourage more people to follow the example of all those we have heard from. His story should resonate with the majority of the self-made wealthy. His example is inspiring but his analysis of the outlook of his peers is a reminder of how difficult it will be to persuade the majority of those who do not give that giving will also be good for them:

There was no particular influence upon me in my childhood that encouraged me to be charitable until I went to university. I came from a working-class Tory background in east London. The ethic is you work hard, you earn money if you can. People were kind but not necessarily charitable. When I went to Cambridge, I became much more aware of the realities of life. On the whole, it is much more difficult to get on if you come from a disadvantaged background. I became aware of the need to promote wider access and more opportunities for more people.

I left university and went into stockbroking. I became indirectly involved with supporting the National Society for Mentally Handicapped Children through the social events I went to. But the next, most important stage in my philanthropy was determined by who I married. My wife has always been charitable, and believed that once we had reached a comfortable lifestyle we should give away the 'surplus', and give our time.

I retired from stockbroking when I was forty-six, devoted my time to volunteering and became a trustee of a number of charities alleviating poverty and supporting the elderly. Although we have supported national charities and I was honorary treasurer of one, we decided we should focus on causes in Essex and east London. There is poverty, disability and disadvantage there and we feel an affinity with the area. And we decided we wanted to remain anonymous. We just want to give the money and not be treated specially.

We set up a charitable trust that does not bear our name. We are able to give away about £200,000 a year and we tend to focus on charities we have given to before with whom we have a relationship.

Why don't other people give? If you look at people from my background, they could come to a completely opposite conclusion. 'I came out of that background through hard work so anyone can. So anyone who doesn't isn't deserving of my support.' If that is a basic principle and you are aged forty or more, you are unlikely to change that point of view. That is a deeply emotional view of their life which they see as a personal struggle that was successful. Many people are simply right-wing. They think people are poor because of a lack of effort. They are sceptical about the meaning of the word disability.

Then there are those who say 'I haven't found the cause that appeals to me' or that charities have too many reserves or cost too much. They don't understand why a charity pays anyone and think they should be run entirely by volunteers. They show very poor judgement because they show no understanding that charities need to be run professionally and be businesslike. This is a very commonly held view. The best chance of persuading an intelligent person is the point about being businesslike, but I am not optimistic because these kinds of views are so entrenched.

A recurrent theme throughout this book is motivation. Our anonymous donor is a classic example of a philanthropist who is motivated by nothing more than wishing to help his less fortunate fellow men and women. He and his wife seek no recognition for this.

※

We must be bold if we are to become a more generous society and persuade more people to give and to give more. The confusion about the government's commitment to philanthropy must end. There is an inherent tension between two fundamental points of view. On the one hand, the Treasury and HMRC argue that everyone should pay a fair share of tax and should not be able to hypothecate their taxes. On the other hand, charities and the voluntary sector argue that you should not be taxed on what is not yours as you have given it away to society. Finding a solution will not be easy, but one must be found.

If our government and 'we' as a society are serious that we wish to maintain our mixed economy and plural funding but that we need to adjust to the challenging economic situation by enhancing the role of the voluntary sector and philanthropists, we need to do so in a way that is most likely to ensure a positive result. That requires politicians to understand that charities need to plan and invest for the long term and that philanthropy flourishes as a result of long-term engagement and commitment. Without apology, because the point requires repetition, government and the civil service must try to understand the motivation of donors and that philanthropy will always be about choice. Donors may decide to spend all their money after they have paid their taxes or choose to give some or all of it away. We must do everything possible to encourage them to do the latter.

Without exception, every donor I have spoken to calls for a consistent, long-term national strategy for philanthropy endorsed by all the main political parties. Sir Roger Carr, President of the Confederation of British Industry, told me and is quoted in the Legacy 10 Review for the DCMS as saying: 'It would be preferable to have a philanthropy policy which enjoys all-party support and is thus depoliticised.'

What should that policy be? Here are my recommendations. Some are based on recommendations already made and published by others, many are endorsed by the philanthropists I interviewed in 2012, but ultimately my recommendations are based on my personal view of how we should recruit more to the cause of philanthropy in order to build a better society.

1. Charities and the state

Charities are the flagships of the voluntary sector; they should continue to do what the state cannot do by acting as pioneers and as beacons of good practice.

Where the state commissions services from charities and is principal funder, it must respect the mission and independence of the charity, not least because any distortion of mission risks the loss of philanthropic support.

The state should not withdraw any further from the funding of public services as there is little evidence that philanthropists have either the capacity or the inclination to contribute more. Some philanthropists are alarmed by reductions in welfare support for the most vulnerable and believe state support is often the most effective and efficient means of alleviating poverty. They believe that is why they are paying tax. Most philanthropists are in favour of a mixed economy and plural funding.

Charities and philanthropists welcome matched-funding challenge grants (where £1 from a donor is matched by £1 from the taxpayer) from government, but believe the restrictions imposed by the Treasury are too restrictive and counterproductive because they remove donor incentives. Charities must be accountable for public money but government must trust charities to use matched funding in ways that will be most effective in attracting private money.

The lack of consistency in government policy concerning the voluntary sector and philanthropy requires one minister who has overall responsibility. The minister should work closely with a charity/philanthropy czar (or a committee representing philanthropists) who will represent the voluntary sector and ensure its voice is heard in government.

The voluntary sector and HMRC should work together to improve data on charitable giving in order to inform government on policies most likely to encourage more philanthropy.

Government and the voluntary sector should jointly examine the need to build fundraising capacity in charities and to consider establishing a training programme funded by the National Lottery, trusts and foundations and other private-sector partners.

Charities should ensure that their trustees and senior executives understand how to engage with philanthropists in order to secure their long-term support. This means charities must be clear about their objectives and how effective they are being in achieving them.

2. Tax and public benefit

All British citizens should pay British taxes wherever they live, as all American citizens do. Many philanthropists who live here and pay either British or US tax feel very strongly in favour of the abolition of non-dom status for UK citizens.

Extend tax relief to full deductions against income on cash donations to motivate those who can make large cash gifts, as recommended in 'The Philanthropy Review' as an alternative to Gift Aid. Only 27 per cent of top-rate taxpayers are recorded as making charitable gifts in Britain. In the US, where tax relief is much simpler to understand and to administer, 98 per cent of top-rate taxpayers make charitable donations.

Encourage top-rate taxpayers by offering a reduction in the rate of tax for a long-term commitment to one charity or charitable project for a fixed term.

Offer tax relief on the gift of all classes of assets and, subject to strict regulation, to gifts in kind.

Harmonise tax relief on all gifts, whether made during life or on death. Introduce the successful US model for planned giving, known as lifetime legacies, whereby donors gift capital to charities during their lifetime and continue to enjoy the income from the capital as if they have an annuity. Government should tighten rules on the creation of charitable trusts to overcome fears of tax evasion.

To overcome concerns about tax relief for donations which may not be considered to be in the public interest, we need a clear definition of public benefit. Policy would need to have all-party endorsement to ensure stability for long-term planning by charities and donors.

In order to understand the contribution made by charitable giving, there should be an independent, comparative study to establish on qualitative and quantitative grounds the value added by investment in the public and voluntary sectors.

3. Building a culture of giving and gratitude

Philanthropy will grow in a warm climate where it refreshed by encouragement and acknowledgement and where giving of time and money is expected and becomes usual practice.

The most effective means of changing our culture is by educating our children to be philanthropic in the widest sense of the word. Government must take a lead by building upon the excellent work being done by the two largest national school programmes, Go-Givers and Giving Nation, and by the Youth and Philanthropy Initiative, which does not have the funds to operate in every school. I recommend that government ensures that the national curriculum includes opportunities for children to commit to voluntary work in their communities, following the example set by the Citizenship Foundation and YPI, and to earn a national diploma, following the example of Atlantic College which pioneered the International Baccalaureate, which would be recognised by higher education and employers.

Business people nominated for national honours must also demonstrate evidence of charitable giving and/or the commitment of time to volunteering before they are entitled to be considered. There should be more honours given for philanthropy. Honours should not be awarded to those who do not pay British taxes.

Chairs of the boards of charitable organisations should set an example by pledging lifetime financial support and legacies, so that it becomes the norm that all trustees commit to giving, in accordance with their means.

Some of these recommendations have been with government for more than a decade. Acceptance of at least some of them would make a significant difference to encouraging more philanthropy. It is up to government to decide whether that is what it wishes. Some, including me, have yet to be convinced that government does want to encourage more philanthropy. However, if ministers mean what they say, all they have to do is pick up the telephone. We are ready to talk and get started.

PART 4

Conclusions

CHAPTER 16

So what are you doing, John?

On 8 May 1883, *The Times* reported a speech made by HRH the Prince of Wales at the opening of the Royal College of Music in London:

Fifty scholarships have been established, of which twenty-five confer a free education in music and twenty-five provide not only a free education but also maintenance of the scholars. Of these scholarships, half are held by boys and half by girls. The occupations of the scholars are as various as the places from which they come. I find that a mill girl, the daughter of a brick-maker and the son of a blacksmith take high places in singing, and the son of a farm labourer in violin playing. The capacity of these candidates has been tested by an examination of unusual severity.

One hundred and thirty years later, the Royal College of Music (RCM) ranks amongst the world's leading conservatoires and remains committed to the admirably progressive values of 1883 by providing scholarships for those unable to afford fees and the expense of living in London. Moreover, the Prince of Wales is an enthusiastic president who patently enjoys his visits to the college.

I am also an enthusiastic supporter of the RCM, as a member

of the governing council and of its capital campaign committee, for we have to raise £30 million in order to bring our building up to scratch and to fund the increasing demand for scholarships in our tough new world of alarmingly high fees. First-time visitors to our building in 'Albertopolis', south Kensington, are immediately struck by the intriguing sounds of multiple instruments and voices in rehearsal and practice. Exiting from a lift, you might have to negotiate around a cellist in a corner. Every corridor pulses with young people making music in the most unlikely places. As the head of percussion says: 'There is a terrific acoustic in the toilets but...'

The need is clear. Conservatoires are responsible for the future of the highest possible quality of professional music-making. Music matters to millions. The questions I have to answer are: given my responsibilities to the college, what am I going to do in terms of supporting the campaign, and should I make my decision public?

I have never given a significant sum to a capital appeal before, so I should put myself into the position of the person we are trying to persuade to be charitable. So what might my motivation be?

Firstly, is the cause good and will it deliver public benefit? The RCM makes an important contribution to the lives of all those who love music. It has a first-class track record and an impeccable international reputation. The college must offer world-class opportunities to young people if it is to maintain its international position, to attract those who are able to pay fees and to provide funded scholarships for those who cannot. The building needs renewal with more high-quality rehearsal and performing space. There needs to be more space and more opportunity for the public to enjoy what the college has to offer to music lovers.

The case for support is strong. I also believe that as a member of the governing body I must make a contribution.

How much should I give? That will be determined by how much I feel about the cause as well as how much I can afford. We know from the evidence presented in this book that all donors feel passionate about the causes to which they devote their generosity.

Music gave me hope during a difficult childhood. Music gave me strength when I was seriously ill in my twenties and nearly went under. I cannot imagine life without music. So that is clear. I have to be as generous as is possible.

I have spent decades asking people to give money, urging them to be acknowledged so that others will be encouraged by their example. The main purpose of this book is to persuade people of the importance and many virtues of giving. Many of those who are being generous have struggled and have found it hard to decide whether to be anonymous or not. Now I understand their dilemma.

I am inclined to keep my decision and the details of my donation private. Why? Am I ashamed? Am I fearful that people would think I was showing off? Do I fear being criticised and having my motivation questioned? These were the concerns felt by Trevor and Lyn Shears when they started giving. Then they decided they should be prepared to talk about their generosity in public, not least because they want to encourage others to be generous. However, Trevor and Lyn also want people to know how fulfilling it is to give.

So I have decided to 'come out' for the second time in my life and I hope that this experience will not be as challenging as the first time. Accordingly, I will be only too pleased to follow the example of John and Lorna Norgrove and I will give to the RCM exactly the same sum that they gave to establish their foundation in memory of their daughter. My gift will go to the college's scholarship fund to help those talented young musicians who could not possibly afford to attend otherwise. In due course, this gift will be followed by a legacy.

I ask government to note that I could not possibly contemplate making a six-figure donation without using Gift Aid and the tax relief it affords. My fellow fundraisers should note that I will not be able to repeat this gift. And I ask those who are not giving and who are so very much richer than I am to join me.

Finally, as a philanthropist said to me when I told him I wanted to write this book: 'Don't forget to tell them what fun giving is.'

CHAPTER 17

What will your legacy be?

'Remembering that I will be dead soon is the most important tool I have ever encountered to help me make the big choices in life … you are already naked. There is no reason not to follow your heart.'
– Steve Jobs

We have heard from those who give, learned what motivates and frustrates them, what will encourage them to give more and what they think of their peers who don't give or give too little. We know how personal generosity can transform lives, bring hope to others and give donors a fulfilment they cannot find by simply making money. Above all, those who give want to do the right thing and make a difference. We have shown government what they need to do to encourage and increase philanthropy.

I agree with Polly Toynbee on the role of charities, I share her concern about tax relief and those charities offering no public benefit, but I disagree with her view that too many donors are vain, self-indulgent and whimsical. I hope the evidence of the donors in this book will help to change her perception and that of the many who share her point of view.

More importantly, have we succeeded in changing the minds of those in the top 1 per cent who are not giving? Despite an astonishing growth in the wealth of the richest, charitable giving in Britain is either falling or stalling. It is understandable that the middle classes feel beleaguered. Life is more expensive. Bringing up children and looking after elderly parents costs more. The very rich have no excuses.

What messages should we be sending to those who do not give and who do not agree with Andrew Carnegie that they should be using their surplus wealth to support the public realm? Or should we be drawing their attention to Carnegie's most quoted saying, 'he who dies rich, dies disgraced'? And would they care if we did?

Let us consider the world view of the rich, who, like the poor, are always with us. Wealth creators often feel as follows: 'I have worked for this, I have taken all the risk, I deserve the money I have made. It is mine and I don't want to give half or even more of it to the government, and I don't want to be told by anyone what to do with my money.' Not all wealthy people feel like this, but many do. The idea that personal wealth is an entirely private matter certainly governed my upbringing.

According to the world view of some of those who are not rich, the wealthy are antisocial pariahs and we do not want them in Britain, paying less tax than anyone else. Let them eat foie gras in tax exile, and if they are bored and miss London, too bad. If they want to stay, let them pay tax, preferably at a rate of 90 per cent.

There is a pragmatic way between these two extremes which acknowledges the concerns of both the wealthy minority who we do need in Britain, and the majority which comprises everyone else.

We should acknowledge that private wealth has been used to the great benefit of the common good. We have the historical evidence and we know it is happening today. I admire friends of mine who retired early to enjoy their good fortune by living abroad and who are devoting their time and money to giving educational opportunities to disadvantaged young people from all over the world. I respect a very private family I know who are British but who were brought up overseas and rarely live here, who are 'offshore' for tax purposes but who have given many millions to health, education and arts projects in Britain, usually anonymously or with their names discreetly placed. I am astonished by the generosity of those who are not British and who have given huge donations to Tate, some anonymously without any discernible benefit to them other than private satisfaction. The public benefit to Tate's 7 million annual visitors is significant. I applaud those who do stay here, pay their taxes and give imaginatively and generously. One such is a friend who prefers to make non-glamorous gifts and who anonymously renovated the women's lavatories at the refurbished Royal Festival Hall in London, a prime example of both private need and public benefit. These donors have a keen sense of obligation to others. Do we wish to discourage them or should we be encouraging more people to follow their example?

We cannot avoid politics in philanthropy, and politics are divisive. In the context of the recent global economic crisis, the rich have become very much richer and increasingly unpopular. The selfish behaviour, tax avoidance and conspicuous consumption of a few has done no favours for the reputation of the wealthy who are generous and there is little public sympathy for those expressing doubts about living here or continuing their financial commitments in Britain. So this may not be the best time for proposing measures that seem to benefit the wealthy and make them feel better about Britain. In order to encourage philanthropy, our government has to balance interests which may appear irreconcilable.

The public realm is having a hard time and some of us are horrified by how cuts in public expenditure affect the poor, both the young and the old. 'The bankers' are not to blame for every aspect of the current financial crisis, although many were clearly culpable, but any government will have to take deeply unpopular and divisive decisions to reduce the massive debts caused by speculation, over-consumption, too much dependence on the state and not enough upon personal responsibility. However, I fear that the current balance of interests is tilted too far towards those of us who have and away from those in need.

Throughout the current financial and political crisis in the USA and Europe, I believe it is vital that all of us, and our politicians in particular, do not lose sight of the powerful force which has made humanity so successful – a sense of mutual obligation towards each other. This means concern for the most vulnerable and encouragement for the rest of us, and the rich in particular, to do more to help others. Now is the time for a new social contract between the citizen, society and the state. Government should take the initiative to secure cross-party agreement on how to strengthen the voluntary sector and how to give us all the 'financial instruments' to encourage more charitable giving. We must think again about how to teach our children that they are blessed to live in a civil society and that they have a responsibility to help sustain it and an obligation to their fellow citizens. We must revive the concept of the common good. This is the only way to create a culture of giving, supported by a culture of gratitude that recognises, acknowledges, thanks and encourages the generous.

Persuading people to start being generous is a challenge because the British are uncomfortable talking about money. Moreover, the concept of 'doing good' makes some queasy. The thought of doing something because it is good for you can be even more irritating depending upon who is saying it. John Ruskin, the Victorian writer and critic, thought great wealth was a curse and said, 'There is no wealth but life,' which prompted a contemporary to complain that listening to Ruskin was like being 'preached to death by a mad governess'.

If Carnegie's warning about the rich dying disgraced has lost its bite, maybe the wealthy of today might be persuaded to listen to the advice of Steve Jobs, one of the greatest entrepreneurs of our own time.

Both refer to death, about which most of us are in denial. It was not always so, and people thought more about their legacies when life was shorter, more people died at home and we were confronted with the reality of our end. Death defines us and yet it has been tidied away and has become almost invisible. Steve Jobs preferred to face up to the inevitable and to focus on using his remaining energy and time in the most fulfilling way he knew how. He was clearly also aware of his legacy.

We should follow Steve Jobs's example and bear in mind the research which shows that the overwhelming emotion felt by those approaching the end of their lives is too often one of regret and frustration about missed opportunities and a failure to fulfil their potential. Have I done everything I could have done? Have I done my best? Could I have done more? How will I be remembered? Will I be remembered as mean or generous? What will be my legacy?

As we face death, surely we should all feel that we have done everything within our power to leave the world a better place than when we entered it? There is no escape from the inevitability of our end. One should always act before it is too late. And so I urge those who have not yet given to discover and fulfil their humanity, to give and to give generously for their own sake, as much as for anyone else.

For those of us like Steve Jobs, who have been forced to face the imminent prospect of our own death, or who have witnessed the last moment of those closest to us, we have to acknowledge the finality of everything. I know because I have experienced both. That moment of finality is almost certainly the most profound in all our lives, the revelation that all that matters is the love we give each other and, to echo Steve Jobs, the need to follow our hearts.

Let us cheer ourselves with a life-affirming thought, remembering that life itself is the result of a gift from one person to another. Every donor who has given intelligently will tell you that generosity brings pleasure and satisfaction like nothing else. I know this to be true from my own personal experience. Money is essential and makes the world go round but the paradox is that money can only make you happy when you give it away.

However, we should heed the warning given by the poet W. H. Auden when he said, 'We must love one another or die.' He makes the point even more powerfully in 'The Shield of Achilles' (see Epilogue), with his vision of hell as a place without civil society.

Are *you* bothered? The wrong answer is too awful to contemplate.

Epilogue

'The Shield of Achilles'
W. H. Auden

She looked over his shoulder
For vines and olive trees,
Marble well-governed cities,
And ships upon untamed seas,
But there on the shining metal
His hands had put instead
An artificial wilderness
And a sky like lead.

A plain without a feature, bare and brown,
No blade of grass, no sign of neighborhood,
Nothing to eat and nowhere to sit down,
Yet, congregated on its blankness, stood
An unintelligible multitude,
A million eyes, a million boots in line,
Without expression, waiting for a sign.

Out of the air a voice without a face
Proved by statistics that some cause was just
In tones as dry and level as the place:
No one was cheered and nothing was discussed;
Column by column in a cloud of dust
They marched away enduring a belief
Whose logic brought them, somewhere else, to grief.

She looked over his shoulder
For ritual pieties,
White flower-garlanded heifers,
Libation and sacrifice,
But there on the shining metal
Where the altar should have been,
She saw by his flickering forge-light
Quite another scene.

Barbed wire enclosed an arbitrary spot
Where bored officials lounged (one cracked a joke)
And sentries sweated, for the day was hot:
A crowd of ordinary decent folk
Watched from without and neither moved nor spoke
As three pale figures were led forth and bound
To three posts driven upright in the ground.

The mass and majesty of this world, all
That carries weight and always weighs the same,
Lay in the hands of others; they were small
And could not hope for help and no help came:
What their foes liked to do was done, their shame
Was all the worst could wish; they lost their pride
And died as men before their bodies died.

She looked over his shoulder
For athletes at their games,
Men and women in a dance
Moving their sweet limbs
Quick, quick, to music,
But there on the shining shield
His hands had set no dancing-floor
But a weed-choked field.

A ragged urchin, aimless and alone,
Loitered about that vacancy; a bird
Flew up to safety from his well-aimed stone:
That girls are raped, that two boys knife a third,
Were axioms to him, who'd never heard
Of any world where promises were kept
Or one could weep because another wept.

The thin-lipped armorer,
Hephaestos, hobbled away;
Thetis of the shining breasts
Cried out in dismay
At what the god had wrought
To please her son, the strong
Iron-hearted man-slaying Achilles
Who would not live long.

Appendix

How to be a good donor, trustee, charity and fundraiser

Whilst speaking at a seminar for aspiring senior arts managers, I was asked this simple question:

'What do you say when you ask someone for money?'

To which I replied:

'What do you say when you want to make love with someone?'

I doubt if this was the expected answer because the questioner showed that she had yet to understand that the essence of a good relationship between those who give and those who receive is trust, mutual interests and a degree of intimacy. Asking a person for money is not the same as asking a company for sponsorship. Personal gifts are rarely business deals. When people give significant sums (say, £1,000 to a small charity and £10,000 or more to a larger one), they will usually not do so before they have formed a relationship with a cause and those who lead it. If the relationship is going well, it may not even be necessary to ask. If the donor and the charity are aligned, the donor will be aware of the need and may make an offer before asking becomes necessary. (NB, Sir John Madejski and his gift of £3 million to the Royal Academy of Arts, page 110.)

For many outside the charity sector, philanthropy and the art of fundraising is a mystery. (I do believe fundraising at its best is an art form as it requires a creative, sensitive and convincing performance to achieve transformation.) Unfortunately, the gift and receipt of donations is also a mystery to people within charities and to their trustees, who too often have unrealistic expectations about what is possible and the time needed to court potential philanthropists.

A good director of development (jargon for fundraising) must be able to manage upwards (chairman, trustees, directors), sideways (senior colleagues) and downwards (the development team) simultaneously, juggling different sets of expectations, maintaining perfect composure to the outside world, being charming and effortlessly articulate with prospective donors, reassuring patrons who may be aware of fluttering and fratricide inside the dovecote, whilst also achieving demanding fundraising targets. This is a tough but fulfilling job. Unfortunately, despite some stars, there are not enough people in Britain who are good at it.

Many books have been written that recommend best practice and I do not intend to add to the pile. However, for those who want to know more, I hope they will have learned something from the people I interviewed in *Giving is Good for You*. I have. For ease of reference, I have made some notes that reflect what I have learned during my career and I hope they will be helpful.

Becoming a philanthropist

Whether you have only recently made or inherited enough money to be philanthropic or have very little to give, the principle is the same. Follow the example of those who are giving and support causes that interest and matter to you. Or as Steve Jobs put it, follow your heart.

If you want to commit more than a modest monthly direct debit, ask yourself, why? What is your motivation and what are your expectations? And having answered the question, what should you do next? John Studzinski makes the point succinctly:

What are you interested in? What do you want to learn about? Who do you want to meet? Who do you want to hang around? Go to a charity and ask them what do they really need. And then do something really transformational for them, which only you can do. Find someone you might like and get to know them really well. Find charities you really believe in and which have visionary leaders.

People who have no intention of giving to charity have invented a myriad of excuses why they should not. Most of these so-called reasons have been debunked in the preceding pages by those who give. However, for those willing to be persuaded, choosing one or two charities to support out of 160,000 could be off-putting. However, if you are serious about committing your money and really want to make a difference then you should be prepared to undertake research and draw your own conclusions about who might deserve your support, just as you would for any other investment. Talk to current donors of a charity and ask them about their experience. Consult your local Community Foundation or the Community Foundation Network at network@ukcommunityfoundations.org.

Not all of us have hundreds of thousands or millions to give. However, annual gifts of £500 or more should enable you to have a relationship with a charity if they are smart enough to know how to look after you. Many arts organisations have become very good at making their friends and patrons feel wanted, welcome and involved. If you feel you are making a difference by giving £1,000 a year, you may feel inclined to give more in due course or leave a legacy.

Becoming a friend or an annual patron is an excellent way to get to know a charity. Moreover, regular commitments are particularly helpful to charities. You will be making a valuable contribution to sustainability. Don't simply write a cheque and disappear.

Most successful philanthropists (by which I mean people who find being philanthropic rewarding and will go on being generous) have set themselves a clear set of objectives and defined a strategy to achieve them. Many will have established a charitable foundation, thus exempting the capital and the income generated from inheritance, capital gains and income tax. Make sure that your gifts are useful to charities and are helping them to fulfil *their* objectives. Do not make gifts that are designed simply to please you.

Do not make unreasonable demands upon charities that will cost them time and money. Charities should look after their donors but not to extent that, by doing so, they are distracted from their main purpose.

Consider supporting a charity's long-term plans by making a commitment to fund its core costs and by helping it to 'build capacity'. This could mean investment in staff and training. Many smaller charities are struggling in the recession. Some have lost public funding and don't have either the resources or skills to raise money from the private sector. Judicious investment in fundraising could transform a charity's finances, but do not expect a return for at least eighteen months. Having read *Giving is Good for You*, you know why. All successful fundraising is the result of long-term relationships rather than a one-night stand.

Allow yourself to be persuaded that your generosity should be acknowledged in public unless you have good reason to protect your identity. One of the most effective ways of encouraging more people to be philanthropic is to show leadership by example. This need not require more than having your name listed on a donor board in a public place or in an annual report.

Most charitable giving offers tax relief to UK taxpayers on the principle that tax should not be paid on money that is given away. The net cost of a donation of £100,000 to a top-rate taxpayer could be £55,000. There is also tax relief on the gift of some assets and on legacies. Ask your financial or legal adviser, or a charity's development department.

Donors often find that a long-term commitment to one charity is more rewarding than supporting a number of causes. John Nash, sponsor of Pimlico Academy, puts this well:

> Our focus on education has been so interesting. Rather than go off and found new schools, we thought we should concentrate on Pimlico and ensure that we really understand the complex issues involved ... experienced business people tend to underestimate the judgement calls required when working with charities. The issues are complex ... what business people can do is to help with strategy and empowerment and give management a shoulder to cry on.

One of the reasons John and Caroline Nash chose to support Pimlico Academy was because they have an affinity with the area. Many donors choose to give back to the people and places that influenced them in childhood or were instrumental in creating their wealth.

Some philanthropists become so committed to the charities they support that their gift of time may be even more valuable than their donations, as John Studzinski's commitment proves. Accordingly, they may be invited to join the board of a charity and serve as a trustee.

Becoming a trustee

All charities should ensure their trustees are informed of their responsibilities and liabilities.

All trustees should be clear about what is expected of them and agree a specific role with the chairman of the board and the charity's chief executive. This is particularly important for donors who join a board and who you hope will continue to be a donor after they are no longer serving as a trustee.

In Britain, there has been a tradition that trustees who give a great deal of time should not be expected to give money. This is becoming untenable. Donors often ask fundraisers if all board members are giving and they may be less inclined to give if the answer is negative. Some board members feel strongly that they should not be expected to give but there is now a powerful tide in favour of the view that all trustees should give something, according to their means. We should not adopt US practice where boards are stuffed with donors. That can lead to biased decisions. Charities need balanced boards and trustees with a range of skills and experience. However, most trustees ought to be able to give £100, or £2 a week. Many can and should give more. And trustees should also set an example by leaving a legacy.

A trustee who does not give is disabling their charity's fund-raising effort.

As fundraising becomes more of a necessity, it is important that all trustees understand philanthropy and how to raise funds, even though they may not need to be involved directly.

After all, successful fundraising is essential for most charities and therefore becomes a board responsibility. All boards should have at least some members who are able to ask for money and this ability should be a requirement for the chairman.

The most important point for trustees to understand is that fundraising requires a significant investment in a senior executive who should be regarded as an essential member of the management team and who should be given whatever resources are required to fulfil the task allotted to them. A good fundraiser should be entitled to the active support of all parts of a charity and particularly its trustees.

How to be a good fundraising charity

The first requirement of any charity in need of external funding is that it has a clear sense of purpose and its activities are in the public interest. Following close behind, charities need to inspire confidence by having strong and inspirational leadership and credible, effective plans to fulfil worthwhile objectives and clear measures of performance.

Theresa Lloyd has described what donors are looking for in her interview on pages 292–6. Donors seek inspiration, engagement and sophisticated communication from people within the charity who understand their needs. The impersonal and the routine are the enemy of philanthropy.

Charities must be prepared to invest and spend money employing high-quality people. A small charity may only need one senior fundraiser as long as he or she has all the administrative support needed, including research, which is essential and not an optional extra, as well as the wholehearted support of colleagues and trustees. At Tate, I took on a fundraising target of a few hundred million in 2005. I was given a blank sheet of paper and invited to submit a request for whatever resources I needed, backed up by a plan. The board accepted my recommendation for a significant expansion of the fundraising department, and that investment is now paying off under the leadership of my successor: more than £200 million of capital has been raised for Tate Britain, Tate Modern and Tate St Ives, and annual giving is up by more than 250 per cent since 2006, despite recession.

It would be tempting to characterise Tate's success as a one-off, given its status and international profile, but that would be to miss the point. Whilst Tate's profile has undoubtedly helped it to raise money, much of its prominence and reputation has been made possible by the huge amounts of money invested in plans for growth, largely from the private sector although public money has also played a significant role. Fundraising at Tate has been successful because inspirational executive leadership has motivated trustees, executive colleagues, curators, collectors and donors to unite behind ambitious and credible plans for the future which are clearly in the public interest.

The basic principles behind Tate's success may be adopted by any charity needing to raise funds, albeit on a modified scale. The key point is that the executive and the trustees agree to invest in, support and work with a fundraiser who is sufficiently experienced to offer leadership to them.

The perfect fundraiser

What kind of person makes a good fundraiser? What skills do they need? The person I am about to describe will be someone who is able to ask anyone for money (companies, trusts and foundations), including the most senior philanthropists. It is true that the more senior the donor, the more likely it is that they will wish to deal with the chairman or chief executive, but the best fundraisers can bring in six- and seven-figure donations and should be expected to do so where these kinds of figures are realistic.

This person may not exist but charities should be looking for at least most of the qualities below:

1. Asking people to give their own money is different from asking businesses and institutional trusts, because money cannot be disentangled from the donor's personal feelings. This means you will sometimes need to get up close and be personal. You must feel comfortable doing so.

2. Accordingly, you must like people and be interested in what motivates them. Donors will soon notice if you are not interested.

3. If you are not interested, why should they be interested in you? You must find a way of making the donor interested in you and *believe* in you if you are to have a meaningful professional relationship.

4. You must research thoroughly in advance of meetings so as not to waste your prospective donor's precious time. Your time is not as important as theirs.

5. You need to be a good listener and to know when to keep quiet. By listening attentively and restraining your own natural enthusiasm you may be rewarded with your cue as to when to ask for money and how.

6. Raising money from donors can be a long game requiring patience and persistence, and success may take eighteen months or a few years. Make sure your colleagues and trustees understand this. They won't want to know but they must be told.

7. Rarely, some donors who are capricious may make a spontaneous offer, so be prepared.

8. Whilst there will be exceptions, most successful fundraising is the result of a team effort. Peer group pressure is often essential and can be very effective. These groups of senior volunteers need to be managed by you. You must keep control of them and retain their confidence. This aspect of your job is one of the most challenging.

9. Most donors will give and want to be involved with a charity because they care and they are interested. Their commitment is there to be nurtured. The majority will be good, generous people. Many donors have dedicated funds to give and will have objectives and priorities in terms of how their charitable funds should be used. Be sure you know what they are.

10. A minority of donors may be difficult and you will meet a few who are obnoxious. Never complain (to them) and always be scrupulously polite and professional whatever the provocation.

11. Most of the super-rich I have met have been delightful and some have been a joy to work with, but at the risk of making sweeping generalisations, please note they tend to:
    - have highly developed egos, high-octane energy levels and low boredom thresholds;
    - have above-average intelligence (but not always!), be sophisticated and keenly aware of self-interest;
    - be supported and protected by gatekeepers and high-powered teams of legal and financial advisers;
    - Have fast-moving, ever-changing and completely unpredictable schedules.

    As a fundraiser, it is your job to find a way to overcome all these challenges.

12. Good fundraisers have to be ambassadors who can go anywhere and speak to anyone. You have to appear to be fearless and also be:

- charismatic and eloquent;
- energetic and enthusiastic;
- charming and warm;
- intuitive and tactful;
- patient and resilient;
- discreet and trustworthy;
- a good host and a good guest.

13. Being a good host means knowing how to organise a breakfast, lunch, drinks or dinner party and how to seat people to the best advantage of your cause and in a way which gives your guests pleasure, enables them to enrich their networks, but not at your expense, and not bore or embarrass them.

14. Everyone has too many events to go to and too many invitations. Only organise an event if there is no alternative. They are time-consuming and expensive.

15. You have to have an excellent memory and look as if you have made an effort regarding your appearance out of respect for those you meet. If your memory for names escapes you, devise a strategy for coping.

16. A good fundraiser must be tough and sensitive enough to persuade all the key players (including your chairman and trustees as well your colleagues) to do whatever is required to help you raise funds. This is often harder than it should be because they may not recognise that a board must take responsibility for fundraising. They may have other priorities. You have to tell them that they are responsible. They should be looking to you for leadership. You must lead so that trustees and your colleagues follow.

17. You must not be the biggest ego on the scene but you cannot afford to be a shrinking violet. You must somehow manage to suppress the demands of your own ego when circumstances demand, if only temporarily. You may need

to defer to donors who have a bigger ego than yours. You must accept that there will be times when it is not appropriate for you to attend a meeting or event.

18. Know your own strengths and weaknesses. Find others to compensate for your weaknesses and then play to your strengths. I have always delegated as much management as possible, partly because I needed people who were better managers than me but also to enable me to be an ambassador and salesperson, which is my strength. Good fundraisers need to be chameleons and be able to adapt immediately to whomever they are with, whatever the circumstances.

19. You must believe absolutely in your cause if you are to convince others but you should not let your conviction carry you away so that you accept money from people of doubtful virtue. Your charity should have a clear policy on what is an acceptable and an unacceptable donation, policed by an ethics committee or similar. Always be sure to know who your donors are and where their money has come from.

20. You must be strong however awful you may feel. You must never give up and always keep on going. Something will turn up if you look hard enough and listen.

21. Always remember that your first port of call should be the people who have supported you before. If you have looked after them well, they will probably give again and give more.

22. Always remember to say 'thank you' and mean it.

In conclusion, my life as a fundraiser and now as a non-executive trustee, mentor and donor has been and continues to be fulfilling, rewarding, inspiring and life-enhancing. I recommend it. I am particularly enjoying my relatively new role as a donor. Giving really is good for you.

Copyright and permissions

Index